From Warfare to Wealth

The economic rise of Europe over the past millennium represents a major human breakthrough. To explain this phenomenon, this book highlights a counterintuitive yet central feature of Europe's historical landscape: warfare. Historical warfare inflicted numerous costs on rural populations. Security was a traditional function of the city. To mitigate the high costs of conflict in the countryside, rural populations migrated to urban centers. Over time, the city's historical role as a safe harbor translated into local economic development through several channels, including urban political freedoms and human capital accumulation. To make this argument, the authors perform a wide-ranging analysis of a novel quantitative database that spans more than one thousand years – from the fall of the Carolingian Empire to today. The book's study of urban Europe's historical path from warfare to wealth provides a new way to think about the process of long-run economic and political development.

Mark Dincecco is Assistant Professor in the Department of Political Science at the University of Michigan. He is the author of *Political Transformations and Public Finances: Europe, 1650–1913* (Cambridge University Press, 2011). In 2016–17, he was the Edward Teller National Fellow at the Hoover Institution at Stanford University.

Massimiliano Gaetano Onorato is a faculty member in the Department of Economics and Finance at the Università Cattolica del Sacro Cuore in Milan. He is the author of several peer-reviewed journal articles. He holds a PhD in Economics from Bocconi University. In 2010–11, he was a postdoctoral research associate at the Leitner Program in International and Comparative Political Economy at Yale University.

POLITICAL ECONOMY OF INSTITUTIONS AND DECISIONS

Series Editors

Jeffry Frieden, *Harvard University*
John Patty, *University of Chicago*
Elizabeth Maggie Penn, *University of Chicago*

Founding Editors

James E. Alt, *Harvard University*
Douglass C. North, *Washington University of St. Louis*

Other books in the series

(*continued after the Index*)

From Warfare to Wealth

The Military Origins of Urban Prosperity in Europe

MARK DINCECCO

University of Michigan

MASSIMILIANO GAETANO ONORATO

Università Cattolica del Sacro Cuore

CAMBRIDGE
UNIVERSITY PRESS

CAMBRIDGE
UNIVERSITY PRESS

One Liberty Plaza, 20th Floor, New York, NY 10006, USA

Cambridge University Press is part of the University of Cambridge.

It furthers the University's mission by disseminating knowledge in the pursuit of education, learning, and research at the highest international levels of excellence.

www.cambridge.org
Information on this title: www.cambridge.org/9781107162358
DOI: 10.1017/9781316677131

First published 2018

Printed in the United States of America by Sheridan Books, Inc.

A catalogue record for this publication is available from the British Library.

Library of Congress Cataloging-in-Publication Data
NAMES: Dincecco, Mark, 1977– author. | Onorato, Massimiliano Gaetano, author.
TITLE: From warfare to wealth : the military origins of urban prosperity in Europe /
Mark Dincecco, University of Michigan, Massimiliano (Gaetano) Onorato, Universita
Cattolica del Sacro Cuore.
DESCRIPTION: Cambridge, United Kingdom ; New York, NY : Cambridge University
Press, 2017. | Includes bibliographical references and index.
IDENTIFIERS: LCCN 2017012405 | ISBN 9781107162358 (hbk : alk. paper) |
ISBN 9781316612590 (pbk : alk. paper)
SUBJECTS: LCSH: War – Economic aspects – Europe – History. | Economic
development – Europe – History. | Urbanization – Europe – History. |
Europe – History, Military. | Europe – Economic conditions.
CLASSIFICATION: LCC HC240.9.D4 D56 2017 | DDC 330.94–dc23
LC record available at https://lccn.loc.gov/2017012405

ISBN 978-1-107-16235-8 Hardback
ISBN 978-1-316-61259-0 Paperback

Contents

Figures

Tables

Acknowledgments

In the preface to his book *Guns, Sails, and Empires* (1965), the great social scientist Carlo Cipolla writes: "The first person to be utterly surprised at having written a book entitled 'Guns and Sails' is definitely the author, and readers may feel confident that the book is neither magnetized by some Freudian attraction for weapons nor biased by an ancestral love for salt water. The book has simply been written because, in studying the history of the early modern period the author was forced, by overwhelming evidence, to recognize, against his tastes and inclinations, the importance of guns and sails."

We now offer a similar – though less eloquent – disclaimer. We share Cipolla's strong natural tendency toward pacifism. Nonetheless, we believe that a true understanding of the economic rise of urban Europe – the main goal of this book – compels us to grapple with warfare, as counterintuitive as that may seem at first glance.

Three key inflection points stand out in this book's development. The first was the two-hour presentation at the Political Institutions and Economic Policy (PIEP) Conference at the Weatherhead Center for International Affairs at Harvard University in December 2014. This seminar provided us with invaluable comments on nearly all facets of our research project. We are very grateful to the conference conveners, Jeffry Frieden and Kenneth Sheplse, the two discussants, Eric Chaney and James Fearon, and the distinguished audience. The second inflection point was a breakfast conversation with Joel Mokyr at Northwestern University in October 2015. This conversation was critical to our thinking about the different channels through which warfare could "translate" into wealth in Europe over the long run. We greatly thank Joel for his insights. The final inflection point was the daylong book workshop at the California Institute of Technology in October 2016. This workshop provided us with many thoughtful comments on ways to improve the book manuscript. We are incredibly grateful to the workshop convener, Jean-Laurent Rosenthal, and to the participants: Lisa Blaydes, Daniel Bogart, Gary Cox, Maura Dykstra, Philip Hoffman, Margaret Peters, Jared Rubin, Richard von Glahn, and R. Bin Wong.

Beyond such turning points, we extend special thanks to Kenneth Scheve and David Stasavage for their helpful comments on our book proposal. Similarly, we thank Robert Dreesen for his attentive and enthusiastic direction of the publication process at Cambridge University Press. We also thank two anonymous readers for their numerous useful suggestions.

A vast number of colleagues have offered valuable comments and data toward this research project over the past several years. We thank Robert Bates, Pablo Beramendi, Timothy Besley, Carles Boix, Roberto Bonfatti, Catherine Boone, Massimo Bordignon, Maarten Bosker, Eltjo Buringh, William Roberts Clark, Daniel Corstange, Christian Davenport, Jeremiah Dittmar, Edward Glaeser, Anna Grzymala-Busse, Nahomi Ichino, Eliana La Ferrara, Horacio Larreguy, Walter Mebane, James Morrow, Tommaso Nannicini, Nathan Nunn, Scott Page, Torsten Persson, Paul Rhode, Frédéric Robert-Nicoud, James Robinson, Hugh Rockoff, Thorsten Rogall, Frances Rosenbluth, David Soskice, Guido Tabellini, Ugo Troiano, Jan Luiten van Zanden, Hans-Joachim Voth, Leonard Wantchekon, Barry Weingast, Warren Whatley, Julian Wucherpfennig, and Daniel Ziblatt.

Similarly, a great many seminar and conference participants have provided perceptive feedback on different parts of this research project. We thank audiences at the University of Birmingham, Bocconi University, the University of Bristol, the California Institute of Technology, UC Berkeley, UC Davis, University College London, the University of Geneva, George Mason University, Harvard University, the London School of Economics, the University of Michigan, the University of Modena, the New Economic School, Northwestern University, the University of Nottingham, the Paris School of Economics, Queen Mary University, Stanford University, the Vancouver School of Economics, the American Economic Association Annual Meeting (2014), the American Political Science Association Annual Meetings (2014, 2015, 2016), the Barcelona GSE Summer Forum (2014), the Conflict and Development Conference at UC Irvine (2016), the Economic History Association Annual Meeting

(2014), the Economic History Society Annual Conference (2014), the European Political Science Association Annual Conference (2015), the European Historical Economics Society Annual Conference (2013), the International Political Economy Society Annual Conferences (2013, 2015), the International Society for New Institutional Economics Annual Conference (2013), the Midwest Political Science Association Annual Conferences (2014, 2015), the One Hundred Flowers Conference at UC Berkeley (2014), the Petralia Sottana Workshop (2013), the Political Economy of Social Conflict Conference at Yale University (2015), the Political Economy Workshop at the Università Cattolica del Sacro Cuore (2014), the PRIN Bologna Workshop (2013), the Spring Meeting of Young Economists (2013), the State-Making Workshop at Lund University (2016), and the World Economic History Congress (2015). In addition, we thank our coauthors on two related projects: Traviss Cassidy and James Fenske. We also thank a host of industrious librarians – Tania Iannizzi, David Medeiros, Nicole Sholtz, and Caterina Tangheroni – and research assistants – Nicola Fontana, Maiko Heller, Giovanni Marin, Corey Miles, and Michael Rochlitz.

We are very fortunate to have received generous funding for this research project from several sources. Without such funding, our project would have never come to fruition. We thank the Department of Political Science at the University of Michigan, and in particular the former and current Department Chairs Charles Shipan and Nancy Burns. Similarly, we thank the Hoover Institution at Stanford University, where Mark was the Edward Teller National Fellow during 2016–17, and in particular Director Thomas Gilligan and Senior Fellows Stephen Haber and Jonathan Rodden. We also thank the National Science Foundation (Grant SES-1227237) and the ADVANCE Faculty Summer Writing Grants Program at the University of Michigan.

We dedicate this book to family: Mark to Kimberly, Julien, and Nico; and Massimiliano to Jessica. Without their love and support, this research project would have been not only impossible but also not worth undertaking. Massimiliano offers special thanks to his late grandfather, Antonio, whose wisdom continues to help guide him through life's challenges.

I

Introduction

The process of modern economic development first began in Europe.[1] Yet modern Europe's most prosperous zones are located exactly where for hundreds of years military conflict was most rampant. Italy exemplifies this paradox. Today, northern Italian regions are wealthy, while many southern Italian regions remain poor.[2] Average per capita GDP is more than 50 percent higher in the north (Table 1.1). However, northern regions saw far more historical warfare than did southern regions. Between 1000 and 1799, there were nearly three times as many recorded major conflicts in the north (Table 1.1). For perspective, the typical modern civil war increases the amount of citizens who live in absolute poverty by 30 percent (Collier et al., 2003: 17). If warfare inevitably spawns a legacy of poverty, however, then how can we explain the robust positive relationship between historical warfare and regional prosperity today in Italy? In our view, any convincing account of Europe's "economic miracle" (Jones, 2003) must make sense of the apparent contradiction between wealth on the one hand and warfare on the other.

This book provides an explanation for Europe's puzzling historical path from warfare to wealth. Our argument runs as follows. The ninth-century fall of the Carolingian Empire gave rise to a high level of political fragmentation in Europe.[3] From (at least) this point onward, warfare was an enduring feature of Europe's historical landscape. Historical warfare inflicted many costs on rural populations. A basic historical function of the city was security. To mitigate the rural costs of conflict, rural populations migrated to urban centers. Following Glaeser and Shapiro (2002: 208), we call this phenomenon the "safe harbor effect." Over time, the city's historical role as a safe harbor translated into local economic

TABLE 1.1 *Historical Warfare and Per Capita GDP Today: Northern versus Southern Italy*

	Total Number of Conflicts, 1000–1799	Average Per Capita GDP (PPS), 2001–5
North	86	27,463
South	30	17,930

Notes: Per capita GDP (purchasing power standard units) is averaged over each NUTS2 region in the north and south, respectively. Historical warfare sums the number of recorded major conflicts over 1000–1799 within each NUTS2 region in the north and south, respectively. We describe our conflict database in detail in Chapter 2. We define the north and the south according to Malanima (1998: 95). "North" refers to the regions of Emilia Romagna, Liguria, Lombardy, Piedmont (including the Aosta Valley), and Veneto (including Friuli Venezia Giulia). "South" refers to the regions of Abruzzo, Apulia, Basilicata, Calabria, Campania, and Lazio.
Sources: Bradbury (2004) and Clodfelter (2002) for historical warfare and Eurostat (http://ec.europa.eu/eurostat) for per capita GDP.

development through several channels: the establishment of local privileges, including self-governance and property rights protections from predatory outside rulers; technological innovation and human capital accumulation; and economic agglomeration effects. We label this process the "warfare-to-wealth effect."

We focus on historical development at the city level (versus the national level) for this reason: urban development underpins national economic development (Glaeser, 2011: 1–2; Glaeser and Millett Steinberg, 2016: 4–7). Figure 1.1 illustrates the strong positive correlation between the urbanization rate and per capita GDP across modern-day nations.[4] Contemporary Europe's economic backbone is the urban belt – the regional urban corridor that runs from southern England to northern Italy through Belgium, the Netherlands, and parts of France and Germany (Figure 1.2). Average per capita GDP today is nearly 40 percent higher in the urban belt than the nonurban belt (Table 1.2). Modern Europe is predominantly urban (United Nations, 2015: 10), but things were not always this way. After the fall of the Carolingian Empire roughly one millennium ago, Europe's urbanization rate was approximately 3 percent (van Bavel, Bosker, Buringh, and van Zanden, 2013: 394). To truly understand the roots of long-run prosperity in

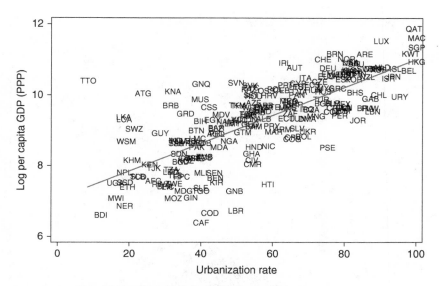

FIGURE I.I Per Capita GDP and the Urbanization Rate, 2015
Notes: Log per capita GDP is based on purchasing power parity (PPP). Urbanization rate is the percentage of the population living in urban zones as defined by national offices of statistics.
Source: World Bank (http://data.worldbank.org).

Europe, therefore, we must explain the historical transformation from countryside to city.

Our book has implications for three long-standing questions in the social sciences. First, which factors explain the economic rise of Europe? Second, where does state capacity come from? Third, are the lessons drawn from the European development experience universal?

To explain, we now trace each step of the book's argument according to the flowchart in Figure 1.3.

POLITICAL FRAGMENTATION

The book's period of analysis starts in the aftermath of the ninth-century fall of the Carolingian Empire, which gave rise to (or restored) a high level of political fragmentation (Strayer, 1970: 15; Hoffman, 2015: 123). Tilly (1992: 45) estimates that there were upward of 500 independent states in late medieval Europe. Average state size was small, at approximately 25,000 square kilometers – roughly equivalent to the size of modern-day

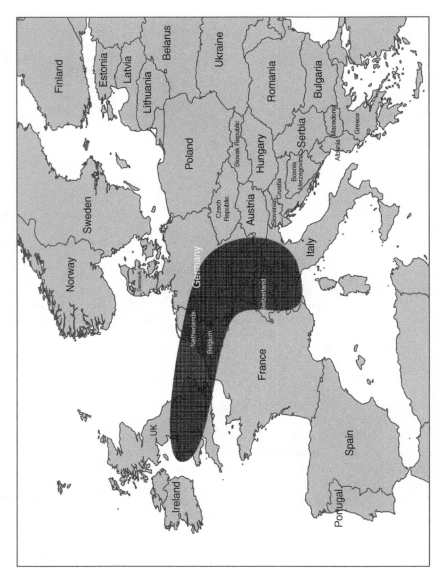

FIGURE 1.2 Europe's Urban Belt
Note: We base this map on Polèse (2009: xv).

TABLE 1.2 *Per Capita GDP: Urban Belt versus Nonurban Belt*

	Urban Belt 2001–5	Nonurban Belt 2001–5
Per Capita GDP (PPS)	26,002	18,907
Observations	56	203

Note: Per capita GDP data for NUTS2 regions is averaged over 2001–5 (using purchasing power standard units).
Source: Eurostat (http://ec.europa.eu/eurostat).

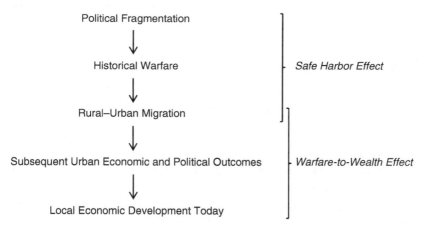

FIGURE 1.3 From Warfare to Wealth: Flowchart

El Salvador or Armenia (Tilly, 1992: 45). The high political fragmentation that resulted from the fall of Charlemagne's empire made instability and warfare more likely (van Zanden, 2009: 34), thereby increasing the city's importance as a safe harbor.

Scholars have analyzed the relationship between political fragmentation and long-run economic and political development in Europe. Jones (2003: 104–26) contends that the high historical dispersion of economic and political power was advantageous, because no central authority could impose policy decisions that would block progress for the "states system" as a whole.[5] According to Landes (1998: 29–44), historical political fragmentation promoted "preemptive" good governance, in order to prevent individuals from switching allegiances from one polity to another.[6] Mokyr (1995: 17–19) relates historical inter-unit competition between states to technological innovations for the states system overall.[7] However, this literature does not study the implications of political fragmentation and warfare for the historical transformation from countryside to city, which we do in this book.

RURAL–URBAN MIGRATION

The economic effects of modern-day migration can be large. Clemens (2011: 85), for example, finds that the potential gains from lifting international policy barriers to labor mobility today range from 50 to 150 percent of world GDP. In European history, de Vries (1984: 222) calls migration the "linchpin of the urban economy and regulator of urban growth." We now review different explanations for historical urbanization in Europe with respect to our argument.

War-Related Migration

Several explanations for urbanization patterns in European history highlight political fragmentation and warfare.

Blaydes and Paik (2016) focus on the role of the Holy Land Crusades over the 1100s and 1200s. According to their argument, Crusader travels between northwest Europe and the Mediterranean Holy Land helped integrate the former region into east–west trade networks, because merchants could exchange textile products for luxury goods, including silk, spices, and porcelain. In turn, urban centers in the northwest (e.g., Bruges) became important trade hubs, promoting city population growth. Voightländer and Voth (2013a, 2013b) highlight the fourteenth-century Black Death (1347–50), which killed at least 30 percent of Europe's total population (Boone, 2013: 229). They contend that, by depleting the rural population, wages in the countryside rose. In turn, there was greater demand for urban manufactured goods, which promoted urbanization and trade. By helping spread disease, warfare kept mortality rates high. Thus, the interactions between disease, urbanization, and warfare help explain medieval Europe's economic takeoff.

Both the Holy Land Crusades and the Black Death were undoubtedly important historical events. Rather than analyze the consequences of a specific historical shock, however, we study the general process by which warfare promoted rural–urban migration in preindustrial Europe as a whole. Furthermore, unlike Blaydes and Paik (2016), we study the consequences of within-Europe or "nearby" warfare – versus overseas or "faraway" warfare – for historical urbanization patterns.

Rosenthal and Wong (2011: 99–128) offer the argument that is the closest in spirit to ours. They contend that historical warfare induced an urban bias to artisanal activity in Europe. In contrast to agricultural activity, artisanal activity was not intrinsically bound to the land. Artisanal capital was not only mobile, but also prone to looting by troops along the war march. Thus, rural artisans under war threats preferred to relocate capital behind the relative safety of urban fortifications. Because of high urban wages and low borrowing costs, new urban manufacturers then had an incentive to substitute capital for labor, thereby promoting technological change.

We go beyond Rosenthal and Wong's contribution in several ways. First, we put forth new types of qualitative evidence to document the city's historical role as a safe harbor. Second, we develop a new conceptual framework to explain the relationship between historical warfare and long-run economic development. In our account, urban capital bias is only one of a handful of channels through which the city's role as a safe harbor could improve local economic performance. Third, we construct a new quantitative database that spans one thousand years, from the aftermath of the fall of the Carolingian Empire to the present day. Our effort to collect such a complete database makes this book stand out relative to much of the previous literature, and not just Rosenthal and Wong. To the best of our knowledge, our database is the first attempt to identify and geocode all major military conflicts fought on land in pre-industrial Europe. Fourth, we favor systematic methods, including statistical analysis, which enable us to reach well-grounded conclusions. In particular, systematic methods enable us to control for many of the alternative explanations put forth by previous scholars. Thus, we can have greater confidence that our results are a true reflection of our argument and are not spurious.

Geographical Endowments

Beyond political fragmentation and warfare, scholars including White (1962: 39–78), Pirenne (1969: 77–105), Rokkan (1975: 575–91), Tilly (1992: 17–19), and Hohenberg and Lees (1995: 18–19) highlight the importance of geographical endowments for historical urbanization in Europe.[8]

According to this classic view, urbanization patterns are at base a function of agricultural conditions and transportation access. To feed a nonagricultural population, the agricultural sector must be productive enough to generate a food surplus. High-quality soil enhances agricultural productivity and makes urban agglomerations possible. Urban agglomerations in turn promote artisanal and entrepreneurial activity. To facilitate commerce, trade routes are important. Urban leaders can build upon early economic success through agglomeration effects, which foster further development. Over time, urban leaders become richer, while places with poor geographical endowments fall behind. In the context of medieval Europe, the geographical endowments hypothesis contends that the central corridor that runs from the Low Countries to northern Italy through eastern France and western Germany was the most favorably endowed, because the soil was high quality and there was easy access to river trade routes. Thus, geographical endowments may explain why this corridor became urbanized from the medieval period onward.

While the focus on geographical endowments is plausible, however, we argue that this hypothesis cannot fully account for historical urbanization patterns. First, this view overlooks the Roman legacy of medieval city locations (Hohenberg and Lees, 1995: 22; Verhulst, 1999: 1, 21–3; Boone, 2013: 221–2). Even if urban centers saw decay after the Roman Empire's fall, they did not typically disappear (Boone, 2013: 222). By serving as a "geographical magnet," Roman fortifications helped determine the location of medieval towns (Verhulst, 1999: 22). Roman towns were typically founded for administrative and military purposes that were no longer relevant by the medieval period (Verhulst, 1999: 23). In this regard, medieval city locations display the "footprint of history" whereby a somewhat obsolete endowment – namely, Roman bureaucratic concerns – continued to influence urban placement (Bleakley and Lin, 2015: 558).

Second, the geographical endowments hypothesis omits the "accidental" way in which the geopolitical partitioning of Charlemagne's empire over the ninth century influenced medieval urbanization patterns (Ganshof, 1971: 289–98; Verhulst, 1999: 155; Stasavage, 2011: 95–100). The ninth-century custom was partible inheritance by the ruler's sons, making dynastic successions vulnerable to idiosyncratic disputes. In the aftermath of the Carolingian partitioning, the former border zones of West and East Francia became relatively large and stable kingdoms, while the former Carolingian core of Lotharingia – the central corridor that forms Europe's urban belt today – became politically fragmented.

The need to split the territory equally between the three heirs was the apparent basis for the Carolingian partitioning – not ethnic, linguistic, political, or religious borders (Ganshof, 1971: 289–98).

Third, the geographical endowments hypothesis discounts the role of endogenous food production in medieval and early modern Europe. According to the geographical endowments view, only locations with the right agricultural conditions could produce enough food to support an urban population. Food production, however, was endogenous in the medium run – if not the short run – because urban centers could make agricultural innovations (Bairoch, 1988: 336–40). An example is convertible husbandry, developed in fifteenth-century urban Flanders, which Mokyr (1995: 11) calls "one of the most important productivity-enhancing innovations in Europe agriculture." Beyond agricultural innovations, city growth itself could facilitate commercial agriculture (Smith, 2008: 257–8; Bates, 2010: 36–7; Rosenthal and Wong, 2011: 46). Furthermore, urban centers could sometimes exchange goods and services for food imports, thereby divorcing themselves from local agricultural limits (Hohenberg and Lees, 1995: 127; Smith, 2008: 254; Rosenthal and Wong, 2011: 46). Describing early modern Europe, de Vries (1984: 244) writes that the "apparently spectacular increase in agricultural productivity suggests that urbanization did not really face a ceiling to its expansion . . ."

Overall, this discussion indicates that the geographical endowments hypothesis, while plausible, does not entirely explain historical urbanization patterns in Europe. Still, our analysis will account for local geographical characteristics in several ways.

FROM WARFARE TO WEALTH

There are several channels through which the city's historical role as a safe harbor could translate into long-run economic development: (1) the establishment of local privileges, including self-governance and property rights protections from predatory outside rulers; (2) technological innovation and human capital accumulation; and (3) economic agglomeration effects. We now describe each channel, one by one.

Local Privileges

The first channel expands Rosenthal and Wong's (2011) argument as recounted earlier. We argue that artisans and entrepreneurs under the threat of warfare could not only move their capital behind the relative safety of urban fortifications, but could also take advantage of local privileges granted as parts of political bargains with sovereign rulers who sought new funds to meet military-related demands (Tilly, 1994: 11, 24; Bates, 2010: 44–6; Blockmans and t'Hart, 2013: 425–7; Hoffman, 2015: 21–2). Such privileges included personal freedoms, self-governance through parliamentary institutions, and legal authorizations that protected private property rights from outside predation (Blockmans and t'Hart, 2013: 426).

Scholars have analyzed the relationship between national-level political institutions that checked royal power and long-run economic development in Europe. De Long and Shleifer (1993) show evidence that preindustrial economic growth was faster under non-absolutist governments – which they argue were better protectors of private property rights, due to institutional checks on royal power – than under absolutist governments. Acemoglu, Johnson, and Robinson (2005) relate economic development in preindustrial Europe to the interaction between the growth of Atlantic trade and the development of parliamentary government at the national level. In nations with relatively non-absolutist medieval political institutions (e.g., England), Atlantic trade enabled merchant elites to become economically powerful enough to demand political reforms that placed even greater checks on royal power. Executive checks made private property rights more secure. In turn, merchant elites were more willing to make new investments and expand trade, thereby promoting economic growth.[9]

The focus by De Long and Shleifer (1993) and Acemoglu, Johnson, and Robinson (2005) on historical development at the national level makes sense. The nation-state is the most common political unit today. Furthermore, historical data – always in rare supply – are more widely available at this level than at the local level. This focus, however, hides regional variations in historical development within nations. As described earlier, modern Europe's economic backbone is the urban corridor that spans southern England, Belgium and the Netherlands, eastern France and western Germany, and northern Italy. Thus, in our view, it is just as important to understand which historical factors influenced *local* development patterns as it is to understand which factors influenced development patterns at the national level.

Scholars have in fact analyzed the historical relationship between local political institutions and economic development within Europe. Van Zanden, Buringh, and Bosker (2012) construct a measure of medieval parliamentary activity at the regional level. They find a positive correlation between regional parliamentary activity – which they argue placed checks on predatory outside rulers – and historical development. Similarly, Stasavage (2014) develops a historical measure of local self-governance. He finds that city autonomy promoted economic growth over the short run but reduced it over the long run. He argues that, over time, merchant elites could implement entry limits into their professions, thereby blocking innovation. We further discuss Stasavage's results in Chapter 3.[10]

De Long and Shleifer (1993), Acemoglu, Johnson, and Robinson (2005), van Zanden, Buringh, and Bosker (2012) and Stasavage (2014) all urbanization rates to proxy for historical development, even if historical urbanization patterns per se are not of principal interest to them. By contrast, we focus on the actual process by which historical warfare promoted rural–urban migration. In our view, historical city population growth is a fundamental outcome in and of itself, because it strikes at the heart of any explanation about the long-run development of the urban belt, modern Europe's economic backbone. Furthermore, unlike van Zanden, Buringh, and Bosker (2012) and Stasavage (2014), we do not take local political institutions as exogenous explanatory variables. As described here, we view local freedoms including self-governance as important parts of political bargains granted by rulers in response to political fragmentation and warfare.

Warfare and State Making

By analyzing how historical warfare promoted rural–urban migration, our book expands our understanding of the relationship between warfare and state making. Warfare is a prominent explanation for nation-state development in Europe.[11] According to Tilly (1992: 67–95), historical governments undertook political and fiscal reforms that enabled them to finance greater military efforts and better defend against survival threats from rival states.[12] Tilly's (1975: 42) well-known expression is "War made the state, and the state made war." Our book shows that, prior to the development of the nation-state, warfare helped "make the city" in literal terms by promoting rural–urban migration. In this regard, we provide a new perspective about how historical warfare drove social change in Europe.

Furthermore, by studying the relationship between historical warfare and rural–urban migration, we improve our overall understanding of the state development process. Dincecco (2011, 2015) evaluates institutional development in Europe at the nation-state level from the seventeenth century onward. He argues that state development proceeded in two major steps. Following a long and arduous process, effective national governments were established by the nineteenth century. Such governments had high extractive and productive powers, enabling them to gather enough revenues to accomplish their intended policy actions, while spending public funds in ways (e.g., transportation infrastructure) that were likely to support economic development. What Dincecco's perspective omits, however, is an analysis of the "front end" of the state-making process in Europe, which our book provides. As described earlier, this book explains how warfare helped "make the city." The rise of the city preceded the rise of the nation-state in important ways (Blockmans, 1994: 220). Institutional developments at the city level were oftentimes historical precursors to nation-state level innovations. City-states pioneered representative government, not nation-states (Stasavage, 2011: 47–68; van Zanden, Buringh, and Bosker, 2012; Blockmans and t'Hart, 2013: 430–3). Similarly, city-states were the first to establish long-term public debts (Stasavage, 2011: 25–46). By studying the relationship between historical warfare and city development, this book sheds new light on the start of the state formation process in Europe. In turn, we gain a more complete view of how the modern state was made (Figure 1.4).[13]

Playing off of Tilly's (1975: 42) well-known expression that "war made the state," Morris (2014: 8) writes that "war made governments, and governments made peace." He argues that warfare created larger states, because the winners had to govern the losers (Morris, 2014: 3–26). To enforce order over larger groups, governments became more powerful. Powerful governments in turn promoted domestic peace, which facilitated economic development.[14] In the context of preindustrial Europe, order and

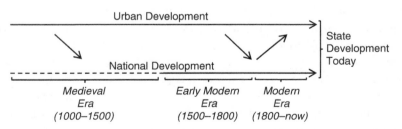

FIGURE 1.4 Historical State Development in Europe: Urban Level versus National Level
Notes: Historical institutional development in Europe took place at the city level from the medieval era onward, influencing institutional development at the national level. Institutional development today in Europe is a product of historical institutional development at both levels. For further details, see the text.

routine was synonymous with the city – and not necessarily with the nation-state (Friedrichs, 1995: 245–6). It seems likely that urban order was at least in part an outgrowth of the city's historical role as a safe harbor. Thus, by studying the process by which historical warfare promoted urban development, our analysis helps illustrate the logic of Morris's argument at the local level. Given that the city could procure internal stability prior to the nation-state, this perspective fleshes out the roots of the process by which government can make society safer and richer.[15]

Some urban centers maintained their autonomy through the 1700s (Stasavage, 2014: 343). By the second half of the eighteenth century, however, the nation-state had become the dominant political unit in Europe (Tilly, 1992: 45–7; Blockmans, 1994: 220; Spruyt, 1994a: 554–7). The nation-state's growing capacity to secure peace over large territorial units reduced the importance of the city's historical role as a safe harbor. Deep changes to the nature of warfare over the 1800s – including technological improvements such as the railway and telegraph and the rise of the mass army (Onorato, Scheve, and Stasavage, 2014) – further weakened the city's ability to fulfill its traditional security role.

By overcoming institutional fragmentation within large territorial units, national governments could promote economic development (e.g., Dincecco and Katz, 2016). We view effective governance at the national level as the continuation of the process of good governance first developed at the city level in Europe (Figure 1.4).

Technological Innovation and Human Capital Accumulation

Regarding the second channel for transformation from safe harbor to economic development, we argue that, due to the advantages of urban density, war-related rural–urban migration could promote both technological innovation and human capital accumulation. Scholars have analyzed the historical relationship between these factors and economic development in Europe. Dittmar (2011) relates the fifteenth-century invention of the moveable type printing press in Mainz to subsequent city population growth. He argues that the printing press promoted the acquisition of valuable business skills, including greater numeracy, entrepreneurial education, and book-keeping improvements. Becker and Woessmann (2009) analyze the relationship between the sixteenth-century Protestant Reformation and subsequent economic development in Prussia. Unlike Max Weber (1992: 13–38), who highlighted the "Protestant work ethic," Becker and Woessmann focus on the effect of

Protestantism on universal education. They contend that widespread literacy among Protestants improved economic productivity. Cantoni and Yuchtman (2014) study the relationship between university legal training and the revival of commerce in medieval Germany. Due to the Papal Schism of 1378, the French academy became intolerant of German faculty and students loyal to the Roman pope. To accommodate them, the pontiff promoted higher education in Germany, which Cantoni and Yuchtman argue improved university access for many Germans. In turn, a greater amount of administrators were trained in Roman law, reducing trade risks and promoting commercial exchange.

Although we acknowledge the historical importance of the printing press, the Protestant Reformation, and university establishment, our book brings to bear on urban development in Europe the role of warfare – an endemic historical feature that does not play a starring role in any of the accounts we have described.

Economic Agglomeration Effects

Regarding the third channel, we argue that war-related rural–urban migration could promote economic agglomeration effects beyond the flow of ideas. Urban density reduces production costs, encourages the division of labor, and fosters thick labor markets (Fujita and Thisse, 2002: 5–11; Glaeser and Joshi-Ghani, 2015: xx–xxi). Our book analyzes the process by which historical warfare promoted urban development. In turn, we improve our understanding of the roots of economic agglomeration effects in Europe today (Ciccone, 2002).

THE GREAT DIVERGENCE

Numerous scholars have analyzed the "Great Divergence" whereby Europe took off economically but China fell behind after 1800. To explain this phenomenon, Pomeranz (2000) highlights the role of colonial exploitation and slavery. Both early modern China and Europe faced ecological limits to further economic growth (e.g., fuel shortages, reduced soil fertility), which European nations solved through colonialization. By holding colonial markets captive, European nations forced the economic periphery in the "New World" to exchange natural resources for manufactured goods, thereby promoting technological change in the European core.[16] Free labor, by contrast, characterized the economic periphery in East Asia, meaning that peripheral nations there could always decide to undertake proto-industrialization of their own. In turn, there was not only lower demand by the Asian periphery for manufactured goods from China, but also a lack of raw materials available for export to it.

Allen's (2009) account of the Great Divergence emphasizes domestic factors specific to eighteenth-century England, where labor costs were very high but energy costs were low. England's unique price environment influenced both the demand and the supply for technological change there. To reduce production costs, English entrepreneurs had a strong incentive to replace labor with machinery and energy (e.g., the steam engine). Moreover, high wages enabled individuals in England to invest in education, increasing literacy and numeracy and making technological innovations more likely. In China, by contrast, labor costs were low and energy costs were high, reducing the impetus for technological change.

Mokyr's (2002) explanation of the Great Divergence focuses on intellectual developments unique to early modern Europe. He argues that there are two types of knowledge: propositional (what we know about natural phenomena) and prescriptive (what we know about techniques). According to Mokyr, the seventeenth-century Scientific Revolution in Europe expanded the base of propositional knowledge. Due to the codification of this new knowledge base, the eighteenth-century "Industrial Enlightenment" reduced the access costs to best-practice techniques. Low access costs, in turn, produced a self-reinforcing spiral of both propositional and prescriptive knowledge, generating a European wave of technological innovations.

Greif and Tabellini (2015) analyze the roots of social cooperation in China and Europe. They contend that religious differences between these two world regions were evident by 1000. Such differences had implications for the diverse ways in which each society thought about morality, promoting kin-oriented morality in China and impersonal-oriented morality in Europe. Under kin-oriented morality, the clan was the most natural way to enforce cooperation, relying on dispute resolution by clan elders. Under impersonal-oriented morality, by contrast, the corporation was the most efficient way, relying on formal procedures such as legal codes. Over time, the initial importance of clans as a cooperation device strengthened kin obligations in China, while the initial importance of corporations reinforced the rule of law in Europe, thereby promoting persistent cultural differences. Kin-oriented morality meant that public goods provision would be better organized within the clan than the city. The share of individuals in society who subscribed to kin-oriented morality was high in China, making the clan attractive as the main public goods provider and thereby reducing city size. In Europe, the opposite chain of logic held, driving up city size.

The arguments made by Pomeranz (2000), Mokyr (2002), Allen (2009), and Greif and Tabellini (2015) provide a sampling of the different ways in which scholars have attempted to explain the Great Divergence. Such arguments significantly improve our understanding of this critical phenomenon. Nonetheless, each downplays important parts of the long-run development experience in Europe relative to other world regions. Pomeranz's (2000) emphasis on core-periphery relations tends to overlook the historical roles of political fragmentation, endemic warfare, and the establishment of local freedoms within Europe itself. Unlike Pomeranz, both Mokyr (2002) and Allen (2009) stress domestic conditions particular to Europe. Yet they too discount the historical importance of warfare and politics. Furthermore, all three works focus their analysis at the level of the nation-state or higher. Greif and Tabellini (2015) explicitly relate their argument to historical trends in city population growth. To explain rural–urban migration, however, they do not leave a clear role for political fragmentation and warfare.[17]

By analyzing the relationship between historical warfare and urban development in comparative perspective, our book provides a new way to think about the economic and political divergence between Europe and other world regions. To illustrate, we now provide a sketch of our comparative argument. We view this argument as a first step in a research agenda that examines the long-run economic consequences of warfare across the globe rather than as the last word in such a debate. We focus on China and sub-Saharan Africa, two world regions that differ economically and politically from Europe but are relatively comparable in terms of physical size.

Europe versus China

Premodern China was not only huge in size, but also faced a largely unidirectional attack threat from nomads from the Eurasian Steppe (Ko, Koyama, and Sng, 2014: 46; Hoffman, 2015: 70–1, 74–5). Relative to China, high political fragmentation in preindustrial Europe induced greater conflict risk in the form of multidimensional attack threats, making city relocation more likely. Rural–urban migration was in fact lower in early modern China than in Europe during the same period (Winter, 2013:

405; Xu, van Leeuwen, and van Zanden, 2015: 15). Furthermore, unlike in China, political fragmentation and warfare often induced European rulers to grant local political and legal privileges to urban elites in exchange for new tax funds, thereby promoting a business environment that was favorable to economic development. Credible threats by urban elites in Europe to switch allegiances from one city or polity to another further enhanced their bargaining power vis-à-vis rulers.

Europe versus Sub-Saharan Africa

According to Akyeampong et al. (2014: 1), sub-Saharan Africa is the "development challenge of our time." Civil conflicts or wars took place in roughly one-third of all sub-Saharan African nations over the 1990s (Blattman and Miguel, 2010: 4). Precolonial sub-Saharan Africa was thinly populated, with only two people per square kilometer in 1500 (Herbst, 2000: 16). Given such a high land-labor ratio, rural inhabitants may have preferred to migrate to faraway virgin land in the face of nearby conflict rather than seek safety behind urban fortifications, a phenomenon that Herbst (2000: 39) calls the "primacy of exit." By contrast, the land-labor ratio in preindustrial Europe was relatively low, making it more likely that the city would function as a safe harbor in wartime. Consistent with this argument, urbanization in precolonial sub-Saharan Africa was low relative to that of Europe (Weil, 2014: 94–5).

The high historical land-labor ratio, moreover, may have contributed to an "enduring-warfare effect" in sub-Saharan Africa (Bates, 2008: 85; Reid, 2012: 10; Besley and Reynal-Querol, 2014). Unlike in Europe, the main goal of warfare in land-rich but labor-scarce sub-Saharan Africa was to capture slaves (Thornton, 1999: 16; Herbst, 2000: 42–3; Reid, 2012: 4–5). Precolonial sub-Saharan Africa's high land-labor ratio – and the traditional "raiding" style of warfare that it spawned – may have been more likely to promote open-ended conflict, particularly in combination with the transatlantic slave trade (Whatley and Gillezeau, 2011).

PLAN

We present our main argument, along with the core questions in the social sciences that we address, in this chapter. The rest of the book proceeds as follows. In Chapter 2 we describe the importance of historical warfare in Europe, drawing on the new conflict database that we have constructed. We make the historical case for the safe harbor effect and the warfare-to-wealth effect, respectively, in Chapter 3. Chapter 4 contains our statistical analysis of the safe harbor effect, while Chapter 5 consists of this analysis for the warfare-to-wealth effect. In Chapter 6 we analyze the European development experience in comparative perspective. The Epilogue provides reflection on the implications of the book's results for economic development today.

2

The Importance of Warfare

This chapter offers a new perspective on historical warfare in Europe. To analyze conflict patterns over time and across space, we construct a comprehensive database of military conflicts that spans 800 years of European history. Our database shows that warfare was a central feature of Europe's historical landscape. The analysis in this chapter provides the basis for our subsequent investigation of the relationship between endemic warfare and urban development.

WARFARE'S DOMINANT ROLE

Scholars argue that warfare was a main feature of European history. Gutmann (1980: 4), for example, writes: "For generations of European men, women, and children, war was an element of almost everyday experience." Similarly, describing Renaissance Europe, Hale (1985: 21) states: "There was probably no single year throughout the period in which there was neither a war nor occurrences that looked and felt remarkably like it." Tilly (1992: 72) estimates that major powers in early modern Europe were at war in more than 90 percent of all years over the 1500s and 1600s and nearly 80 percent of all years during the 1700s.[1] Relative to the early modern period, he writes that "European states concentrated even more exclusively on the making of war" over the first half of the millennium (Tilly, 1992: 74).

Government expenditure patterns further illustrate the historical importance of warfare in Europe. Hoffman (2015: 21–2) estimates that early modern governments spent 40–80 percent of total yearly funds on the military.[2] Such percentages increase if one includes funds spent on subsidizing allies and on servicing debts for past wars. For example, median yearly military expenditures exceeded 80 percent in seventeenth-century France, eighteenth-century England, and eighteenth-century Prussia (Hoffman, 2015: 23). In 1780s England, military spending accounted for more than 10 percent of GDP (Hoffman, 2015: 20). By comparison, the United States spent just 5 percent of GDP on the military during the latter part of the Cold War (Hoffman, 2015: 20).

Beyond government expenditures, the development of public credit also reflects warfare's key historical role in Europe. Stasavage (2011: 31–2) shows that city-states were the first to establish long-term public debts (relative to nation-states). In 1241, Arras became the first such polity to take out a long-term loan, followed by Venice (1262), Siena (1290), Bremen (1295), and Douai (1295). By 1400, many city-states had created long-term debts (Stasavage, 2011: 31–2). Warfare was the main reason for this innovation (Stasavage, 2011: 26–9).[3] Stasavage (2011: 29) writes: "Faced with the need to raise finance quickly to respond to military challenges (or opportunities), states found that access to public credit was a critical ingredient for survival and success."

This short overview suggests that warfare was a central feature of European history. We now analyze which factors help explain why historical warfare was so prevalent.

WHY WARFARE?

We focus on three "fundamental" factors that help explain why historical warfare was endemic in Europe. The key factor was the demise of Charlemagne's empire and the political fragmentation that resulted from it. Two other important factors were the quest for glory by rulers and scarce territory.

Fall of the Carolingian Empire

A first fundamental factor was the high level of political fragmentation that resulted from the demise of Charlemagne's empire. This demise took place in multiple steps.[4] Charlemagne died in 814. Only one legitimate son, Louis the Pious, outlived him. The death of Louis the Pious in 840 led to civil war between his three heirs. The Treaty of Verdun of 843 ended this conflict and divided the empire into three kingdoms: (1) West Francia, centered on modern-day France; (2)

Middle Francia, the corridor that ran from the Low Countries to northern Italy; and (3) East Francia, centered on modern-day Germany. Lothar I, ruler of Middle Francia, divided his kingdom between his three heirs in 855 in the face of serious illness. One heir received northern Italy; the second, the French region of Provence; and the third, the northwestern territory called Lotharingia that ran from the Low Countries into western Germany. The Treaty of Meersen of 870 divided Lotharingia between West and East Francia. Airlie (1998) argues that Lotharingia was short-lived because of a royal marital dispute. Lothar II, king of Lotharingia from 855 to 869, wished to divorce his wife and marry his mistress, but he died of fever before this marriage was declared legitimate, leading to the division of his kingdom.

This account of the fall of the Carolingian empire suggests that there was a role reversal by the start of the tenth century. While the former border zones of West and East Francia became relatively large and stable kingdoms, the former Carolingian core of Lotharingia became politically fragmented. Indeed, Stasavage (2011: 102) finds a positive correlation between a city's location in Lotharingia and its subsequent status as an autonomous political unit. Strayer (1970: 15) writes, "Fragmentation proceeded at different rates and to different degrees in each part of the old Frankish realm, but it went so far that by the year 1000 it would have been difficult to find anything like a state anywhere on the continent of Europe (except for the Byzantine Empire)."

The high level of political fragmentation that resulted from the fall of Charlemagne's empire was long lasting.[5] Hale (1985: 14), for example, describes the political geography of the Holy Roman Empire in 1450 as follows: "In spite of the border which a cartographer can draw around the area which opinion in the mid-fifteenth century accepted as within the Holy Roman Empire, that is the chiefly Germanic zone between France and Hungary, and Denmark and northern Italy, he cannot color in the multitude of cities, princely enclaves and military ecclesiastical territories that saw themselves as actually or potentially independent, without giving the readers an impression that he is suffering from a disease of the retina." There were up to 500 independent states in Europe circa 1500 (Tilly, 1992: 45). At approximately 25,000 square kilometers (e.g., the size of modern-day El Salvador or Armenia), average state size was small (Tilly, 1992: 45). Thus, attack threats could emanate from multiple directions. Overall, high political fragmentation made instability and warfare more likely (van Zanden, 2009: 34).

Quest for Glory by Rulers

Another fundamental factor was the quest for glory by rulers. Hoffman (2015: 25) writes: "For the major monarchs of early modern Europe, victory was thus a source of glory or a way to enhance their reputation." From a young age, future rulers were encouraged to focus nearly all of their time and energy on thoughts of war (Hoffman, 2015: 19, 24–5). To illustrate this mind frame, Hoffman (2015: 19, 26) cites historical scholarship by Niccoló Machiavelli and Thomas Hobbes. Machiavelli (1998: 58) states: "Thus, a prince should have no other object, nor any other thought, not take anything else as his art but that of war and its orders and discipline; for that is the only art which is of concern to one who commands." Similarly, Hobbes (1950: 103) writes: "So that in the nature of man, we find three principal causes of quarrel. First, Competition; Secondly, Diffidence; Thirdly, Glory." Importantly, glory was non-divisible. To accrue it, rulers not only had to go to war, but they had to be victorious, thereby reducing the attractiveness of peaceful resolutions (Hoffman, 2015: 28).

Royal ministers could (and did) offer foreign policy advice. However, the decision to go to war was wholly the ruler's to make, prompting Galileo to refer to warfare as "royal sport" (Hale, 1985: 29). Hale (1985: 33) relates the story of Thomas Cromwell, the well-known chief minister of King Henry VIII of England during the 1530s. In 1523, Cromwell – then a member of the House of Commons – wrote a speech to deliver in front of Parliament. This speech made a rational argument against an invasion of France, emphasizing the high monetary costs and England's small capacity to occupy a relatively large polity. Cromwell's points did not dissuade Henry VIII, however, who decided to invade France with England's largest army ever (at the time), in 1544.

This example highlights a fundamental governance dilemma in European history, which Cox (2011: 133–4) labels the "problem of royal moral hazard in warfare." Rulers could gain a great deal from victory in warfare, including glory and war spoils, but did not bear the full weight of war-related losses (Hoffman, 2015: 26–7). Hoffman (2015: 27) shows that, incredibly, major monarchs in Europe never lost their thrones after defeat in war between 1498 and 1789.[6] Thus, rulers had a strong incentive to choose war over peace. Religious fervor – against Muslims, non-European "heathens," and other Christians after the Protestant Reformation – gave European rulers even more incentive to opt for belligerence (Hoffman, 2015: 25).[7]

Scarce Territory

A final fundamental factor was scarce territory. Herbst (2000: 16) estimates that population density in Europe was relatively high, at 14 individuals per square kilometer in 1500. By way of comparison, sub-Saharan Africa did not reach this level of population density until the 1970s (Herbst, 2000: 16). In the context of Renaissance Europe, Hale (1985: 23) writes: "Land, and the 'glory' it brought with it, was a far more potent motive for war than any anticipated economic profit." There was a strong link between social status and land ownership, through both the legal rights and the opportunity for patronage that came with it (Hale, 1985: 22).[8] Sovereign rulers were the largest landowners and acted accordingly. In the words of Hale (1985: 22), "Political Europe was like an estate map, and war was a socially acceptable form of property acquisition."

NEW CONFLICT DATABASE

To quantify historical warfare patterns over time and across space, we construct a new database of major military conflicts fought on land in Europe between 1000 and 1799. This database represents the first attempt to identify and geocode all such conflicts. The start year of our database (1000) occurs in the aftermath of the ninth-century fall of Charlemagne's empire, which splintered Europe into hundreds of independent states (Strayer, 1970: 15; Hoffman, 2015: 123). High political fragmentation made instability and warfare more likely, thereby increasing the city's importance as a safe harbor. The end year of our database (1799) occurs (1) amidst the nation-state's growing ability to secure peace across large territorial units and (2) just before fundamental nineteenth-century changes to the nature of warfare, including technological improvements in communication (e.g., telegraph) and transportation (e.g., railway) and the establishment of the mass army, all of which reduced the city's ability to fulfill its traditional role as a safe harbor (see Chapter 1).

To construct our database, we rely on two comprehensive works by military historians: *The Routledge Companion to Medieval Warfare* (2004) by Bradbury and *Warfare and Armed Conflicts: A Statistical Encyclopedia of Casualties and Other Figures, 1500–2000* (2002) by Clodfelter. These works are among the most exhaustive and detailed sources available for historical warfare. Also, there are several reasons why we prefer Bradbury and Clodfelter to potential alternatives.

The Bradbury text spans the whole medieval period (it stops in 1525) and the entire geographical area of Europe (including Eastern Europe).

Each chapter of Bradbury covers a different geographical zone of medieval warfare. For example, chapter 6 covers "The Holy Roman Empire and Central Europe, 850–1500," while chapter 7 covers "The Byzantine Empire and Eastern Europe, 400–1453." Within each chapter, Bradbury presents short overviews of each major military conflict, including the location, date, and conflict type (e.g., battle). Our database includes all of the conflicts described by Bradbury between 1000 and 1499. Later we provide an example from the Bradbury text.

The Clodfelter text is organized by century and geographical zone worldwide. We focus on warfare in the geographical zones that Clodfelter labels "Western Europe," "Eastern Europe," and the "British Isles." Unlike Bradbury, Clodfelter categorizes individual conflicts under war headings such as the "Thirty Years' War: 1618–48." To identify the major conflicts that make up each war, we read through each war heading in Clodfelter and compose a list of all individual conflicts therein. For example, Table 2.1 presents the 37 major individual conflicts that make up the Thirty Years' War, according to Clodfelter. Our database includes all of the conflicts described by Clodfelter between 1500 (when his data start) and 1799 for the three geographical zones listed earlier. We offer an example later from the Clodfelter text.

In subsequent chapters, we will perform statistical analyses of the safe harbor effect and the warfare-to-wealth effect, respectively. Both analyses call for measures of local conflict exposure. To compute such measures, we must geocode the location of each historical conflict in our database.[9] For geocoding, we make use of the accounts in Bradbury and Clodfelter to identify the settlement – the hamlet, village, town, or city – nearest to each conflict. This method is practical, given that historical accounts cannot always pinpoint exact conflict locations. Furthermore, it is intuitive, because individual conflicts were typically named after nearby settlements.

To illustrate our historical conflict data and construction methods, we now provide two examples of battles – one from Bradbury and the other from Clodfelter. Providing an example from each work also enables us to show that the sorts of conflicts found in the texts are similar in nature.

According to Bradbury (2004: 148), the Battle of Cannae was fought in 1018 between the aristocrat Melus of Bari and Boiannes, the head of the Catepanate of Italy (a province of the Byzantine Empire).[10] Norman mercenaries fought under Melus, while Greeks and the elite Varangian Guard fought under Boiannes, who was victorious. Amatus, an eleventh-century Benedictine monk who wrote an important contemporary history of the Normans in southern Italy, writes that the "Greeks swarmed over

TABLE 2.1 *Major Military Conflicts That Comprise the Thirty Years' War,
1618–48*

No.	Conflict Name	Year	Nearby Settlement	Country
1	Sablat	1619	Budweis	Czech Republic
2	White Hill	1620	Prague	Czech Republic
3	Fleurus	1622	Fleurus	Belgium
4	Hochst	1622	Frankfurt am Main	Germany
5	Wimpfen	1622	Bad Wimpfen	Germany
6	Stadtlohn	1623	Stadtlohn	Germany
7	Breda	1624–5	Breda	Netherlands
8	Bridge of Dessau	1625	Dessau	Germany
9	Lutter	1626	Lutter am Barenberge	Germany
10	Stralsund	1626	Stralsund	Germany
11	Wolgast	1628	Wolgast	Germany
12	Madgeburg	1630–1	Madgeburg	Germany
13	Breitenfeld	1631	Leipzig	Germany
14	Frankfurt (Oder)	1631	Frankfurt (Oder)	Germany
15	Werben	1631	Werben (Elbe)	Germany
16	Lützen	1632	Lützen	Germany
17	Nuremberg	1632	Nuremberg	Germany
18	River Lech	1632	Rain	Germany
19	Nordlingen	1634	Nordlingen	Germany
20	Tornavento	1636	Oleggio	Italy
21	Wittstock	1636	Wittstock	Germany
22	Breda	1637	Breda	Netherlands
23	Leucate	1637	Leucate	France
24	Breisach	1638	Breisach	Germany
25	Fuenterrabia	1638	Hondarribia	Spain
26	Rheinfelden	1638	Rheinfelden	Switzerland
27	Casale	1640	Casale Monferrato	Italy
28	2nd Breitenfeld	1642	Leipzig	Germany
29	Lérida	1642	Lérida	Spain
30	Rocroi	1643	Rocroi	France
31	Freiburg	1644	Freiburg im Breisgau	Germany
32	Allerheim	1645	Allerheim	Germany
33	Jankau	1645	Jankov	Czech Republic
34	Mergentheim	1645	Bad Mergentheim	Germany
35	Lérida	1647	Lérida	Spain
36	Lens	1648	Lens	France
37	Zusmarshausen	1648	Zusmarshausen	Germany

Source: Clodfelter (2002).

the battlefield like bees from an over-full hive" (Bradbury, 2004: 148). This battle took place on the right bank of the Ofanto River, roughly five miles from the Adriatic coast, at Canne della Battaglia, now a ward of the city of Barletta. We therefore assign to it the coordinates of Canne della Battaglia (41° 30' N, 16° 15' E).

The Thirty Years' War started as a religious conflict between Catholic and Protestant powers. The Protestant majority of the kingdom of Bohemia (the predecessor to the modern-day nation of the Czech Republic) did not recognize the newly elected Holy Roman Emperor Ferdinand II, a devout Catholic (Clodfelter, 2002: 35). The war began when two of the emperor's envoys were thrown out of a third-floor window of Hradschin Castle by members of the Diet of Prague – a practice called defenestration. According to Clodfelter (2002: 35), the Battle of White Hill was fought on November 8, 1620, between the Catholic Count of Tilly, Johann Tserclaes, and the Protestant Prince of Anhalt-Bernburg, Christian I. Five thousand Protestant troops were captured or killed, while only 250 Catholic troops were (though hundreds were wounded). In response to this defeat, King Frederick I of Bohemia fled Prague. This battle took place at White Hill, situated on the outskirts of Prague. We therefore assign the coordinates of Prague (50° 08' N, 14° 44' E) to it.

Given the historical nature of the conflict data, there may be measurement error. We address this concern in two ways. First, even if Bradbury and Clodfelter are unable to record all historical conflicts, it is likely that they include the main historical conflicts (as first documented by contemporary scholars such as Amatus). Appendix Table A.1, which presents all sample conflicts from 1000 to 1799 in our database, suggests that the main historical conflicts are well represented. Second, it may still be the case that the quality of data coverage of historical conflicts differs by geographical zone and century. Our statistical analyses in Chapters 4 and 5 will account for local differences in data quality in a variety of ways.

Beyond Bradbury and Clodfelter, Brecke (1999) and Jaques (2007) are two potential alternative sources for historical conflict data. Many scholars, including Iyigun (2008), Pinker (2011), Zhang et al. (2011), Besley and Reynal-Querol (2014), and Morris (2014), have made use of Brecke's data. Specifically, Brecke constructs data for violent conflicts worldwide from 1400 to today. To compute local conflict exposure measures for our statistical analyses, we must geocode the location of each historical conflict (as described earlier). The main shortcoming of Brecke's data in this respect is that his conflict details are somewhat vague. For example, entry number 1297 reads "Emperor-Palatinate, 1618–20." Brecke does not provide any information regarding the specific location (or locations) of this conflict, but Clodfelter does (e.g., the Battle of White Hill of 1620 as described previously). For the purposes of geocoding specific conflict locations, therefore, Bradbury and Clodfelter are superior to Brecke.[11]

Jaques (2007) is a dictionary of battles and sieges worldwide from antiquity to today. Unlike Brecke, Jaques provides specific conflict locations that could in theory be geocoded. The main shortcoming of Jaques's dictionary for our purposes is his laser-beam focus on battles and sieges only. Clodfelter (2002: 1), by contrast, attempts to include every sort of military conflict: "[I]nternational wars and civil wars, internationalized civil wars, limited wars and unlimited wars, border wars and miniwars – as well as those less organized and less sustained, or wholly one-sided outbreaks of mass human violence – riots, revolutions, massacres, bloodbaths, and pogroms." Bradbury's approach is also wide ranging – he includes revolts and sacks in addition to battles and sieges. Bradbury and Clodfelter therefore provide a more complete "universe" of historical conflicts in Europe than Jaques, which is important to our inquiry.[12]

CONFLICT PATTERNS

Table 2.2 presents the descriptive statistics for the historical conflict data. In total, there were more than 850 recorded major conflicts between 1000 and 1799, which averages to more than 100 such conflicts per century. The 1200s experienced the least conflict over this period, with just less than 30 recorded conflicts, while the 1700s experienced the most conflict, with more than 300 recorded conflicts. Overall, the descriptive statistics help substantiate the claims by Hale (1985: 21), Tilly (1992: 72), Parker (1996: 1), Hoffman (2015: 22), and others who argue that warfare was a main feature of European history.

Figure 2.1 maps the locations of all recorded major conflicts over this period. There is a clear overlap between the locus of historical conflicts and today's urban belt, the corridor of urban regions that runs from southern England to northern Italy through the Low Countries and parts of France

TABLE 2.2 *Major Military Conflicts by Century, 1000–1799*

1000–99	1100–99	1200–99	1300–99	1400–99	1500–99	1600–99	1700–99	Total
51	35	29	57	75	122	164	323	856

Note: Land-based conflicts in Europe.
Sources: Bradbury (2004) and Clodfelter (2002).

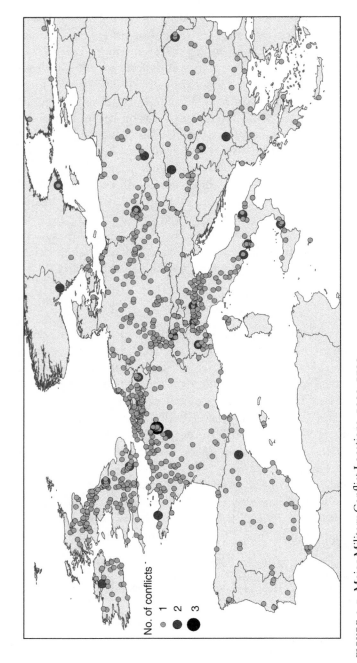

FIGURE 2.1 Major Military Conflict Locations, 1000–1799

Notes: Land-based conflicts. Dot sizes indicate the number of conflicts geocoded to each specific location.

Sources: Bradbury (2004) and Clodfelter (2002).

TABLE 2.3 *Major Military Conflicts by Type,*
1000–1799

Battles	Sieges	Other	Total
492	317	47	856

Notes: Land-based conflicts in Europe. "Other" category includes revolts and sacks.
Sources: Bradbury (2004) and Clodfelter (2002).

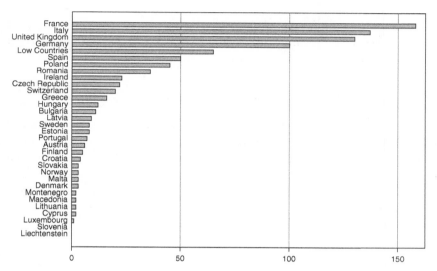

FIGURE 2.2 Major Military Conflicts by Country, 1000–1799
Note: Land-based conflicts in Europe.
Sources: Bradbury (2004) and Clodfelter (2002).

and Germany (see Figure 1.2). To complement this figure, Figure 2.2 breaks down the historical conflict data by modern-day country borders. France experienced the most recorded conflicts within its borders over 1000–1799, with more than 150. Next was Italy, with nearly 140; followed by Britain, with nearly 130; Germany, with 100; and the Low Countries (Belgium and the Netherlands), with more than 60.

Tables 2.3 and 2.4 display recorded major conflicts by type and duration. Battles and sieges account for more than 90 percent of all sample conflicts (Table 2.3). Battles are the most common conflict type, with nearly 500, followed by sieges, with more than 300. Revolts and sacks (labeled

TABLE 2.4 *Major Military Conflicts by Duration,*
1000–1799

	> One Day but ≤ One Year	> One Year	Total
≤ One Day			
456	360	40	856

Note: Land-based conflicts in Europe.
Sources: Bradbury (2004) and Clodfelter (2002).

"Other") account for the other 40-plus recorded conflicts. The majority of recorded conflicts endured one day or less (Table 2.4). Fewer than 5 percent of recorded conflicts endured for more than one year.

CHAPTER SUMMARY

This chapter presents new quantitative evidence that warfare was a central feature of Europe's historical landscape. Fundamental factors including the political fragmentation that resulted from the fall of the Carolingian Empire, the quest for glory by rulers, and scarce territory all help explain why warfare was so prevalent. In the following chapters, we will analyze the implications of endemic warfare for urban development in Europe.

3

Europe's Urban Rise

From 1000 to 1800, there was a dramatic increase in urbanization in Europe. This chapter presents a new argument to explain this historical phenomenon. Rural–urban migration played a fundamental role in historical city population growth. We show evidence that warfare – a main feature of Europe's historical landscape – played, in turn, an important role in rural–urban migration patterns. Warfare inflicted many costs on rural inhabitants. In this context, the city was a "safe harbor" due to two historical defensive advantages over rural areas: fortification and scale. We provide numerous historical examples of the safe harbor effect. Furthermore, we show evidence that urban destruction due to warfare was rare. Finally, we discuss different channels through which the city's historical role as a safe harbor could translate into local economic development. We call this process the "warfare-to-wealth effect." In subsequent chapters, we will perform statistical analyses of both the safe harbor effect and the warfare-to-wealth effect.

URBAN POPULATION PATTERNS

In the year 1000, there were very few large towns in Europe (van Bavel, Bosker, Buringh, and van Zanden, 2013: 392). Rome, for example, was only 5–10 percent of its size as under the Roman Empire (van Bavel et al., 2013: 392). Other large towns – Córdoba, Palermo, and Seville – were under Muslim rule (van Bavel et al., 2013: 392).[1] The urbanization rate in Western Europe at the end of the first millennium was approximately 3 percent (van Bavel et al., 2013: 394).[2] By comparison, the urbanization rate in the Middle East, the world's most urbanized region at this time, was approximately 7 percent (van Bavel et al., 2013: 392, 394). By 1800, however, Western Europe had become highly urbanized. The urbanization rate had risen to nearly 13 percent, and there were nearly 14 million urban inhabitants (van Bavel et al., 2013: 394). The urbanization rate in the Middle East, by contrast, had only risen to 9 percent by 1800 (van Bavel et al., 2013: 394).

This short overview illustrates the dramatic increase in European urbanization over 1000–1800. In what follows, we further explore historical urbanization patterns in Europe.

THE IMPORTANCE OF RURAL–URBAN MIGRATION

In theory, there are two ways to account for greater historical urbanization in Europe (de Vries, 1984: 231). The first concerns the urban rate of natural increase, whereby urban birth rates exceeded urban death rates. The second concerns an influx of new urban inhabitants from the countryside (enabled by a positive rural rate of natural increase).

In practice, we can rule out the first possibility due to the widely recognized "urban graveyard effect" in European history (de Vries, 1984: 231; Friedrichs, 1995: 131; Moch, 2003: 44–5; Winter, 2013: 404). This effect was a combination of high urban death rates with low urban birth rates. Epidemics such as the bubonic plague were responsible for the high death rates (Friedrichs, 1995: 130; Moch, 2003: 45; Winter, 2013: 404). Life expectancy at birth was up to 50 percent higher for rural versus urban inhabitants in early modern Europe (Woods, 2003: 43).

Thus, the second possibility – namely, rural–urban migration – must have accounted for (the bulk of) the dramatic increase in historical urbanization. Migration is another widely recognized fact of European history (de Vries, 1984: 213; Hohenberg and Lees, 1995: 128; Moch, 2003: 22–59). De Vries (1984: 213) writes, "One of modern historical demography's key findings is that the preindustrial European population was highly mobile."

One important migration pattern was from the countryside to the city. Winter (2013: 404) states that "influxes of new residents from the countryside represented nothing less than the lifeline" for urban growth. According to Blondé and van Damme (2013: 250), early modern towns skimmed off a "considerable part" of the rural demographic surplus. For there to have been a one-unit increase in the total urban population, approximately two times as many individuals had to permanently migrate from the countryside to the city (Winter, 2013: 404). Winter (2013: 404) claims that even in an early modern city with a relatively flat population over time, approximately 30 percent of urban inhabitants on average were born in the countryside.[3] For example, approximately half of the sixteenth-century urban inhabitants of Aix-en-Provence in southern France were not born there (Friedrichs, 1995: 133). Similarly, approximately half of the citizens (and two-thirds of noncitizens) of Frankfurt am Main in 1700 were migrants (Hohenberg and Lees, 1995: 90; Moch, 2003: 44). Finally, nearly 20 percent of all births in seventeenth-century England were "earmarked" for migration to London (Blondé and van Damme, 2013: 250). The vast majority of urban migrants were young, single, and childless adults (Winter, 2013: 404).

In the face of the urban graveyard effect, why would individuals want to leave the countryside for the city? Infant mortality was a major contributor to the rural–urban mortality differential in early modern Europe (Voightländer and Voth, 2013b: 780). The bulk of urban migrants – young, single, and childless – may have unwittingly downplayed the importance of the urban graveyard effect when deciding whether to relocate, naively thinking that infant mortality rates in the city were as low as they were in the countryside. Describing medieval Europe, Boone (2013: 234) writes, "Indeed, even in the harsher times of demographic crisis, the city continued to attract newcomers, despite the urban graveyard effect it exercised. To many, therefore, the advantages of living in a city clearly outweighed the disadvantages and inherent risks." Our formal model in the Model Appendix explicitly accounts for the sort of cost-benefit analysis that potential urban migrants may have undertaken. We will summarize the predictions of this model ahead.

In the aftermath of the fourteenth-century Black Death, feudal lords in Eastern Europe put new limits on personal mobility, reducing the ability of individuals to migrate to urban centers (Brenner, 1976: 41; Winter, 2013: 406–7, 412; Peters, 2015: 6–14). By 1800, the urbanization rate in Eastern Europe was only 5 percent (van Bavel, Bosker, Buringh, and van Zanden, 2013: 394).[4] Our statistical analysis of the safe harbor effect in Chapter 4 will distinguish between Western and Eastern Europe.

THE CITY AS SAFE HARBOR

The previous section shows that rural–urban migration played a fundamental role in historical city population growth in Europe. We now discuss the importance of warfare for rural–urban migration.

A basic – if not *the* basic – historical function of the city was security.[5] Near the start of Henri Pirenne's (1969: 57) chapter "City Origins," he writes, "Populations have to prepare refuges where will be found momentary protection from the enemy in case of invasion. War is as old as humanity, and the construction of fortresses almost as old as war." Similarly, Glaeser and Shapiro (2002: 208) state, "The first, and probably most important, interaction between warfare and urban development is that historically cities have provided protection against land-based attackers . . . Indeed, the role of cities in protecting their residents against outside attackers is one of the main reasons why many cities developed over time."

Urban centers held two historical defensive advantages over rural areas: fortification and scale (Glaeser and Shapiro, 2002: 208–10). Urban fortifications including outer rings of conjoined dwellings, defensive palisades or ramparts, fortified (single or double) walls, or bastioned traces were difficult to overcome (Tracy, 2000b: 79–80). In the words of Mumford (1961: 250), "Against sudden raids a wall, on guard at all hours, was more useful than any amount of military courage." Because of urban fortifications, even small groups of defenders could fend off large groups of attackers. Furthermore, urban fortifications created a scale economy. As the urban population grew, there was a sharp decline in the required amount or length of fortifications per inhabitant.[6] Adam Smith (2008: 250) summarizes the historical defensive advantages of urban centers as follows: "The inhabitants of cities and burghs, considered as single individuals, had no power to defend themselves: but by entering into a league of mutual defence with their neighbours, they were capable of making no contemptible resistance."

Landowning rural elites in medieval Europe could enhance security in the countryside by providing food and lodging in exchange for peasant labor and muscle (Bates, 2010: 37–40). Due to the advantages of fortification and scale as we have described, however, urban centers could defend themselves better than rural power centers, particularly after the revolution in military tactics, strategy, army size, technology, and impact from the fifteenth century onward (Parker, 1996: 1–2; Bates 2010: 41–2). Thus, rural landlords could not typically offer security levels as high as those provided by urban centers.

Indeed, warfare inflicted numerous costs on rural inhabitants. Describing Renaissance Europe, Hale (1985: 196) writes, "In terms of personal impact the burdens of war certainly afflicted the rural more than the urban population." A first cost to rural inhabitants was violence and destruction by soldiers along the war march (Gutmann, 1980: 32–5; Hale, 1985: 182–3, 186–7; Hoffman, 1996: 186, 202–3; Caferro, 2008: 186–7).

In the words of Gutmann (1980: 33), "Soldiers' actions read like a textbook outline of criminal practices: burning, looting, assault, rape, murder, thievery, and desecration of churches." Villagers feared the loss of property that warfare could bring (Rosenthal and Wong, 2011: 105, 107). Gutmann (1980: 31) states, "The onset of war led people to assume the worst – that their lives, homes, and property would be damaged, with a safe return to normal life perhaps years away. A generation's work of accumulating property for the future could be easily wiped out by just a year or two of warfare." Similarly, Hoffman (1996: 186) writes, "If animals were seized, buildings put to flame, or fields left to grow over because of the fear of attack – if, in short, capital goods were damaged – then recovery might also be long delayed. Clearing away the brush and small trees that sprouted on abandoned fields was a particularly slow and arduous task; it might continue for years." In his well-known diary, Luca Landucci describes the destruction that French troops inflicted upon the Tuscan countryside in November 1494. The French destroyed Landucci's house, drank his wine and ate his corn, and stole household items. In another village, they killed 11 men, leaving them to rot in the fields.[7] In anticipation of military conflict, villagers often burned their homes and farms prior to evacuation as a "scorched-earth" policy (Hale, 1985: 185). Rural dwellers in early modern Lorraine in northeastern France, for example, decided to starve their horses in order to produce animals of such poor quality that soldiers would not wish to seize them (Hoffman, 1996: 186).

A second cost to rural inhabitants was the lodging and feeding of soldiers (Gutmann, 1980: 36–39; Hale, 1985: 187–91, 196–7). Prior to the seventeenth century, there were few army barracks. The traditional system called for villagers to house troops in preparation for battle, in garrison or during winter, or for rest after battle's end (Gutmann, 1980: 36; Hale, 1985: 197). Furthermore, soldiers expected villagers to provide them food and utensils such as wood, candles, bedding, bowls, and pots (Gutmann, 1980: 38). Such costs could drive villagers into debt (Gutmann, 1980: 38–9). In theory, soldiers purchased food from villagers (Gutmann, 1980: 38–9; Hale, 1985: 182–3, 197). Still, villagers had to secure and deliver large amounts of food on quick notice, using valuable manpower and making upfront cash outlays (Gutmann, 1980: 38–9). For short stays, troops camped on village fields, destroying agricultural production (Gutmann, 1980: 36).

A third cost to rural inhabitants was money raising (Gutmann, 1980: 41–6; Hale, 1985: 185). An army could raise funds in foreign territory in two ways (Gutmann, 1980: 41). The first was the right of expropriation in areas under military occupation. The second was the right to collect contributions in nearby areas. In the words of Gutmann (1980: 41–2), "The power to collect contributions is a clear example of might-makes-right; anything the army could get was deemed legal. Raiding parties entered nearby or unoccupied territory and made demands punctuated by violence ... The troops might burn a house or two as a warning or kidnap a few men, to be ransomed by the village." If villagers did not pay such ransoms, then troops had the right to raze the village (Gutmann, 1980: 42). Overall, war-related money raising was a major expense for villagers (Gutmann, 1980: 45; Hoffman, 1996: 186, 202–3). To meet war-related demands, rural inhabitants often had to borrow funds from urban lenders (Gutmann, 1980: 50–2; Caferro, 2008: 189). As villagers repaid their debts, there was a wealth transfer from the countryside to the city. Furthermore, to prevent default, rural landowners sometimes had to sell their property, increasing land ownership by urban inhabitants.

A fourth cost to rural inhabitants was the loss of local manpower (Gutmann, 1980: 39–41; Hale, 1985: 196). The military had major if short-lasting needs for simple labor. Villagers were used to dig trenches and erect defenses (Gutmann, 1980: 40; Hale, 1985: 196). For example, King Louis XIV of France called on 20,000 peasants to construct his siege works at Maastricht in 1673 (Gutmann, 1980: 40). Furthermore, villagers had to provide wagons, animals, and drivers to cart military baggage (Gutmann, 1980: 39–40; Hale, 1985: 196; Hoffman, 1996: 186). Finally, peasants were more likely than urban inhabitants to be recruited for the military (Hale, 1985: 196). Overall, this manpower drain could severely disrupt agricultural production. As Hale (1985: 196) writes, "At the very times when cultivation for food was most crucially important, the labor force might be drastically reduced."

In an effort to mitigate the many costs of warfare, rural inhabitants migrated to urban centers, a phenomenon that Glaeser and Shapiro (2002: 208) call the "safe harbor effect." Describing medieval Europe, Rosenthal and Wong (2011: 115) state, "By the Renaissance the most urbanized parts of Europe were also those where conflict had raged most often: the band of territories from Flanders to Rome, including the Burgundian estates, western Germany, and northern Italy." Similarly, Moch (2003: 26) writes of early modern Europe that "... the politics of war and intolerance motivated more migration in this period than they would at any time before the twentieth century." In practice, the safe harbor effect could be (1) anticipatory, taking place under impending conflict threats, or (2) reactionary, taking place either during or in the immediate after-math of conflict. Furthermore, sustained conflict threats could influence the migration decisions of rural inhabitants not just day-to-day, but also across several generations. To illustrate the different forms that the safe harbor effect could take, the next section provides a wide variety of historical examples.

SAFE HARBOR EXAMPLES

There are numerous historical examples of the safe harbor effect, which we now describe in detail.

An anonymous inhabitant of fifteenth-century Paris provides a fascinating first-hand journal account of the city's role as safe harbor during the Hundred Years' War (1337–1453) and the civil war between the Armagnacs and the Burgundians (1407–35). In the summer of 1419, the English ransacked the countryside near Paris. The anonymous journal-ist describes the arrival of rural refugees at the city gates of Paris as follows (Shirley, 1968: 140):

Twenty or thirty people appeared at the Porte Saint-Denis, panic-stricken, like men who have just escaped death – and so evidently they had. Some were wounded, some had collapsed from terror, from the heat, and from hunger; they looked more dead than alive ... Whilst they were talking, and the gate-keepers were looking toward Saint-Lazare, they saw great crowds coming, men, women, and children, some of them wounded, some stripped, another carrying two children in his arms or on his back ... And all the following week they keep coming, from Pontoise and the villages nearby; whole bewildered troops of them were all over Paris.

Similarly, the anonymous journalist documents the role of Paris as a safe harbor during the thick of the Armagnac-Burgundian Civil War. In 1420, he states (Shirley, 1968: 148), "The Armagnacs still infested the country round Paris, stealing, looting, fire-raising, murdering, raping women, girls, and nuns. For ten leagues around Paris not a soul remained in the villages; all were in good towns." Similarly, describing the state of this conflict nine years later, he writes (Shirley, 1968: 238), "When the inhabitants of the villages around Paris heard how they [the Armagnacs] were gaining ground everywhere, they took their belongings into the good towns; they harvested their corn before it was ripe and brought it into the good town of Paris."

High-frequency historical migration data in wartime prove difficult to uncover. The best historical demographic data are for Italy (Hohenberg

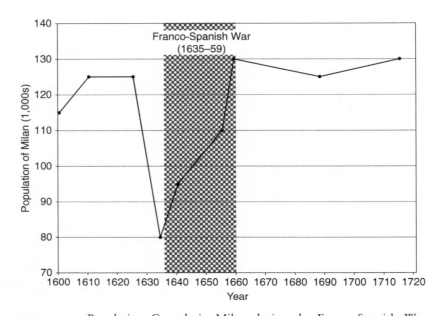

FIGURE 3.1 Population Growth in Milan during the Franco-Spanish War, 1635–59
Sources: D'Amico (1994) for city populations 1600–55 and D'Amico (2012) for city populations 1659–1715.

and Lees, 1995: 75). For example, city population data for Milan from D'Amico (1994, 2012) are available at regular intervals before, during, and after the Franco-Spanish War (1635–59). Figure 3.1 displays this time series. Milan's population at the start of the seventeenth century was roughly 125,000 (D'Amico, 2012: 13) and was relatively stable until the plague of 1630, when approximately 45,000 Milanese inhabitants died (D'Amico, 1994: 165). The Franco-Spanish War endured more than two decades, from the mid-1630s to the end of the 1650s. This war devastated the countryside, driving rural inhabitants to seek safety in Milan (D'Amico, 2012: 14). As a result, the city's population grew dramatically: by the war's end in 1659, the Milanese population was 130,000 – an increase of more than 60 percent from 1630 (D'Amico, 2012: 14). Milan's population was relatively stable for decades thereafter (D'Amico, 2012: 14). This example suggests that – via the safe harbor effect – the Franco-Spanish War was a boon to Milan's population over the seventeenth century, enabling it to not only recover from, but even surpass, pre-plague city population levels.

TABLE 3.1 *Baptisms of Children of Rural Immigrants in Pisa during Wartime, 1495–1509*

Period	Name	Baptisms by Rural Immigrants
1	Domination by Florence (1457–94)	4%
2	Florentine-Pisan War (1495–1509)	40–45%
3	Domination by Florence (1510–27)	12%
Percent change between periods 1 and 3		200%

Note: Baptisms by rural immigrants is the share of baptisms in Pisa of children whose immigrant parents originally hailed from the Pisan countryside.
Source: Luzzati, Baldi, and Puccinelli (2009).

The medieval Tuscan rivalry between Florence and Pisa is another historical example for which (somewhat) high-frequency migration data are available. To analyze migration patterns in Pisan history, Luzzati, Baldi, and Puccinelli (2009) make use of nearly 30,000 baptismal records over 1457–1527. Table 3.1 summarizes these data. Prior to 1495, Pisa was under stable Florentine rule. Roughly 4 percent of baptized children in Pisa over this period had immigrant parents that originally hailed from the Pisan countryside (Luzzati, Baldi, and Puccinelli, 2009: 10–11). Between 1495 and 1509, Pisa fought Florence in an attempt to regain its independence. In response, the scale of migration to Pisa grew rapidly, as rural inhabitants sought refuge from military conflict within the city's walls. Up to 45 percent of baptized children in Pisa over this period had immigrant parents that originally hailed from the Pisan countryside (Luzzati, Baldi, and Puccinelli, 2009: 10). Meanwhile, the share of migrants from Florence or its hinterlands plunged (Luzzati, Baldi, and Puccinelli, 2009: 10). From 1510 onward, through 1527, Pisa was once again under stable Florentine rule. Though some wartime migrants returned to the Pisan countryside, many decided to remain permanently in the city (Luzzati, Baldi, and Puccinelli, 2009: 10). Approximately 12 percent of baptized children in Pisa in the postwar period had parents who had migrated from the Pisa countryside – roughly three times greater than in the pre-1495 period of Florentine rule (Luzzati, Baldi, and Puccinelli, 2009: 10–11). This example suggests that – working through the safe harbor effect – the Florentine-Pisan War brought about significant permanent relocation from the countryside to the city.

A fourth group of historical examples of the safe harbor effect concerns the French Protestants known as the Huguenots. Although the Huguenots made up a relatively small share of the total French population, their economic importance went beyond their numerical strength (Scoville, 1951: 355; Treasure, 2013: 3). The Huguenots were skilled artisans and entrepreneurs (Scoville, 1951: 355; Moch, 2003: 28; Treasure, 2013: 3; Hornung, 2014: 86) who furthermore tended to be rural dwellers.[8] During the French Wars of Religion (1562–98) between Catholics and Protestants, Huguenot refugees found safety in urban centers such as Strasbourg in northeastern France (Moch, 2003: 26–8). In the aftermath of the Third War of Religion (1568–70), the Peace of Saint Germain established specific "safe towns" for Huguenots in wartime (Wolfe, 2009: 104). Other urban centers such as Paris became Catholic safe towns (Wolfe, 2009: 104). Beyond war-related migration within France, Huguenots took refuge abroad, in nations such as England, Holland, Germany, and Switzerland (Scoville, 1951: 354; Hohenberg and Lees, 1995: 95; Moch, 2003: 26–8). In Geneva, for example, sixteenth-century Huguenot newcomers helped make clock- and watchmaking the city's main industry (Scoville, 1951: 354). Similarly, they established textile plants in urban centers such as Cologne in western Germany (Scoville, 1951: 354).

A related example concerns the Dutch Revolt against Spanish rule (1566–87), which drove approximately 100,000 Protestants from the southern Netherlands into urban centers in the Dutch Republic (Moch, 2003: 26–7; Winter, 2013: 406). Such migrants were typically highly skilled (Cipolla, 1965: 34; Verhulst, 1999: 154–5; Winter, 2013: 406). Though roughly 40 percent came from Antwerp (Moch, 2003: 29), a good number came from small towns (Verhulst, 1999: 154–5). Moch (2003: 29) relates the arrival of skilled labor to the subsequent economic success of the Dutch Republic.

Other historical examples of the safe harbor effect include the following. According to the thirteenth-century friar Salimbene da Parma, inhabitants of the village of Roncolo in northern Italy took their belongings and fled to the stronghold of Parma, leaving their village empty, as a result of the ongoing military conflict between Frederick II and local communes.[9] In response to medieval Ottoman conquests, migrants from the Balkan Peninsula fled to coastal strongholds on the Adriatic Sea, including Venice (Del Panta et al., 1996: 57–8). During the Thirty Years' War (1618–48), the southwestern German city of Esselingen was "often full of refugees from villages which had been occupied or destroyed by undisciplined soldiers" (Friedrichs, 1995: 118). Finally, Gutmann (1980: 35) describes the migration of clergy in Belgium from the village of Visé to the city of Liège during the Dutch War (1672–9).

Migration Decisions across Generations

The historical examples described previously indicate that conflict threats and/or actual conflict often made quick migration from the countryside to the city necessary. Beyond such rapid relocation, sustained conflict threats could influence the migration choices of rural inhabitants across multiple generations. In the central Italian region near Orvieto circa 1300, for example, there were 170 inhabited rural villages, or roughly one every six square kilometers (Pinto, 1988: 252; Del Panta et al., 1996: 55). Yet, over the next 200 years, many such villages were vacated in pursuit of greater security (Pinto, 1988: 252; Del Panta et al., 1996: 55–6). Similarly, rural dwellers near the Tuscan city of Siena opted to relocate behind the relative safety of the city's walls over the 1300s and 1400s, abandoning once-thriving villages (Pinto, 1988: 251). Although the municipal government in Siena attempted to induce such migrants to return to the countryside, this effort failed, as most stayed permanently in the city (Pinto, 1988: 251). Finally, in the central Italian region near Perugia throughout the fifteenth century, several small inhabited zones adjacent to historical castles were vacated in favor of the largest and most important towns, each of which constructed city walls shortly thereafter (Pinto, 1988: 250; Del Panta et al., 1996: 55–6). Overall, these examples help illustrate how the city's function as a safe harbor could influence migration decisions across several generations, and not just day-to-day.

URBAN DESTRUCTION IN WARTIME

The previous two sections call to mind a natural question. Even if the historical evidence indicates that (1) the costs of warfare were greater in the countryside than in the city and (2) urban centers served as safe harbors, didn't warfare destroy cities too? Glaeser and Shapiro (2002: 210) call this possibility the "target effect." Indeed, there are well-known examples of urban sacks. In 1527, mercenary troops under the (nominal) allegiance of Holy Roman Emperor Charles V pillaged Rome. Friedrichs (1995: 295) writes of this event that "... atrocities of every sort were reported and most such stories were probably well-founded ..." Another dramatic sack took place in Antwerp in 1576 during the Dutch Revolt (Hale, 1985: 195; Friedrichs, 1995: 296; Hohenberg and Lees, 1995: 121). Spanish troops killed 7,000 and blunted the city's economic dynamism (Hale, 1980: 195; Friedrichs, 1995: 296; Moch, 2003: 29). A third example is the sack of Magdeburg by Catholic forces in 1631 as part of the

Thirty Years' War (Friedrichs, 1995: 296). This attack – including a widespread fire – destroyed nearly all of the city's buildings, leaving Magdeburg uninhabitable for months (Friedrichs, 1995: 296).

Although spectacular, such sacks were rare historical events (Friedrichs, 1995: 296; Hohenberg and Lees, 1995: 121).[10] It was not only challenging for an army to capture a city, but there were few benefits involved, because urban dwellers could always move their wealth, whether from centralized storage locations to various private vaults run by goldsmiths in town or to new urban locations altogether (Bates, 2010: 42). Still, our statistical analysis of the safe harbor effect in Chapter 4 will account for the possibility of the target effect in a variety of ways.

Postwar urban regeneration, moreover, was common. For example, Rome was able to regain a sense of normalcy after the sack of 1527, even if it took more than a year (Friedrichs, 1995: 295). Although the textile hub of Hondschoote – then part of the Spanish Netherlands – lost more than 95 percent of its population between the 1560s and the mid-1580s due to warfare, it became prosperous once more after the start of the 1600s (Hale, 1985: 180).[11] To make up for population losses during the Thirty Years' War (1618–48), King Frederick William of Prussia encouraged highly skilled French Huguenots to migrate, through the Edict of Potsdam (Hornung, 2014: 89–96).[12] Hornung (2014: 92) describes the impact of French immigration as follows: "When asked if his goal of restoring Magdeburg to its former prosperity had been met, the king answered that the town had been idle for 40 years after the war, but when the refugees came, all buildings filled up within 18 years. New manufactories were established, foreign money had come to town, and hundreds of citizens were employed and contributing to consumption."[13]

Fire and Plague

Beyond warfare, fire and plague could wreak havoc on the early modern city. Even Venice, located across more than 100 islands in the Venetian Lagoon, saw many severe fires (Friedrichs, 1995: 277). There were more than 300 major urban fires in early modern England, the most famous of which was the Great Fire of London in 1666 in which 13,000 houses burned (Friedrichs, 1995: 277–8). According to Friedrichs (1995: 277), however, the number of severe fires was "dwarfed" by the number of those that were quickly dealt with.

Unlike fire, which would always burn out in days, epidemics such as the bubonic plague could endure a whole summer (Friedrichs, 1995: 127–31;

281–5).[14] The most well-known historical epidemic is the Black Death (1347–50), which killed at least 30 percent of Europe's total population (Boone, 2013: 229). Urban populations, however, quickly sprung back after major epidemics. In the words of de Vries (1984: 218), "Most cities that suffered severe crises of mortality, suddenly losing 20–40 percent of their populations in outbreaks of plague or other epidemic diseases, attracted sufficient replacement migrants to regain their precrisis population levels within a matter of years." For example, the 35,000-plus inhabitants that London lost to plague in 1625 were replaced by migrants from the countryside within two years (de Vries, 1984: 218). Smaller urban centers also saw high levels of replacement migration from the countryside in the aftermath of plague (de Vries, 1984: 218; Boone, 2013: 229).[15]

FROM WARFARE TO WEALTH

We now discuss different channels through which the city's historical role as a safe harbor could translate into local economic development – a process that we call the warfare-to-wealth effect. We focus on three potential channels: (1) the establishment of local privileges, including self-governance and property rights protections from predatory outside rulers; (2) technological innovation and human capital accumulation; and (3) economic agglomeration effects.

Local Privileges

As described earlier, rural inhabitants feared the loss of property that warfare could bring. Rosenthal and Wong (2011: 105–10) argue that warfare induced an urban bias to artisanal activity. Unlike agricultural activity, artisanal activity was not inherently bound to the land. Furthermore, troops along the war march were inclined to plunder artisanal capital. Rural artisans under threat of conflict therefore had an incentive to move their capital behind the relative safety of urban fortifications. Indeed, urban centers were the locus of nonagrarian activity in preindustrial Europe (van Bavel, Bosker, Buringh, and van Zanden, 2013: 385).

Rural manufacturing did in fact occur in preindustrial Europe, but only to a relatively small extent (van Bavel, Bosker, Buringh, and van Zanden, 2013: 385). If rural security improved, then rural manufacturing would become more attractive. For example, Rosenthal and Wong (2011: 118–19) relate the growth of the putting-out industry in England – whereby urban entrepreneurs advanced raw materials to rural craft workers and then bought their output at predetermined prices – to the extended period of domestic stability following the end of the Civil War (1642–51). More generally, the city's traditional importance as a safe harbor in Europe fell over the nineteenth century, due to the nation-state's growing capacity to secure peace across large territorial units, along with deep changes to the nature of warfare (see Chapter 1). In this context, the relative attractiveness of rural (versus urban) manufacturing would increase.

Overall, however, the foregoing discussion suggests that urban centers were generally safer places for capital enterprises than were rural areas in preindustrial Europe. Beyond the safety of urban fortifications, moreover, urban centers could often offer artisans, entrepreneurs, and other residents local privileges, including personal freedoms, self-governance through parliamentary institutions, and legal authorizations that protected private property rights from outside predation (Blockmans and t'Hart, 2013: 426). Max Weber (1958: 181–90) argues that such institutional benefits were a defining characteristic of the medieval city. In the words of Postan (1972: 212), "[The medieval towns] were non-feudal islands in the feudal seas; places in which merchants could not only live in each other's vicinity and defend themselves collectively but also places which enjoyed or were capable of developing systems of local government and principles of law and status exempting them from the sway of the feudal regime." Similarly, Adam Smith (2008: 253) writes, "Order and good government, and along with them the liberty and security of individuals, were, in this manner, established in cities at a time when the occupiers of land in the country were exposed to every sort of violence."

Why did absolutist rulers grant local privileges to urban centers? One prominent answer revolves around political fragmentation and warfare. Early modern governments in Europe spent vast amounts on the military (see Chapter 2). To secure new funds, sovereign rulers could repress domestic populations, seek external revenues via colonialization, or bargain domestically (Tilly, 1994: 11, 24). The latter option – bargaining with well-off urban entrepreneurs – was a common solution, the "price" of which was the granting of local freedoms (Tilly, 1994: 11, 24; Hohenberg and Lees, 1995: 41; Bates, 2010: 44–6).[16] For example, Møller (2016) analyzes local political development in Aragon (1100–1327), a parliamentary first-mover. He shows that war-related tax needs were a major reason why Aragonese rulers convoked local parliaments. Similarly, warfare plays a key role in Boucoyannis's (2015) account of parliamentary development in England, which was another early mover.

In our account, the logic of the local privileges channel runs as follows. Political fragmentation and warfare played an important role in rural–urban migration, and in particular for artisans and entrepreneurs who could transport capital behind the relative safety of urban fortifications. Once there, artisans, entrepreneurs, and other urban migrants could take advantage of local privileges – including self-governance and property rights protections from predatory outside rulers – the granting of which by such rulers were themselves a function of war-related needs for new funds. Local governance by business-oriented elites who regularly met face-to-face may have promoted a legal environment conducive to investment and trade.[17] To increase local autonomy, furthermore, urban elites could play sovereign rulers off against each other by threatening to switch allegiances from one polity to another if their demands for greater local control over regulation and taxation went unmet (Gelderblom, 2013: 1–18; Cox, 2016b). The Investiture Controversy is an early example of this phenomenon, in which urban elites in medieval Italy (e.g., in Milan) played the Holy Roman Emperor against the Pope over the authority to appoint bishops (Blumenthal, 1988: 113–26; Hohenberg and Lees, 1995: 41). For all of the reasons given here, the city's role as a safe harbor could promote local economic development. In the absence of political fragmentation and warfare, this chain of logic would be wholly undercut, reducing long-run growth prospects.

Technological Innovation and Human Capital Accumulation

Beyond the relative security of urban fortifications and local privileges, urban centers could offer migrants new incentives to make technological innovations. To start with, urban wages were higher than rural wages, but urban borrowing costs were lower (Rosenthal and Wong, 2011: 105–10). Thus, to reduce costs, urban producers would have an incentive to replace labor with capital through technological innovations (Rosenthal and Wong, 2011: 105–10). Local governance by business-minded elites, along with property rights protections from outside predation, could help undergird this incentive to innovate.

Furthermore, urban density could promote the generation and adoption of new ideas (Bairoch, 1988: 336; Mokyr, 1995: 9–10; Fujita and Thisse, 2002: 7–8; Glaeser and Joshi-Ghani, 2015: xxii). This urban advantage held for two reasons (Mokyr, 1995: 9–10). First, invention called for an exchange of ideas across diverse fields (Mokyr, 1995: 9). Mokyr (1995: 9) writes, "Urban areas, because of the higher frequency of human interaction, were clearinghouses for ideas and information, and so invention was facilitated further by the continuous interface of different types of knowledge." Second, invention depended on repeated interactions between "savants" and "fabricants" (Mokyr, 1995: 10; Mokyr, 2002: 28–77). In the words of Mokyr (1995: 10), "In towns it was easier to find the skilled artisans and engineers that could transform a technical idea from blueprint to reality." Put differently, urban density reduced the access cost of exploiting best-practice techniques, which could facilitate innovation (Mokyr, 1995: 10; Mokyr, 2002: 28–77).

Urban density could also promote human capital accumulation. Glaeser and Joshi-Ghani (2015: xxii) state that "when the workers learn from the people around them, their human capital increases, and that makes them more productive." In medieval Europe, urban guilds promoted skill training and knowledge exchange between members (de Moor, 2008: 203). There may have been a feedback loop through which more skilled workers demanded new technology (Acemoglu, 2009: 382). Finally, urban centers may have attracted individual types with a greater ability and willingness to learn and innovate. Bairoch (1988: 336) describes this possibility as follows: "... the urban milieu provides a natural refuge for original spirits ill at ease in rural areas, where the pressure to conform is as a rule stronger."[18]

Urban centers were important hubs for innovation in European history. Medieval urban centers in Italy were innovators in high-end textiles, metalwork, chemicals, printing, clockmaking, optical utensils, cartography, and gunmaking (Mokyr, 1995: 8). Medieval German towns such as Augsburg and Nuremberg were renowned for instrument making (Mokyr, 1995: 8). The first moveable type printing press was invented in Mainz (Dittmar, 2011: 1133). Urban centers in the early modern Dutch Republic were "at the technological cutting edge of the world," making innovations in shipping, textiles, papermaking, hydraulics, and medicine (Mokyr, 1995: 8–9).[19]

Moreover, urban centers were places of education and learning. Van Zanden (2009: 86) writes as follows of medieval Europe: "There were however large regional variations, and often the difference between town and countryside ... was substantial. Literacy was probably highest in the urban belt that ran from Northern Italy to the Low Countries ..." Similarly, Friedrichs (1995, 259) states this of the early modern period: "Literacy was always higher in towns than in the countryside." Van Zanden (2009: 86) estimates that literacy grew from approximately

1 percent in the eleventh century to 12 percent by the end of the fifteenth century. By the mid-eighteenth century, the ability to read and write was "entirely normal" among the urban middle class (Friedrichs, 1995, 260). Furthermore, urban centers were home to institutions of higher education (Mokyr, 1995: 10–11). The first university in Europe was established at Bologna in the eleventh century (Cantoni and Yuchtman, 2014: 824). There are several historical examples of skilled urban migration in response to warfare (as described previously).

This discussion highlights the different ways in which urbanization could promote technological innovations and human capital accumulation. However, we must acknowledge an important counterargument, which Mokyr (1995: 14) calls "Cardwell's Law." Mokyr (1995: 14) writes, "Technological progress, in true dialectical fashion, has tended to create the forces that eventually destroyed it." The historical evidence suggests that urban creativity in any particular city was relatively short-lived (Mokyr, 1995: 14). Mokyr (1995: 14–17) and Stasavage (2014) both argue that urban property rights were the root of this problem: while urban property rights promoted innovation in the short run, they reduced it over the long run as local capital owners implemented entry limits to preserve the local technological status quo. Although Cardwell's Law could have negative long-run economic consequences for an individual city (Stasavage, 2014), we should be careful to distinguish between individual growth effects on the one hand and the overall growth effect of technological competition between urban centers on the other (Mokyr, 1995: 17–19). In the words of Mokyr (1995: 17), "It can be shown that with sufficient inter-unit competition, a competitive system of interdependent units can do what each individual unit cannot do for itself." Thus, even if individual urban centers were subject to capture by a local oligarchy, urban innovation for the whole of Europe was of key importance. Mokyr (1995: 19) describes this phenomenon as follows: "The contribution of the totality of all European urban centers taken together, however, was enormous, even if each individual unit contributed only for a limited period of time."

In our account, the logic of the technological innovation channel is as follows. War threats were an important catalyst for rural–urban migration. Thus, relative to more peaceful zones, there would be more individuals living side by side – including artisans and entrepreneurs – to exploit the advantages of urban density for technological innovation and human capital accumulation. To an extent, this argument fleshes out the statement by the character Harry Lime (played by Orson Welles) in the 1949 film *The Third Man*: "In Italy, for thirty years under the Borgias, they had warfare, terror, murder and bloodshed, but they produced Michelangelo, Leonardo da Vinci and the Renaissance." In turn, technological progress and human capital formation – or, as Romer (1990: S72) describes them, "improvement in the instructions for mixing together raw materials" – could promote local economic growth.[20] Without warfare, this chain of logic would be blunted, weakening the prospects for long-run economic development.

Economic Agglomeration Effects

Beyond promoting the flow of ideas, urban density created other economic agglomeration affects. Urban density reduces the exchange costs for goods and labor (Fujita and Thisse, 2002: 5–11; Glaeser and Joshi-Ghani, 2015: xx). If an input supplier locates near a final goods producer, then both firms can improve productivity by saving on transportation costs. Similarly, urban density promotes an efficient division of labor (Glaeser and Joshi-Ghani, 2015: xxi). As Adam Smith (2008: 26) writes, "There are some sorts of industry, even of the lowest kind, which can be carried on nowhere but a great town." By contrast, in rural areas "every farmer must be butcher, baker, and brewer for his own family" (Smith, 2008: 26). Furthermore, urban density promotes thick labor markets (Glaeser and Joshi-Ghani, 2015: xxi). If a particular firm fails, then thick labor markets imply that former employees may quickly find productive new work. Finally, the potential economic gains from agglomeration effects are increasing in urban populations and density (Glaeser and Joshi-Ghani, 2015: xviii).[21]

It nearly goes without saying that agglomeration effects were a main feature of urban centers in European history. Sir John Hicks (1969: 42) defined the classic city-state as follows: "The core of the city-state, regarded as a trading entity, is a body of specialized traders engaged in external trade." Early modern towns displayed diverse occupational structures (Blondé and van Damme, 2013: 249). Urban artisans, shop-keepers, and professionals produced a host of goods, including "food, shoes, pots and pans, paintings, entertainment, professional services, and religious comfort" (Blondé and van Damme, 2013: 249). Each major sector of the early modern urban economy was subdivided into numerous specializations (Friedrichs, 1995: 94–5).[22]

In our account, the logic of the economic agglomeration channel runs as follows. Rural–urban migration was an important response to warfare. Once in the city, urban migrants – including artisans and entrepreneurs –

could take advantage of agglomeration effects to reduce production costs. Local governance by business-oriented elites, along with property rights protections from predatory outside rulers, could further promote agglomeration effects. Similarly, urban migrants could take advantage of thick labor markets to find productive work. As historical urban centers grew larger and denser due to war-related migration, the potential economic gains from agglomeration effects rose. In such ways, the safe harbor effect could translate into local economic development. Max Weber (1958: 77) called the medieval European city the "fusion of fortress and market." Without warfare, this chain of logic would be undermined, decreasing the potential for long-run economic growth.

Section Summary

This section describes three potential channels through which the warfare-to-wealth effect could be transmitted: (1) the establishment of local privileges, including self-governance and property rights protections from outside predation; (2) technological innovation and human capital accumulation; and (3) economic agglomeration effects. While each potential channel is distinct, the warfare-to-wealth effect could be transmitted through multiple channels simultaneously. Put differently, such channels were not mutually exclusive. We will perform a statistical analysis of this effect in Chapter 5.

MODELING WARFARE TO WEALTH

In the previous sections, we have argued that warfare played an important role in the dramatic increase in urbanization in Europe between the fall of Charlemagne's empire and the start of the Industrial Revolution. Namely, we have argued that the historical city was a safe harbor that mitigated the high rural costs of military conflict, due to its dual defensive advantages of fortification and scale. Furthermore, we have argued that the city's historical role as a safe harbor could translate into local economic development, a process we call the warfare-to-wealth effect.

To further elucidate the main points of our argument, we develop a simple formal model, which we now summarize (we leave the technical details to the Model Appendix). Our model produces predictions about optimal migration decisions that corroborate the historical argument and evidence from previous sections. We will draw on such predictions to help guide our statistical analyses in subsequent chapters.

Our model analyzes the optimal migration decisions of an individual – call her individual j – that lives in the countryside and produces some sort of economic output such as an agricultural good or an artisanal one. This individual must make two sequential migration decisions for a given likely threat of nearby conflict. First, she must decide whether to migrate from the countryside to the city. Second, if this individual does in fact decide to migrate to the city, then she must decide whether to remain there temporarily or permanently.

Both decisions carry historically relevant costs and benefits. First, we assume that there is a relocation cost for rural–urban migration (and vice versa, if urban migration is only temporary). Second, given that warfare inflicted high costs on rural populations, we assume that any individual that did not migrate to the city in response to nearby conflict is subject to a conflict-related production loss.[23] Third, we assume that any individual that decides to remain permanently in the city must pay an urban grave-yard cost, since urban life expectancy was on average lower for urban (versus rural) inhabitants because of epidemics. Finally, because of the different economic and political benefits that the city may offer (e.g., the establishment of local privileges, including self-governance and property rights protections from predatory outside rulers), we assume that the output of any permanent urban migrant may increase by a positive productivity factor.

We now summarize the model's predictions about the individual's optimal migration decisions in light of such costs and benefits.

A first prediction of the model is that, even in peacetime, the urban productivity gain for the individual can make permanent relocation to the city an attractive choice, so long as this gain outweighs the urban graveyard cost. This prediction corroborates the historical evidence that the economic and political benefits of preindustrial urban life in Europe may have sometimes outweighed the costs, thereby promoting rural–urban migration.

A second prediction of the model is that nearby conflict makes *temporary* migration to the city more likely. For example, any individual with a low-enough urban productivity gain relative to the urban graveyard cost will always prefer to stay in the countryside in peacetime. When there is nearby conflict, however, this individual will relocate to the city – at least temporarily – so long as the rural costs of conflict are high enough. This prediction (along with the next one) corroborates the city's historical role as a safe harbor.

A third prediction of the model is that nearby conflict makes *permanent* relocation to the city more likely. The rural costs of conflict will induce an individual to permanently relocate to the city when the urban productivity gain and/or the conflict-induced production loss is high enough. This prediction corresponds with the warfare-to-wealth effect through which the city's historical role as a safe harbor could translate into local economic development.[24]

In particular, this prediction illustrates how nearby conflict could make permanent urban relocation by artisans and entrepreneurs more likely. Historically, artisanal capital was prone to looting by troops along the war march (Rosenthal and Wong, 2011: 105–10), implying that the conflict-induced rural production loss may have been larger for artisans relative to farmers. Furthermore, unlike agricultural activity, which was intrinsically bound to the land, artisanal capital was moveable (Rosenthal and Wong, 2011: 105–10), implying that the rural–urban relocation cost may have been relatively small for artisans. Finally, artisans and entrepreneurs may have been more likely to take advantage of urban economic and political benefits than were farmers. Thus, the urban productivity factor may have been relatively large for such individuals. For all of these reasons, artisans and entrepreneurs may have been the most likely to prefer permanent urban migration in the face of high threats of nearby conflict, thereby amplifying the warfare-to-wealth effect.[25]

CHAPTER SUMMARY

This chapter shows evidence that warfare played an important role in rural–urban migration in preindustrial Europe. In this context, the city was a safe harbor that mitigated the high rural costs of conflict. We identify a warfare-to-wealth effect through which the city's historical role as a safe harbor could translate into local economic development. In the next two chapters, we will rigorously test the main predictions of our argument using statistical methods.

4

Evaluating the Safe Harbor Effect

The historical evidence in Chapter 3 highlights the city's historical role as a safe harbor that mitigated the large rural costs of warfare in preindustrial Europe. This chapter brings together the evidence on warfare and city population growth to perform a rigorous statistical analysis of the safe harbor effect. Although the historical evidence strongly supports the safe harbor argument, there may still be confounding factors (e.g., geographical endowments) that influenced urban development. To maximize informative content, we combine historical data on city populations, conflict exposure, and local characteristics into a single panel database. Statistical methods enable us to exploit the variation within this database across time and space, systematically disentangling the safe harbor effect from other potential explanations for historical city population growth.

The main results of this statistical analysis show strong support for the safe harbor effect. We find that conflict exposure was associated with a roughly 10 percent average increase in city populations per century between 1000 and 1800. This estimate suggests that conflict-related city population growth accounted for approximately 15–20 percent of average per-century city population growth over this period. Our statistical analysis always controls for local geographical characteristics as well as common shocks over time. Furthermore, we typically control for time-varying "national level" features such as nation-state building and pre-existing city population trends.

Although the main analysis accounts for numerous potential confounders, we still test the robustness of our statistical results in many ways. First, we control for a wide range of time-varying observable local characteristics that may have influenced city populations, including the "returns" to local geography, soil suitability for different crops, international trade, and the strength of urban networks. Second, we evaluate several alternative samples. Finally, we test alternative grid sizes and conflict exposure measures. Our main results are robust to all such checks.

The historical evidence in Chapter 3 indicates that, although there are well-known examples of spectacular urban sacks (e.g., Magdeburg in 1631), such events were rare. Still, our statistical analysis controls for reverse causation from city populations to conflict exposure in several ways. To further verify that a target effect – whereby large urban centers made for the most attractive targets – does not bias our results, we perform a number of additional tests, all of which offer more evidence that reverse causation is not a major concern.

To conclude this chapter, we analyze conflict types and evidence from city walls, both of which further establish the historical importance of the city as a safe harbor.

HISTORICAL DATA

The statistical analysis calls for two main types of historical data: city populations and conflict exposure.

City Populations

We rely on historical city population data constructed by three economic historians: Bairoch, Batou, and Chèvre (1988). To the best of our knowledge, this database is the most comprehensive source available for historical city populations in Europe. Ahead, we justify why we prefer Bairoch, Batou, and Chèvre to de Vries (1984), a potential alternative.

Bairoch, Batou, and Chèvre provide data for all urban centers in Europe that ever reached 5,000 inhabitants at 100-year intervals between 800 and 1700 and at 50-year intervals between 1750 and 1850.[1] To maintain estimation intervals of equal lengths, we focus on the 100-year intervals. The start year of our city population data (1000) occurs in the aftermath of the ninth-century fall of the Carolingian Empire, which gave rise to a high level of political fragmentation (see Chapter 1). In turn, instability and warfare became more likely, increasing the city's importance as a safe harbor. The end year (1800) occurs just prior to the Industrial Revolution in Continental Europe. By the nineteenth century, the nation-state's growing capacity to secure peace over large territorial units – along with deep changes to the nature of warfare – reduced the city's traditional role as a safe harbor (see Chapter 1). We linearly inter-polate – but never extrapolate – any missing city population observations over 1000–1800.[2]

De Vries (1984) provides an alternative database to that of Bairoch, Batou, and Chèvre for historical city populations in Europe. His data do not start until 1500, however, reducing their appeal for our research project. In any case, Bosker, Buringh, and van Zanden (2013: data appendix, 5) compare the Bairoch, Batou, and Chèvre database and the de Vries database for each century from 1500 to 1800. They show that the two databases are very similar: the correlation coefficients are 0.99. Thus, it is very unlikely that the use of de Vries over Bairoch, Batou, and Chèvre would significantly alter the statistical results to be described ahead.

Conflict Exposure

For the second type of data, we must proxy for the risk of local exposure to historical conflicts. To compute such a proxy, we first locate each sample city within 150 km × 150 km grid-scale cells using a cylindrical equal-area map projection with a geometric center near Davos, Switzerland (46° 76' N, 10° 01' E).[3] We then compute a binary variable that indicates whether there was at least one recorded major military conflict in the same grid cell as each sample city for each century between 1000 and 1800. This approach makes sense because nearly 90 percent of grid cell-centuries experienced 0 or 1 conflicts. Furthermore, this approach reduces the potential influence of any unobservable character-istics that would affect a sample city's total conflict exposure. Still, for robustness, our statistical analysis that follows will test an ordered conflict variable as an alternative.

The 150 km × 150 km grid size is appropriate for our purposes for two reasons. The first reason is as follows. Eurostat is the official statistical office of the European Union. Eurostat's units of economic territory are called NUTS (nomenclature of territorial units for statistics). There are three such units, of which NUTS2 is the main unit. Our statistical analysis of the warfare-to-wealth-effect in Chapter 5 will make use of NUTS2 data. The 150 km × 150 km grid size is roughly comparable in size to the NUTS2 unit. For example, the Lombardy region in northern Italy is approximately 150 km × 150 km. Thus, the use of this size of grid cell promotes analytic consistency across both chapters. The second reason is that the 150 km × 150 km grid size makes sense in terms of historical travel times. A horseback traveler in medieval Europe could cover 50–60 kilometers per day (Reyerson, 1999: 54, 56). Thus, we estimate that the medieval travel time between a city such as Bergamo, located in the center of the Lombardy region, and a city such as Cremona, located approximately 75 kilometers away (as the crow flies) near Lombardy's southern border, would have taken roughly one to two days. Still, our statistical analysis will test alternative grid sizes as a robustness check.

Figure 4.1 maps the locations of the military conflicts and city locations that our statistical analysis will exploit. Historical conflict locations do not appear to be randomly distributed throughout Europe. One particular concern is that the central corridor that runs from the Low Countries to northern Italy through eastern France and western Germany may have favorable geographical endowments, including good agricultural conditions and easy waterway access, that promoted both historical conflict and city population growth (see Chapter 1). To analyze the relationship between local characteristics (i.e., geographic, economic, political, and social) and historical conflict exposure, we estimate a logit model (we leave the technical details to Appendix Table B.1). There are positive and significant correlations between (1) soil suitability for barley cultivation, soil suitability for potato cultivation, and sovereign capital status and (2) the historical likelihood of local conflict. Meanwhile, there are significant negative correlations between (1) riverports and city elevations and (2) this likelihood. Of equal importance, there are no significant correlations for seaports (Atlantic or non-Atlantic), Roman road hubs, terrain ruggedness, the general likelihood of cultivation, urban networks, local self-governance, archbishop seats, or university seats. Thus, to summarize the results of this exercise, some local characteristics did in fact influence historical conflict exposure, but many others did not. Regardless, our statistical analysis will account for the local correlates of conflict in a wide variety of ways.

STATISTICAL METHODOLOGY

To statistically analyze the relationship between conflict exposure and city population size in preindustrial Europe, we estimate the following OLS model.

$$P_{i,g,t} = \alpha + \beta \, Conflict_{i,g,t-1} + \mu_i + \lambda_t + \varepsilon_{i,g,t} \qquad (4.1)$$

Here we model the log population for city i in grid cell g at century t as a function of $Conflict_{i,g,t-1}$, the binary variable that equals 1 if there was at

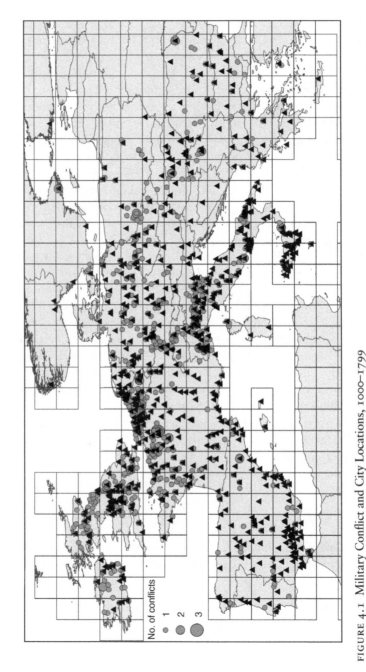

FIGURE 4.1 Military Conflict and City Locations, 1000–1799

Notes: Military conflict locations are indicated by circles and those of cities by triangles. Data displayed in projection of analysis. Dot sizes indicate the number of conflicts geocoded to each specific location. Squares refer to 150 km × 150 km grid cells.

Sources: Bradbury (2004) and Clodfelter (2002) for military conflicts and Bosker, Buringh, and van Zanden (2013) for city locations.

No. of conflicts
1
2
3

least one recorded major military conflict in the same 150 km × 150 km grid cell as sample city i over the previous century $t - 1$.[4] To control for local characteristics that were time invariant – for example, soil suitability for barley or potato cultivation, riverport status, and elevation – we always include city fixed effects μ_i. Similarly, to account for widespread shocks across time such as the fourteenth-century Black Death and the fifteenth-century military revolution, we always include century fixed effects λ_t. The random error term is $\varepsilon_{i,g,t}$. We report robust standard errors, clustered at the grid cell level to account for any within-grid serial correlation in the error term. Appendix Table B.2 shows the descriptive statistics for the regression variables.

MAIN RESULTS

Table 4.1 presents the main regression results for the safe harbor effect. The specification in column 1 includes city and century fixed effects. As predicted, there is a significant relationship (at the 1 percent level) between conflict exposure and city populations. The point estimate for $Conflict_{i,g,t-1}$ is 0.105.

City fixed effects help account for unobserved features specific to a city that did not vary over time, while century fixed effects help account for unobserved features that were common across all units at a given point in time. However, there may still be unobserved "national level" features such as total population, economic growth, and nation-state building that

TABLE 4.1 *Safe Harbor Effect: Main Results*

	(1)	(2)	(3)
	Dependent variable: log city population		
Conflict exposure	0.105	0.112	0.079
	(0.040)	(0.041)	(0.034)
	[0.010]	[0.007]	[0.021]
City FE	Yes	Yes	Yes
Century FE	Yes	Yes	Yes
Country × century FE	No	Yes	Yes
Initial log city pop × century FE	No	No	Yes
R-squared	0.257	0.408	0.546
Observations	3,293	3,293	3,293

Notes: Estimation method is OLS. All regressions include city and century fixed effects. Robust standard errors clustered at grid cell level in parentheses, followed by corresponding p-values in brackets.

changed over time and influenced city populations. For example, the nation-state's growing ability to secure peace over large territorial units may have promoted domestic trade and urban development (see Chapter 1). To account for "national level" trends, we include country-century interaction effects in column 2 for each of the 26 present-day nations in our sample.[5] The relationship between conflict exposure and city populations remains similar in magnitude and significance as before.

Country-century interaction effects account for "national level" demographic changes over time. However, urban centers with smaller or larger initial populations may still have grown at different rates. Column 3 includes initial log city population-century interaction effects that help control for both preexisting city population trends and reversion to the mean – the tendency for a city's population to move back toward the average urban population level over time.[6] This approach is demanding (Acemoglu, Cantoni, Johnson, and Robinson, 2011: 3299), yet the coefficient for conflict exposure remains highly significant. The point estimate is now 0.079.

Overall, the Table 4.1 results provide robust statistical support for the safe harbor effect. Conflict exposure was associated with an 8–11 percent average increase in city populations per century over 1000–1800. To put such magnitudes into perspective, city population growth averaged 53 percent per century over this period.[7] Thus, our main estimates suggest that conflict-related city population growth accounted for 15–21 percent of average per-century city population growth in preindustrial Europe.

For another perspective, we compare the magnitudes of our coefficient estimates to the results of two other statistical analyses that use historical city population size as an outcome: Dittmar (2011) and van Zanden, Bosker, and Buringh (2012). We review both works in Chapter 1. Van Zanden, Bosker, and Buringh analyze the relationship between regional parliamentary activity and city population growth in Europe between 1188 and 1789. They find that each additional year of parliamentary activity was associated with a 0.20 percent increase in city populations per century (van Zanden, Bosker, and Buringh, 2012: 855). Given that regional parliaments met 20 years per century on average (van Zanden, Bosker, and Buringh, 2012: data appendix), their estimate translates into a benchmark per-century city population increase of 4 percent. This magnitude is smaller than our result that conflict exposure was associated with a roughly 10 percent average increase in city populations per century. Dittmar analyzes the effect of the fifteenth-century invention of the moveable type printing press on city population growth. According to his estimate (Dittmar, 2011: 1150), the printing press accounted for 18 percent of city population growth between 1500 and 1600. This magnitude is similar in size to our result that conflict-related city population growth accounted for 15–21 percent of average per-century city population growth over 1000–1800.[8]

ROBUSTNESS

The main results in the previous section are robust to controls for local geographical characteristics, widespread shocks, "national level" features, and preexisting city population trends. This section further tests the robustness of our results. We first control for a wide range of observable characteristics that may have influenced city populations. We then evaluate alternative samples, grid sizes, and conflict exposure measures. All robustness checks use the most stringent main specification (i.e., column 3 of Table 4.1).

Returns to Local Geography

City fixed effects help account for local geographical features. However, the "returns" to geography may have changed over time. For example, White (1962: 39–78) argues that the medieval introduction of the heavy plow promoted urbanization in European zones with fertile clay soils. The prior plow, called the "scratch plow," was better suited for dry and light Mediterranean soils (White, 1962: 42–3). Column 1 of Table 4.2 controls for this agricultural improvement by interacting local soil suitability for barley – a heavy-plow-positive crop – with century fixed effects.[9] The point estimate for conflict exposure is 0.075, with p-value 0.026.

Nunn and Qian (2012) find that the widespread introduction of the potato from the Americas from the late 1600s onward promoted European urbanization, while Iyigun, Nunn, and Qian (2010) find that adoption of the potato reduced violent conflict in Europe.[10] To help account for the potato's impact on city population growth and historical warfare, column 2 of Table 4.2 interacts local soil suitability for potato cultivation with century fixed effects.[11] The coefficient for conflict exposure resembles the previous specification in magnitude and significance.

Finally, to help control for time-varying geographical returns in general, we draw on the database of Bosker, Buringh, and van Zanden

TABLE 4.2 *Safe Harbor Effect: Controls for Observables*

	(1)	(2)	(3)	(4)	(5)	(6)
	Dependent variable: log city population					
Conflict exposure	0.075	0.078	0.064	0.076	0.078	0.070
	(0.033)	(0.034)	(0.030)	(0.033)	(0.034)	(0.031)
	[0.026]	[0.022]	[0.037]	[0.020]	[0.022]	[0.027]
Barley suitability × century FE	Yes	No	No	No	No	No
Potato suitability × century FE	No	Yes	No	No	No	No
Local geography × century FE	No	No	Yes	No	No	No
Atlantic port × century FE	No	No	No	Yes	No	No
Hanseatic city × century FE	No	No	No	No	Yes	No
Urban network	No	No	No	No	No	Yes
R-squared	0.532	0.551	0.582	0.563	0.548	0.555
Observations	3,134	3,293	3,293	3,293	3,293	3,293

Notes: Estimation method is OLS. All regressions include city and century fixed effects, country-century interaction effects, and initial log city population-century interaction effects. Local geographic controls are for riverports, seaports, Roman road hubs, terrain ruggedness, and elevations. Robust standard errors clustered at grid cell level in parentheses, followed by corresponding p-values in brackets.

(2013). They code a wide variety of city-level characteristics at century intervals for hundreds of historical urban centers in Europe, including whether each city is a riverport, a seaport, or a Roman road hub and features such as terrain ruggedness and elevation. Column 3 of Table 4.2 interacts each of these geographical variables with century fixed effects. The point estimate for $Conflict_{i,g,t-1}$ is 0.064, with p-value 0.037.

Overall, these robustness checks provide further evidence that local geographical characteristics do not drive our main results.

Trade

Acemoglu, Johnson, and Robinson (2005) find that Atlantic trader nations – Britain, France, the Netherlands, Portugal, and Spain – saw faster urban development after 1500. To help account for the role of Atlantic trade, we code Atlantic seaports according to Bosker, Buringh, and van Zanden (2013) and interact them with century fixed effects (column 4 of Table 4.2). The result for conflict exposure is robust to the inclusion of these interaction effects. The point estimate is 0.076.

Beyond Atlantic trade, the federation of north German merchants called the Hanseatic League was an important historical trade network in Europe (Ogilvie, 2011: 25–6). To help control for the role of the German Hanse, we code Hanseatic towns according to Dollinger (1964: ix–x) and interact them with century fixed effects (column 5 of Table 4.2). The point estimate for $Conflict_{i,g,t-1}$ is similar in magnitude and significance to the previous specification.

City fixed effects control for distances between urban centers. To further account for urban trade networks, column 6 of Table 4.2 controls for the number of towns with populations greater than 10,000 located within 100 km of each sample city per century according to Bosker, Buringh, and van Zanden (2013).[12] The coefficient for conflict exposure remains highly significant.

Taken together, these exercises provide additional evidence that historical trade patterns do not drive our main results.

Eastern Europe

Feudal lords in Eastern Europe put new restrictions on personal mobility in the aftermath of the Black Death (1347–50). Scholars argue that such mobility limits reduced the scope for rural–urban migration (Brenner, 1976: 41; Winter, 2013: 406–7, 412; Peters, 2015: 6–14). To test for the role of the Second Serfdom, column 1 of Table 4.3 restricts the city sample to Eastern European nations according to the United Nations geoscheme.[13]

TABLE 4.3 *Safe Harbor Effect: Alternative Samples*

	(1)	(2)	(3)	(4)	(5)
	Dependent variable: log city population				
Conflict exposure	0.013	0.103	0.067	0.100	0.094
	(0.061)	(0.043)	(0.037)	(0.038)	(0.034)
	[0.832]	[0.018]	[0.072]	[0.010]	[0.007]
Eastern Europe only	Yes	No	No	No	No
1500–1800 only	No	Yes	No	No	No
1300–1700 only	No	No	Yes	No	No
Exclude historical capitals	No	No	No	Yes	No
Exclude archbishop seats	No	No	No	No	Yes
R-squared	0.705	0.546	0.415	0.571	0.595
Observations	281	1,818	2,010	2,598	2,913

Notes: Estimation method is OLS. All regressions include city and century fixed effects, country-century interaction effects, and initial log city population-century interaction effects. Robust standard errors clustered at grid cell level in parentheses, followed by corresponding p-values in brackets.

The point estimate for $Conflict_{i,g,t-1}$ falls to 0.013 (p-value = 0.832), suggesting that, as the scholarly literature would predict, the city's historical role as safe harbor was less important in the context of Eastern Europe.

Military Revolution

Parker (1996: 1–2) argues that a revolution in military tactics, strategy, army size, technology, and impact in early modern Europe made it much more likely that rulers would go to war rather than seek peaceful resolutions. Our conflict data support Parker's argument: more than 70 percent of recorded sample conflicts took place between 1500 and 1800 (see Table 2.2). Given greater belligerence, the safe harbor effect should have been more pronounced over this period, ceteris paribus. In column 2 of Table 4.3, we restrict the sample to 1500–1800. The result is consistent with our intuition: the point estimate for conflict exposure increases to 0.103 relative to the most stringent main specification (i.e., column 3 of Table 4.1).

Eighteenth-Century Conflicts

The 1700s experienced the most recorded conflicts over the sample period (see Table 2.2). To evaluate the role of the eighteenth century, column 3 of Table 4.3 restricts the sample to 1300–1700. The point estimate for conflict exposure remains relatively similar in size and significance to previous specifications.[14] Thus, eighteenth-century conflicts do not drive our main results.

Seats of Political Power

Did historical seats of political power make for the most important safe harbors? We address this question by testing for the influence of capital city status and archbishop seats, respectively. Column 4 of Table 4.3 excludes all historical sovereign capitals according to Bosker, Buringh, and van Zanden (2013). Relative to the most stringent main specification (i.e., column 3 of Table 4.1), the point estimate for conflict exposure increases from 0.079 to 0.100 (it is significant at the 1 percent level). Similarly, column 5 of Table 4.3 excludes all historical archbishop seats. The point estimate for conflict exposure is now 0.094 (p-value = 0.007). Overall, these results indicate that the safe harbor effect was not limited to historical seats of political power.

Local Self-Governance

Local self-governance may have promoted fiscal and military strength (Glaeser and Shapiro, 2002: 211). For example, Stasavage (2011: 70–93) finds that historical city-states in Europe could issue long-term public debt prior to territorial states and at lower interest rates. Military defense was the main reason for this fiscal innovation (Stasavage, 2011: 26–9). To assess the role of local self-governance, we restrict the city sample to self-governing communes for at least one century according to Bosker, Buringh, and van Zanden (2013). The results (not shown) support this hypothesis. The coefficient for $Conflict_{i,g,t-1}$ for self-governing communes is in fact more significant than for non-self-governing communes (p-value = 0.094 versus p-value = 0.290).

Exclude Nations One by One

City fixed effects control for time-invariant features specific to each sample city. In this respect, they subsume country-level fixed effects. To further test for the importance of any particular country, Figure 4.2 excludes modern-day nations one by one.[15] The point estimates and confidence intervals are relatively stable across subsamples. Thus, no single outlier nation drives our results.

Alternative Grid Sizes

As described in a previous section, the 150 km × 150 km grid size is appropriate for two reasons. This grid size (1) is roughly comparable in size with Eurostat's main unit of economic territory (NUTS2), which our statistical analysis of the warfare-to-wealth-effect in Chapter 5 will exploit, and (2) makes sense in terms of historical travel times. For robustness, we halve the grid size (i.e., 75 km × 75 km) in column 1 of Table 4.4. The coefficient for conflict exposure is highly significant. The point estimate is 0.111 (p-value = 0.001).[16]

Nonlinear Effect

The relationship between conflict exposure and city populations may have been nonlinear. Namely, urban centers that underwent "too much" warfare may have experienced depopulation. To evaluate this possibility,

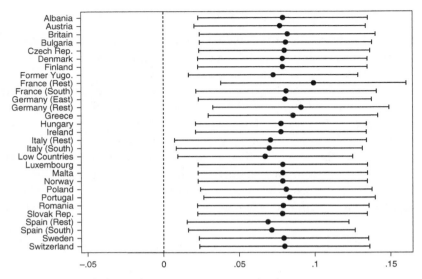

FIGURE 4.2 Exclude Modern-Day Nations One by One

Notes: Black dots are point estimates for most stringent specification (i.e., column 3 of Table 4.1) when we exclude each country one by one. Horizontal bars indicate 90 percent confidence intervals. "Southern France" refers to the regions of Southwest (NUTS1 unit FR6) and Mediterranean (FR8). "Rest of France" refers to all other French regions. "Eastern Germany" refers to the regions of Brandenburg (DE4), Mecklenburg-Vorpommern (DE8), Saxony (DED), Saxony-Anhalt (DEE), and Thüringen (DEG). "Rest of Germany" refers to all other German regions. "Southern Italy" refers to the regions of South Italy (ITF) and Islands (ITG). "Rest of Italy" refers to all other Italian regions. "Southern Spain" refers to the region of Andalusia (ES6). "Rest of Spain" refers to all other Spanish regions.

column 2 of Table 4.4 replaces the main conflict variable (i.e., binary) with the number of conflicts and squared number of conflicts.[17] The point estimate for the number of conflicts is 0.034 and is highly significant. The point estimate for the squared number of conflicts is negative and significant. However, (1) the magnitude of the squared term is very small (−0.002), and (2) the negative effect does not take over until a city was exposed to at least eight conflicts over a single century. This quantity is very large. The vast majority of urban centers saw at most one conflict per century. Thus, this exercise suggests that urban depopulation due to very high conflict exposure was a relatively rare historical phenomenon (also see the analysis in the next section).

TABLE 4.4 *Safe Harbor Effect: Further Robustness*

	(1)	(2)	(3)
	Dependent variable: log city population		
Conflict exposure	0.111 (0.033) [0.001]		
Number of conflicts		0.034 (0.012) [0.004]	
Number of conflicts (squared)		−0.002 (0.001) [0.006]	
Conflict exposure (ordered)			0.049 (0.021) [0.022]
75 km × 75 km grid cell	Yes	No	No
R-squared	0.547	0.547	0.546
Observations	3,293	3,293	3,293

Notes: Estimation method is OLS. All regressions include city and century fixed effects, country-century interaction effects, and initial log city population-century interaction effects. Column 1 uses 75 km × 75 km grid cells, while columns 2 and 3 use the benchmark grid cell size (i.e., 150 km × 150 km). Robust standard errors clustered at grid cell level in parentheses, followed by corresponding p-values in brackets.

Ordered Variable

As described previously, the binary conflict variable approach makes sense because (1) 89 percent of grid cell-centuries experienced 0 or 1 conflicts over 1000–1799, and (2) this approach reduces the potential influence of any unobservable characteristics that would affect a sample city's total conflict exposure. Ninety-five percent of grid cell-centuries experienced 0, 1, or 2 conflicts over this period. Thus, as another way to measure conflict exposure, we construct an ordered variable that equals 0 for each century that a grid cell experienced no conflict, 1 for a single conflict, and 2 for at least two conflicts. The result for conflict exposure is robust to this alternative (column 3 of Table 4.4).

TARGET EFFECT

To this point, we have statistically analyzed the city's historical role as a safe harbor, arguing that the causal relationship runs from military conflict to city population size. However, it is possible that the causal logic runs in the other direction. Put differently, there may be a "target effect" (Glaeser and Shapiro, 2002: 210) whereby large urban centers made for the most attractive targets for would-be attackers. The logic of the target effect is as follows: given that urban density promotes plunder, would-be attackers should have preferred large urban agglomerations, ceteris paribus. In our statistical framework, country-century interaction effects and initial log city population-century interaction effects help control for reverse causation from city populations to conflict exposure. To further verify that a target effect does not bias our results, we now perform several additional tests.

Urban Plunders

Although spectacular, urban sacks were rare historical events (see Chapter 3). To quantitatively support this claim, we identify the number of times per century that a sample city was plundered between 1000 and 1800 according to Bosker, Buringh, and van Zanden (2013).[18] Table 4.5 presents the results of this test. Out of 5,408 city-century observations over 1000–1800, just 2 percent were urban plunders. This result suggests that the target effect was not a widespread historical phenomenon in Europe.

Placebo Tests

Another way to analyze whether larger urban centers made for more attractive targets is to generate a conflict exposure "placebo" that

TABLE 4.5 *Urban Plunders, 1000–1800*

Number of plunders	Frequency	Percent
0	5,286	97.74
1	116	2.14
2	5	0.09
4	1	0.02
Totals	5,408	100.00

Note: "Frequency" refers to the number of city-century observations.
Source: Bosker, Buringh, and van Zanden (2013).

TABLE 4.6 *Safe Harbor Effect: Placebo Tests*

	(1)	(2)	(3)	(4)
	Dependent variable: log city population			
Conflict exposure (placebo)	0.039	0.026	0.039	0.034
	(0.039)	(0.038)	(0.038)	(0.044)
	[0.311]	[0.498]	[0.304]	[0.450]
Exclude 10 largest cities	No	Yes	No	No
Exclude historical capitals	No	No	Yes	No
Self-governing communes only	No	No	No	Yes
R-squared	0.435	0.477	0.454	0.431
Observations	2,620	2,546	2,052	1,786

Notes: Estimation method is OLS. All regressions include city and century fixed effects, country-century interaction effects, and initial log city population-century interaction effects. Robust standard errors clustered at grid cell level in parentheses, followed by corresponding p-values in brackets.

equals the first lead of our main conflict variable in equation (4.1). For example, if the dependent variable $P_{i,g,t}$ measures the log population for city i in grid cell g in 1600, then the conflict exposure placebo measures conflict exposure for this city over 1600–1699, in contrast to the actual conflict variable, which measures conflict exposure over 1500–1599. If the placebo coefficient is positive and significant, then this analysis indicates that a city's population at the start of a given century increases the likelihood that it will be exposed to conflict over the subsequent 100 years (i.e., a target effect).

Table 4.6 shows the results of the placebo analysis. The point estimate for the conflict placebo in column 1 is small (0.039) relative to the main results in Table 4.1 and is not significant (p-value = 0.311). In column 2, we repeat this analysis after excluding the 10 largest historical urban centers each century. The placebo coefficient falls to 0.026. The p-value is now 0.498. In column 3, we exclude historical sovereign capitals. The placebo result is unchanged. Finally, column 4 restricts the city sample to self-governing communes for at least one century. The placebo coefficient remains small (0.036) and is not significant (p-value = 0.450).

Overall, the results of the placebo tests indicate that larger urban centers were not significantly more likely than their smaller counterparts to be exposed to subsequent conflict, casting further doubt on the importance of the target effect in Europe over 1000–1800.

TABLE 4.7 *Alternative Target Effect Test*

	(1)	(2)	(3)	
	Dependent variable: conflict exposure			
Log city population (first lag)	0.029	0.023	0.028	0.015
	(0.026)	(0.029)	(0.029)	(0.030)
	[0.274]	[0.431]	[0.334]	[0.630]
Exclude 10 largest cities	No	Yes	No	No
Exclude historical capitals	No	No	Yes	No
Self-governing communes only	No	No	No	Yes
R-squared	0.316	0.319	0.313	0.351
Observations	2,717	2,637	2,123	1,863

Notes: Estimation method is OLS. All regressions include city and century fixed effects, country-century interaction effects, and initial log city population-century interaction effects. Robust standard errors clustered at grid cell level in parentheses, followed by corresponding p-values in brackets.

Alternative Test

As an alternative way to evaluate whether there was a target effect, we now regress our main conflict variable on lagged log city populations.

$$Conflict_{i,g,t} = \alpha + \beta P_{i,g,t-1} + \mu_i + \lambda_t + \varepsilon_{i,g,t} \qquad (4.2)$$

If β is positive and significant, then this analysis indicates that a city's population at the start of a given century increased the subsequent likelihood that it would be exposed to conflict. Table 4.7 shows the results of this analysis for the same four specifications as for the previous table. The β coefficients again are small; they range from 0.015 to 0.029 and are not significant (the p-values range from 0.274 to 0.630).

Similarly, to test for a "short run" target effect, we regress $Conflict_{i,g,t}$ on $P_{i,g,t-1}$ in equation (4.2), where $Conflict_{i,g,t}$ now equals 1 if there was at least one recorded major military conflict in grid cell g over the first z years of century t, where $z = 10, 20, 30, 40, 50$. The coefficients (not shown) are never significant.

Overall, the results of the alternative target effect tests provide further evidence that reverse causation does not bias our results.

Lagged Dependent Variable

A final way to evaluate the importance of a target effect in European history is to include lagged log city populations as a control and rerun the most stringent main specification (i.e., column 3 of Table 4.1).[19] The coefficient for $Conflict_{i,g,t-1}$ (not shown) remains highly significant, with point estimate 0.069. Thus, including the lagged dependent variable does not alter the main results by much.

FURTHER EVIDENCE FOR SAFE HARBOR EFFECT

To conclude this chapter, we now present two further types of evidence for the safe harbor effect: conflict types and city walls.

Conflict Types

Battles and sieges account for more than 90 percent of all conflicts (see Table 2.3). Battles typically took place in the countryside, while sieges typically took place just outside urban centers (and inside, if successful). We may think that the safe harbor effect would have been more pronounced for battles, which took place relatively far from urban centers. By contrast, the safe harbor effect may have been less pronounced for sieges, which took place near urban centers, making urban destruction relatively more likely and city population growth in turn less likely.[20] To test such predictions, Table 4.8 divides the conflict data into battles only and sieges only across (1) the whole period (1000–1800) and

TABLE 4.8 *Safe Harbor Effect: Conflict Types*

	(1)	(2)	(3)	(4)
	Dependent variable: log city population			
Battle exposure	0.048		0.097	
	(0.030)		(0.034)	
	[0.106]		[0.005]	
Siege exposure		0.053		0.017
		(0.038)		(0.036)
		[0.166]		[0.625]
1000–1800	Yes	Yes	No	No
1500–1800 only	No	No	Yes	Yes
R-squared	0.545	0.545	0.545	0.542
Observations	3,293	3,293	1,818	1,818

Notes: Estimation method is OLS. All regressions include city and century fixed effects, country-century interaction effects, and initial log city population-century interaction effects. Robust standard errors clustered at grid cell level in parentheses, followed by corresponding p-values in brackets.

(2) the "unusually belligerent" (Parker, 1996: 1) early modern period (1500–1800). For the whole period, the results for conflict exposure hardly differ across conflict types (columns 1 and 2). For the early modern period, however, there is a clear difference. The point estimate for battles only is 0.097, with p-value 0.005 (column 3), while the point estimate for sieges only is 0.017, with p-value 0.625 (column 4). This evidence is consistent with the logic of the safe harbor effect, which may have been more pronounced for battles than for sieges.

Evidence from City Walls

Fortified walls made of stone did not encircle every city in preindustrial Europe (Friedrichs, 1995: 23, Tracy, 2000b: 77). A city without fortified walls could still have outer rings of conjoined dwellings, defensive palisades, or ramparts or be situated in a naturally protected location (Tracy, 2000b: 79–80).[21] The high cost of wall construction in terms of labor and materials was the main reason why urban centers sometimes decided to forego this type of fortification (Pepper and Adams, 1986: 30–1; Parker, 1996: 12, 39; Tracy, 2000a: 3).[22] For example, the "modest" wall (3,700 meters long) in medieval Leiden took 50 million bricks to build (Tracy, 2000b: 71). The far-bigger wall in medieval Florence (12 meters tall and 8,500 meters long) took nearly 50 years to finish (Tracy, 2000b: 71). Medieval Lille spent approximately half of its yearly budget on the construction and maintenance costs of its wall (Wolfe, 2009: 65) Rome quit its sixteenth-century plan to build nearly 20 bastions after the construction of just one cost more than 40,000 ducats (Pepper and Adams, 1986: 30; Parker, 1996: 12).[23] Parker (1996: 12) claims that Siena lost its independence to Florence in the sixteenth century after it undertook a fortification scheme that it could not afford, leaving it vulnerable to attack.

Improved security was the main reason why urban leaders decided to construct walls in the face of such high costs. In the words of Tracy (2000a: 3), "No matter how 'natural' it may have seemed for a town to have walls, the sheer labor and expense involved means that wall builders must have had compelling reasons. Most often, it was a matter of defense against anticipated attack." For example, urban centers in France undertook significant wall-building efforts after the outbreak of the Hundred Years' War in the mid-fourteenth century (Reyerson, 2000: 89; Wolfe, 2009: 60–1). Similarly, the start of the religious wars in France in the 1560s began a "frenzy" of new wall-building activity (Wolfe, 2000: 328).

Urban centers in England "quickly rediscovered" the value of walls during the civil wars of the 1640s and 1650s (Friedrichs, 1995: 23).

It is difficult to systematically evaluate which urban centers were walled in preindustrial Europe (Tracy, 2000b: 77). Germany represents the best-documented case (Tracy, 2000b: 77). Tracy (2000b: 85) computes the share of urban centers that were walled between 1000 and 1800 by German province.[24] According to Tracy's estimate, 576 out of 1,083 urban centers – or just over 50 percent – were walled. To analyze the historical relationship between warfare and wall building in Germany, we combine Tracy's walled city data with our database on historical conflicts, as described in Chapter 2. To compute conflict exposure, we first sum the number of recorded major conflicts over 1000–1799 for each historical German province, which we then map to the corresponding modern-day German state.[25] To control for state size, we scale the historical conflict sum by the area (in 1,000 square kilometers) of each modern-day state.

Figure 4.3 plots the relationship between warfare and wall building in the history of Germany. As the safe harbor effect would predict, there is a positive correlation between conflict exposure and the presence of city walls. Rhineland, located in western Germany, is the historical province

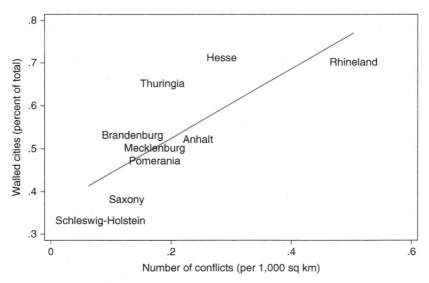

FIGURE 4.3 Historical Warfare and City Walls in Germany, 1000–1799
Sources: Bradbury (2004) and Clodfelter (2002) for historical warfare and Tracy (2000b) for city walls.

TABLE 4.9 *Historical Warfare and City Walls in France circa 1600*

	Non-Walled City	Walled City
Average # of conflicts, 1000–1599	4.54	8.46
Observations	92	13

Notes: There is a significant difference in mean conflict exposure over 1000–1599 between walled and non-walled cities. This difference is 3.92, with standard error 2.12 and p-value 0.068.
Sources: Bradbury (2004) and Clodfelter (2002) for historical warfare and Wolfe (2000) for city walls.

with the highest conflict exposure (more than 0.5 conflicts per 1,000 square km). This province displays the second-highest percentage of walled towns – 51 out of 73, or 70 percent (Hesse has the highest percentage of walled towns, at 71 percent). By contrast, Saxony and Schleswig-Holstein, located in the northwest and north of Germany, respectively, are the historical provinces with both the lowest historical conflict exposure and the lowest percentages of walled towns.

To complement the historical city wall evidence for Germany, we turn to France. Wolfe (2000: 319) provides a map of fortified towns in France at the end of the sixteenth century. We compare conflict exposure between 1000 and 1599 for French sample cities that had walls circa 1600 versus those that did not. To compute local conflict exposure, we build on the method used in the statistical analysis. Namely, we sum the number of recorded major conflicts over 1000–1599 that took place in the same 150 km × 150 km grid cell as each French sample city. Table 4.9 presents the results of this test. Consistent with the safe harbor effect, walled towns in France circa 1600 were exposed to nearly two times as many conflicts over 1000–1599 as non-walled towns.

To add a cross-country element to our analysis, we rely on Stoob's (1988) map of historical fortifications in Central Europe.[26] This map codes urban centers by fortification type. We use this map to identify which sample cities in the modern-day Austria, Czech Republic, Germany, Hungary, Poland, Slovak Republic, and Switzerland had historical walls. Following Tracy (2000b: 79), we define a "walled city" to include (single or double) stone walls or bastioned traces (including bulwarks). To compute local conflict exposure, we sum the number of recorded major conflicts between 1000 and 1799 that took place in the

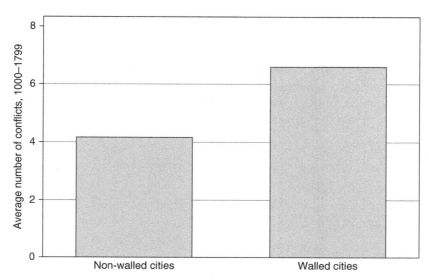

FIGURE 4.4 Historical Warfare and City Walls in Central Europe, 1000–1799
Notes: There is a significant difference in mean conflict exposure over 1000–1799 between walled and non-walled cities. This difference is 2.44, with standard error 1.30 and p-value 0.063.
Sources: Bradbury (2004) and Clodfelter (2002) for historical warfare and Stoob (1988) for city walls.

same 150 km × 150 km grid cell as each sample city. Figure 4.4 presents a bar chart for the historical relationship between conflict exposure and the presence of city walls in Central Europe. In line with the safe harbor effect, walled cities were exposed to nearly 60 percent more conflicts over 1000–1799 than non-walled cities.

Overall, the evidence from city walls lends additional support to our argument for the city as a safe harbor in European history. We find a positive correlation between historical warfare and wall building, which is consistent with the hypothesis that – relative to the countryside – individuals viewed urban centers as safe harbors that would mitigate war-related costs.

CHAPTER SUMMARY

This chapter performs a rigorous statistical analysis of the city's role as a safe harbor in preindustrial Europe. This approach allows us to systematically disentangle the safe harbor effect from other potential explanations for historical city population growth. The results of this analysis show strong statistical support for the safe harbor effect. Our results are robust to a wide range of tests for omitted variables and reverse causation.

The statistical analysis helps "ratify" the evidence from Chapter 3 about the historical importance of the city as a safe harbor. Did the safe harbor effect translate into local economic development? In Chapter 5 we rigorously test the warfare-to-wealth effect.

5

Evaluating the Warfare-to-Wealth Effect

The statistical analysis from Chapter 4 shows strong support for the city's historical role as a safe harbor in Europe. Namely, conflict exposure was associated with a significant average increase in city populations per century over 1000–1800. This chapter systematically evaluates whether the city's role as safe harbor translated into local economic development. Put differently, did the safe harbor effect "turn into" the warfare-to-wealth effect?

The main results of our statistical analysis strongly support the warfare-to-welfare effect. We find that a one standard deviation increase in historical conflict exposure predicts a 5–9 percent increase in regional per capita GDP today. Our analysis accounts for historical demographic conditions, local geographical characteristics, and fixed country-level features. To further test the robustness of our results, we perform a wide range of robustness checks. First, we control for local crop suitability measures – barley, potato, and wheat – beyond general cultivation likelihood itself. Second, we control for historical regional differences in human capital related to the invention of the printing press, the Protestant Reformation, and university access. Third, we analyze alternative samples, by excluding regions that contain modern-day national capitals and by recomputing our conflict exposure measure for different historical periods. Fourth, we test whether the warfare-to-wealth effect is nonlinear. Fifth, we evaluate several regional economic outcomes beyond GDP, including geophysically based economic activity, population density, the high-tech employment share, and R&D expenditures. Sixth, we analyze conflict types. The main results remain robust to all such checks.

To conclude our analysis, we study channels through which the warfare-to-wealth effect was transmitted over time. Given the lack of systematic historical data available at the regional level across Europe, we focus the channel analysis on Italy. Italy displays remarkable historical variety in regional economic, political, and social characteristics, making it a unique laboratory to analyze potential channels. Of equal importance, historical regional data are widely available for Italian regions. Based on our historical argument in Chapter 3, we focus on three potential channels for which such data are available: (1) local political institutions, (2) human capital accumulation, and (3) economic agglomeration effects. We find evidence that the city's historical role as a safe harbor translated into local economic development in Italy through all three mechanisms. Furthermore, our analysis sheds new light on the roots of the north-south economic divide in Italy.

DATA

The statistical analysis of the warfare-to-wealth effect calls for two main types of data: current economic activity and historical conflict exposure.

Current Economic Activity

Systematic city-level economic activity data are not readily available across European nations.[1] Thus, we focus our benchmark analysis at the NUTS2 regional level, Eurostat's main unit of economic territory. To proxy for regional wealth today, we make use of a wide variety of economic indicators. First, we average per capita GDP data between 2001 and 2005 for each available region.[23] We measure these data in purchasing power standard units (PPS) to account for price-level differences across nations. Second, as an alternative to conventional GDP, we use the gross cell product (GCP) for 1 degree longitude x 1 degree latitude grid cells (roughly 100 km x 100 km) in 2005 from Nordhaus et al. (2011), whose project was the first to develop geophysically based economic activity data. To compute per capita GCP, we divide the gross cell product by the population of each grid cell. The GCP data are measured in 2005 US dollars at purchasing power parity exchange rates in 2005. Finally, we use three other regional (NUTS2) economic outcomes in 2005: (1) log population density, (2) the share of high-technology sector employment in total employment, and (3) overall per capita R&D expenditures (in PPS).[4]

Historical Conflict Exposure

To measure historical conflict exposure, we build on the variable used in Chapter 1. First, we sum the number of recorded major conflicts between 1500 and 1799 within each 150 km × 150 km grid cell g. Here we focus on warfare in the early modern period (1500–1800) for two reasons. According to Parker (1996: 1), this period was "unusually belligerent." In our database, the early modern period accounts for 70 percent of all historical conflicts between 1000 and 1800 (see Table 2.2). Furthermore, our proxy for initial demographic conditions (to be described ahead) is more precise for 1500 than for 1000, because there are far fewer missing population observations.[5] Second, we average these sums over all grid cells that overlap with each NUTS2 region. This approach helps account for differences in physical size between NUTS2 regions, particularly for small nations. For example, the Slovak Republic has four NUTS2 regions: Central, Eastern, Western, and Bratislava. The Central, Eastern, and Western regions are very similar in size, at approximately 15,500 square kilometers each; however, the Bratislava region is more than seven times smaller, at approximately 2,000 square kilometers. By averaging historical conflict sums over all grid cells that overlap with the (particularly small) Bratislava region, we are able to incorporate conflicts in neighboring zones that may have influenced its long-run development. Finally, to measure historical conflict exposure for the Nordhaus et al. data, we simply sum the number of recorded major conflicts between 1500 and 1799 within each (equally sized) 1 degree longitude × 1 degree latitude grid cell.

Spatial Patterns

Figure 5.1 maps historical conflict exposure by region.[6] Regions in the top quintile have the darkest shade, while regions in the bottom quintile have the lightest. This figure suggests that historical conflict exposure was highest in Europe's urban belt, the corridor that spans southern England, Belgium and the Netherlands, eastern France and western Germany, and northern Italy.[7] Similarly, Figure 5.2 maps regional per capita GDP today, which also tends to be highest in the urban belt. Taken together, Figures 5.1 and 5.2 highlight the spatial correlation between historical conflict exposure and current regional economic development. Put differently, they highlight the warfare-to-wealth effect. To account for confounding factors that may drive the variation in both historical conflict exposure and modern-day development, we now perform a statistical analysis.

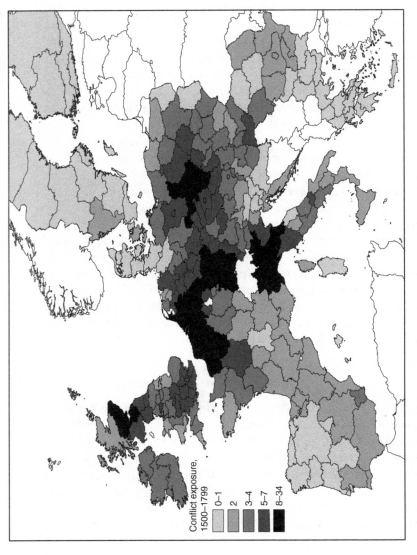

FIGURE 5.1 Historical Conflict Exposure by (NUTS2) Region

Notes: Historical conflict exposure (1) sums the number of recorded major conflicts over 1500–1799 within each 150 km × 150 km grid cell and (2) averages this sum over all grid cells that overlap with each NUTS2 region. We restrict our sample to regions for which per capita GDP data are also available (see Figure 5.2).

Sources: Bradbury (2004) and Clodfelter (2002) for military conflicts and Eurostat (http://ec.europa.eu/eurostat) for NUTS2 regions.

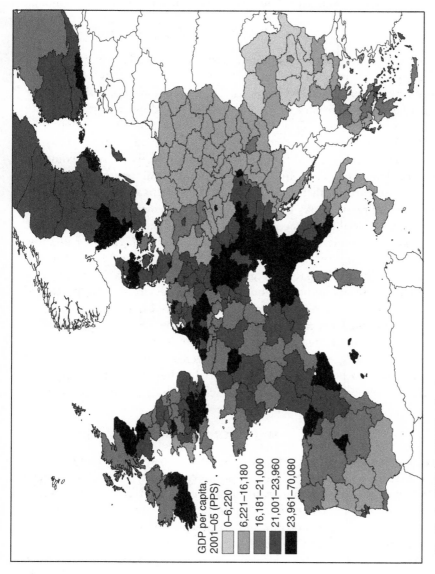

FIGURE 5.2 Per Capita GDP by (NUTS2) Region
Note: GDP data averaged over 2001–5.
Sources: Eurostat (http://ec.europa.eu/eurostat).

STATISTICAL METHODOLOGY

To statistically analyze the relationship between historical conflict exposure and regional economic activity today, we estimate the following OLS model.

$$Y_{r,c} = \alpha + \beta ConflictHistory_{r,c} + \mathbf{X}'_{r,c}\gamma + \mu_c + \varepsilon_{r,c} \tag{5.1}$$

Here we model current economic activity in (NUTS2) region r and country c as a function of $ConflictHistory_{r,c}$ – the measure of historical conflict exposure described earlier, a vector of regional controls $\mathbf{X}_{r,c}$ to be described ahead, country fixed effects μ_c, and random error term $\varepsilon_{r,c}$.

$\mathbf{X}_{r,c}$ is a vector of (NUTS2) regional controls for initial demography and geographical characteristics. We focus on "good controls" (Angrist and Pischke, 2009: 64–8) that are themselves unlikely to be outcomes of historical warfare. First, initial demographic conditions may have promoted historical conflict and economic development alike. To account for this possibility, we proxy for regional population density in 1500.[8] To an extent, this variable helps control for initial local conditions more generally (i.e., economic, political, and social conditions). As we will show ahead, the main results are robust to different start dates. Second, Europe's urban belt may have geographical advantages – for example, good agricultural conditions and easy waterway access – that promoted both historical warfare and economic growth (see Chapter 1). To account for geographical characteristics, we mimic the variables described in Chapter 4 – land area, primary rivers, landlockedness, Roman road hubs, terrain ruggedness, elevation, and general cultivation likelihood.[9] We report robust standard errors, clustered at the country level. Appendix Table C.2 shows the descriptive statistics for the regression variables.

MAIN RESULTS

Table 5.1 presents the main results for the warfare-to-wealth effect. The first specification controls for current economic, political, and social institutions at the national level through country fixed effects. There is a positive and significant relationship (at the 1 percent level) between historical conflict exposure and regional per capita GDP today. The point estimate for $ConflictHistory_{r,c}$ is 0.015.

According to the geographical endowments hypothesis (see Chapter 1), regional development patterns are at base a function of agricultural conditions and transportation access. Local agricultural conditions, moreover, may have influenced historical outbreaks of violence (e.g., Iyigun, Nunn,

TABLE 5.1 *Warfare-to-Wealth Effect: Main Results*

	(1)	(2)	(3)
	Dependent variable: log per capita GDP		
Historical conflict exposure	0.015	0.013	0.008
	(0.005)	(0.005)	(0.003)
	[0.009]	[0.020]	[0.022]
Geography	No	Yes	Yes
Log population density, 1500	No	No	Yes
Country FE	Yes	Yes	Yes
R-squared	0.105	0.129	0.345
Observations	258	258	258

Notes: Estimation method is OLS. Unit is NUTS2 region. All regressions include country fixed effects and land area control. Log per capita GDP is averaged over 2001–5 (purchasing power standard units). Geographic controls are for primary rivers, landlockedness, Roman road hubs, terrain ruggedness, elevation, and general cultivation likelihood. Robust standard errors clustered at country level in parentheses, followed by corresponding p-values in brackets.

and Qian, 2010). To help account for this possibility, column 2 adds the geographic controls in $X_{r,c}$. The relationship between historical conflict exposure and regional per capita GDP today remains similar in magnitude and significance as before.

Finally, to account for initial local demographic conditions that may have promoted both historical warfare and economic development, column 3 adds the variable log population density in 1500. The coefficient for historical conflict exposure remains highly significant, and the point estimate is now 0.008.

Taking stock, the Table 5.1 results provide robust statistical support for the warfare-to-wealth effect. According to the point estimates, a one standard deviation increase in historical conflict exposure predicts a 5–9 percent increase in regional per capita GDP today. To illustrate the economic significance of such magnitudes, we compare two regions in Italy: Lombardy, a wealthy region in the north that is a manufacturing powerhouse (Fortis, 2015), and Calabria, a poor region that is representative of the south. According to our conflict exposure measure, Lombardy experienced 13 major conflicts between 1500 and 1799, while Calabria experienced just 1. Our coefficient estimates predict that, if Calabria had the same historical conflict exposure as Lombardy, then per capita GDP there would be 1,465–2,868 PPS higher today – a size increase that amounts to 9–18 percent of the actual per capita GDP difference between the two regions.[10]

ROBUSTNESS

The main results in the previous section are robust to omitted variable concerns related to historical demographic conditions, local geographical characteristics, and fixed country-level features. To further test the robustness of our results, this section mimics several robustness checks from Chapter 4.

Crop Suitability

The second and third specifications in Table 5.1 control for a wide variety of local geographical characteristics – primary rivers, landlockedness, Roman road hubs, terrain ruggedness, elevation, and general cultivation likelihood. To further account for local agricultural conditions that may have influenced both historical conflict and economic growth, Table 5.2 replaces the general cultivation likelihood variable with controls for local soil suitability for barley (column 1), potato (column 2), and wheat (column 3) in the most stringent main specification (i.e., column 3 of Table 5.1).[11] The results remain similar in magnitude and significance as before. The point estimates for $ConflictHistory_{r,c}$ range between 0.010 and 0.012, with p-values that range between 0.003 and 0.008.

TABLE 5.2 *Warfare-to-Wealth Effect: Crop Suitability*

	(1)	(2)	(3)
	Dependent variable: log per capita GDP		
Historical conflict exposure	0.010	0.012	0.010
	(0.003)	(0.004)	(0.003)
	[0.008]	[0.003]	[0.007]
Barley suitability	Yes	No	No
Potato suitability	No	Yes	No
Wheat suitability	No	No	Yes
R-squared	0.273	0.271	0.267
Observations	246	246	246

Notes: Estimation method is OLS. Unit is NUTS2 region. All regressions include country fixed effects, geographic controls, and log population density in 1500. Log per capita GDP is averaged over 2001–5 (purchasing power standard units). Geographic controls are for land area, primary rivers, landlockedness, Roman road hubs, terrain ruggedness, and elevation. Robust standard errors clustered at country level in parentheses, followed by corresponding p-values in brackets.

Human Capital

Unobserved historical differences in human capital accumulation across regions may affect our main results, particularly if human capital was highest in the urban belt (see Chapter 1). Dittmar (2011) argues that the invention of the moveable type printing press in Mainz in the mid-fifteenth century promoted the attainment of useful business skills. To help account for the historical role of the printing press in human capital accumulation, column 1 of Table 5.3 includes the geodesic distance from the centroid of region *r* to Mainz. This variable is very similar to the one that Dittmar himself uses to measure the historical adoption of the printing press across space. Similarly, Becker and Woessmann (2009) argue that widespread literacy among Protestants improved economic productivity. To help account for the role of Protestant-related literacy, column 2 includes the geodesic distance from the centroid of region *r* to Wittenberg, the birthplace of the Protestant Reformation. This variable follows directly from Becker and Woessmann's original measure of the historical geographic diffusion of Protestantism. Finally, Cantoni and Yuchtman (2014) argue that greater access to university-level legal training in Germany after the Papal Schism of 1378 promoted commercial activity. To help account for the role of university access, column 3 includes the geodesic distance from the centroid of region *r* to the nearest university in 1500 (the start date of

TABLE 5.3 *Warfare-to-Wealth Effect: Human Capital*

	(1)	(2)	(3)
	Dependent variable: log per capita GDP		
Historical conflict exposure	0.008	0.006	0.006
	(0.003)	(0.003)	(0.004)
	[0.011]	[0.070]	[0.107]
Distance to Wittenberg	Yes	No	No
Distance to Mainz	No	Yes	No
Distance to nearest university	No	No	Yes
R-squared	0.351	0.372	0.361
Observations	258	258	258

Notes: Estimation method is OLS. Unit is NUTS2 region. All regressions include country fixed effects, geographic controls, and log population density in 1500. Log per capita GDP is averaged over 2001–5 (purchasing power standard units). Geographic controls are for land area, primary rivers, landlockedness, Roman road hubs, terrain ruggedness, elevation, and general cultivation likelihood. Robust standard errors clustered at country level in parentheses, followed by corresponding p-values in brackets.

our statistical analysis) according to Bosker, Buringh, and van Zanden (2013). The coefficient estimates across all three specifications are relatively similar in magnitude and significance to the most stringent main specification (i.e., column 3 of Table 5.1). Overall, these robustness checks provide evidence that historical regional differences in human capital accumulation do not drive our main results.

Alternative Samples

Regions that include national capitals such as London or Paris tend to be prosperous (Eurostat, 2015). To test whether capital city status drives our results, column 1 of Table 5.4 excludes all regions that contain modern-day national capitals, of which there are more than 20. The point estimate for historical conflict exposure is the same as for the most stringent main specification (i.e., column 3 of Table 5.1), with p-value 0.024.

Column 2 recomputes the historical conflict exposure measure over the whole sample period from the fall of Charlemagne's empire to the start of the Industrial Revolution (i.e., 1000–1799). The benefit of extending the conflict sample farther back in time is that we can include more historical conflicts, while the drawback is that our proxy for initial demographic conditions becomes less precise, because there are more missing population observations in 1000 than in 1500. In any case, the point estimate for historical

TABLE 5.4 *Warfare-to-Wealth Effect: Alternative Samples*

	(1)	(2)	(3)
	Dependent variable: log per capita GDP		
Historical conflict exposure	0.008	0.011	0.018
	(0.003)	(0.004)	(0.007)
	[0.024]	[0.011]	[0.022]
Exclude modern-day capitals	Yes	No	No
Conflict exposure, 1000–1799	No	Yes	No
Conflict exposure, 1300–1699	No	No	Yes
R-squared	0.258	0.235	0.324
Observations	234	258	258

Notes: Estimation method is OLS. Unit is NUTS2 region. All regressions include country fixed effects, geographic controls, and log population density in 1500 (column 1), 1000 (column 2), or 1300 (column 3). Log per capita GDP is averaged over 2001–5 (purchasing power standard units). Geographic controls are for land area, primary rivers, landlockedness, Roman road hubs, terrain ruggedness, elevation, and general cultivation likelihood. Robust standard errors clustered at country level in parentheses, followed by corresponding p-values in brackets.

conflict exposure as measured over 1000–1799 is greater in magnitude and significance than in the most stringent main specification (i.e., column 3 of Table 5.1).

The 1700s saw the most recorded conflicts in preindustrial Europe (see Table 2.2). To test whether this century drives our results, the specification in column 3 recomputes the historical conflict exposure measure over a different sample period (1300–1699) that extends farther back in time but excludes eighteenth-century conflicts. The point estimate more than doubles relative to the most stringent main specification (i.e., column 3 of Table 5.1) and remains highly significant.

Nonlinear Effect

The relationship between historical conflict exposure and regional economic development today may be nonlinear. For example, "too much" historical conflict may have had negative long-run economic consequences. To test for this sort of possibility, we include the squared historical conflict exposure measure $ConflictHistory^2_{r,c}$. The results (not shown) support our use of the linear specification. The point estimate for $ConflictHistory_{r,c}$ is 0.019, with p-value 0.030, in the most stringent main specification (i.e., column 3 of Table 5.1). By contrast, the point estimate for the squared term is negative and significant but exceedingly small. This analysis suggests that regions do not pay an economic penalty today for undergoing "too much" historical warfare.

Gross Cell Product

As an alternative to conventional GDP, Table 5.5 reestimates the main specifications for the geophysically based economic activity variable – the gross cell product (GCP) – from Nordhaus et al. (2011).[12] The relationship between historical conflict exposure and regional per capita GCP today is positive and significant (at the 1 percent level). Thus, our results do not appear to be contingent on any specific measure of economic output.

Alternative Economic Outcomes

Table 5.6 presents the results for the three alternative NUTS2 regional economic outcomes – population density, the high-tech employment share, and per capita R&D expenditures – for the most stringent main specification (i.e., column 3 of Table 5.1). Consistent with our predictions

TABLE 5.5 *Warfare-to-Wealth Effect: Gross Cell Product*

	(1)	(2)	(3)
	Dependent variable: log per capita GCP		
Historical conflict exposure	0.027	0.027	0.022
	(0.005)	(0.004)	(0.006)
	[0.000]	[0.000]	[0.000]
Geography	No	Yes	Yes
Log population density, 1500	No	No	Yes
Country FE	Yes	Yes	Yes
R-squared	0.059	0.110	0.119
Observations	998	998	998

Notes: Estimation method is OLS. Unit is 1 degree longitude × 1 degree latitude grid cell. All regressions include country fixed effects and land area control. Log per capita GCP is for 2005 (2005 USD at purchasing power parity exchange rates in 2005). Geographic controls are for primary rivers, landlockedness, Roman road hubs, terrain ruggedness, elevation, and general cultivation likelihood. Robust standard errors clustered at country level in parentheses, followed by corresponding p-values in brackets.

TABLE 5.6 *Warfare-to-Wealth Effect: Alternative Outcomes*

	(1)	(2)	(3)
Dependent variable:	Log population density	High-tech employment	Log per capita R&D spending
Historical conflict exposure	0.054	0.102	0.062
	(0.010)	(0.033)	(0.024)
	[0.000]	[0.007]	[0.021]
R-squared	0.545	0.215	0.200
Observations	176	176	176

Notes: Estimation method is OLS. Unit is NUTS2 region. All regressions include country fixed effects, geographic controls, and log population density in 1500. All outcome variables are for 2005. High-technology sector employment is share in total employment. Log per capita R&D expenditures are in purchasing power standard units. Geographic controls are for land area, primary rivers, landlockedness, Roman road hubs, terrain ruggedness, elevation, and general cultivation likelihood. Robust standard errors clustered at country level in parentheses, followed by corresponding p-values in brackets.

about the warfare-to-wealth effect (see Chapter 3), the results indicate that regions that were exposed to greater historical conflicts are not only significantly more densely populated today (column 1), but also have significantly more high-tech employment (column 2) and spend significantly more on R&D (column 3).

TABLE 5.7 *Warfare-to-Wealth Effect: Conflict Types*

	(1)	(2)
	Dependent variable: log per capita GDP	
Historical battle exposure	0.019	
	(0.008)	
	[0.023]	
Historical siege exposure		0.009
		(0.005)
		[0.088]
R-squared	0.354	0.334
Observations	258	258

Notes: Estimation method is OLS. Unit is NUTS2 region. All regressions include country fixed effects, geographic controls, and log population density in 1500. Log per capita GDP is averaged over 2001–5 (purchasing power standard units). Geographic controls are for land area, primary rivers, landlockedness, Roman road hubs, terrain ruggedness, elevation, and general cultivation likelihood. Robust standard errors clustered at country level in parentheses, followed by corresponding p-values in brackets.

Conflict Types

Recall that battles and sieges account for more than 90 percent of all conflicts (see Table 2.3). To test how conflict types influence our results, Table 5.7 recomputes the main historical conflict measure for (1) battles only and (2) sieges only and reestimates the most stringent main specification for each (i.e., column 3 of Table 5.1). The magnitude and significance of the point estimate for $BattleHistory_{r,c}$ is greater than for $SiegeHistory_{r,c}$: 0.019 (p-value = 0.023) versus 0.009 (p-value = 0.088). These results are consistent with the statistical evidence from Chapter 4 that suggests that the safe harbor effect was more pronounced for historical battles than for historical sieges, because battles took place relatively far from urban centers, while sieges took place relatively near them, making urban destruction more likely (and in turn making city population growth less likely).

CHANNELS: EVIDENCE FROM ITALY

The statistical evidence from the previous two sections shows robust support for the warfare-to-wealth effect. To conclude our analysis, we now analyze channels through which the warfare-to-wealth effect was transmitted over time, which we view as a quantitative complement to the historical discussion in Chapter 3.

Chapter 3 describes three potential channels: (1) the establishment of local privileges, including self-governance and property rights protections from predatory outside rulers; (2) technological innovation and human capital accumulation; and (3) economic agglomeration effects. Systematic historical data for such variables are not readily available at the NUTS2 regional level. As a way to operationalize our analysis, we draw on Vecchi (2011), who assembles late nineteenth-century data for 15-plus regions in Italy.[13] Italy provides a unique testing ground to analyze different channels because of long-standing variety in economic, political, and social characteristics at the regional level (Epstein, 2000: 10–11). Political fragmentation in medieval Italy was high in the north but low in the south following the twelfth-century establishment of the Norman kingdom (Putnam, 1993: 121–37; Chittolini, 1994: 28–9). Figure 5.3 maps north-south differences in historical fragmentation levels. Numerous small states made up the political geography of northern Italy, while the Kingdom of Naples dominated southern Italy. Unlike many other nations in Europe, Italy did not become a single sovereign political unit – the Kingdom of Italy, a constitutional monarchy – until 1861 (Dincecco, 2010: 309–11; Dincecco, Federico, and Vindigni, 2011: 896).[14] The unification process in Italy was a major change to the geopolitical landscape of Europe. Today, regions in northern Italy (including Emilia-Romagna, Liguria, Lombardy, and Piedmont) form part of Europe's prosperous urban belt, while many regions in southern Italy (e.g., Apulia, Basilicata, Calabria) remain poor; average per capita GDP is more than 50 percent higher in the north than in the south (see Table 1.1).

Importantly, Vecchi's data are available for 1871, just after political unification in Italy. Thus, features related to national-level economic and political institutions, which in the 1870s were only just being established, are unlikely to influence the results of our channel analysis. Our focus on late nineteenth-century outcomes, moreover, enables us to study the consequences of historical warfare at an "intermediate" point in time between the preindustrial era and today. This time period is about when we would expect the warfare-to-wealth channels to have fully manifested themselves (see Figure 1.3).

Figure 5.4 provides an overview of the relationship between historical warfare and economic development at the regional level in late nineteenth-century Italy. As the warfare-to-wealth effect would predict, there is a

FIGURE 5.3 Political Borders in Sixteenth-Century Italy
Note: Political borders as of 1559.
Source: Hearder (2001: 137).

positive correlation between historical conflict exposure over 1500–1799 and per capita GDP in 1871. In the north, where historical political fragmentation and instability was high, regions including Liguria, Lombardy, and Piedmont experienced a great deal of historical conflict. These regions were among the richest in late nineteenth-century Italy. The south, by contrast, experienced early bureaucratic centralization under the Normans,

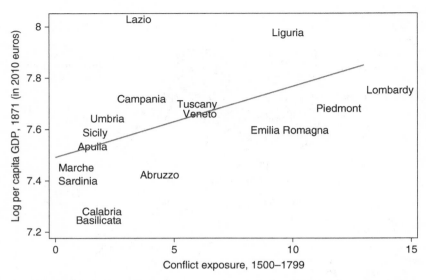

FIGURE 5.4 Historical Warfare (1500–1799) and Per Capita GDP (1871) in Italy
Notes: Per capita GDP is in 2010 euros. Historical conflict exposure (1) sums the number of recorded major conflicts over 1500–1799 within each 150 km × 150 km grid cell and (2) averages this sum over all grid cells that overlap with each NUTS2 region. "Abruzzo" refers to the regions of Abruzzo and Molise. "Piedmont" refers to the regions of Piedmont and the Aosta Valley.
Sources: Clodfelter (2002) for historical warfare and Vecchi (2011: 428) for per capita GDP.

which may help explain why historical conflict exposure was lower. Regions including Apulia, Basilicata, and Calabria saw few recorded major conflicts. Such regions were relatively poor in the late nineteenth century.

Human Capital Accumulation

We first analyze the channel that concerns technological innovation and human capital accumulation. We are not aware of any systematic historical data available to proxy for technological innovation at the regional level. However, Vecchi provides two variables to proxy for human capital accumulation in late nineteenth-century Italy: (1) the regional literacy rate in 1871 and (2) the primary school enrollment ratio. Figures 5.5 and 5.6 plot the relationships between historical warfare and late nineteenth-century literacy and school enrollment in Italy, respectively. There is a clear north-south divide. At one extreme, northern regions (e.g., Liguria, Lombardy, Piedmont) display both high

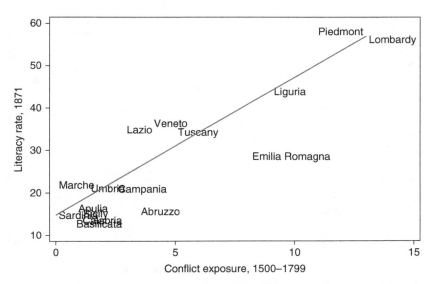

FIGURE 5.5 Historical Warfare (1500–1799) and the Literacy Rate (1871) in Italy
Notes: Literacy rate is the percentage of the regional population aged 15 and over that could read and write. Historical conflict exposure (1) sums the number of recorded major conflicts over 1500–1799 within each 150 km × 150 km grid cell and (2) averages this sum over all grid cells that overlap with each NUTS2 region. "Abruzzo" refers to the regions of Abruzzo and Molise. "Piedmont" refers to the regions of Piedmont and the Aosta Valley. "Veneto" refers to the regions of Veneto and Friuli Venezia Giulia.
Sources: Clodfelter (2002) for historical warfare and Vecchi (2011: 425) for the literacy rate.

historical conflict exposure and high subsequent human capital accumulation. At the other extreme, southern regions (e.g., Apulia, Basilicata, Calabria) exhibit low historical conflict exposure and low subsequent human capital accumulation. In line with the historical discussion in Chapter 3, these results suggest that human capital accumulation was in fact a channel through which historical warfare could translate into local economic development in Italy.

To complement the within-Italy evidence, we draw on Tabellini (2010), who constructs data on the literacy rate in 1880 at the regional level across eight nations in Western Europe.[15] To help account for historical determinants of human capital accumulation beyond warfare, such as the Protestant Reformation (Becker and Woessmann, 2009), we control for country fixed effects. More generally, such effects help account for other potential sources of unobserved country-level

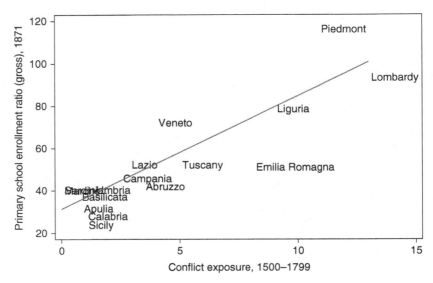

FIGURE 5.6 Historical Warfare (1500–1799) and School Enrollment Ratio (1871) in Italy
Notes: Primary school enrollment ratio (gross) is the number of children enrolled in the primary level of education regardless of their age divided by the population of the age group that officially corresponds to the same level of education (i.e., ages 6–10). Historical conflict exposure (1) sums the number of recorded major conflicts over 1500–1799 within each 150 km × 150 km grid cell and (2) averages this sum over all grid cells that overlap with each NUTS2 region. "Abruzzo" refers to the regions of Abruzzo and Molise. "Piedmont" refers to the regions of Piedmont and the Aosta Valley. "Veneto" refers to the regions of Veneto and Friuli Venezia Giulia.
Sources: Clodfelter (2002) for historical warfare and Vecchi (2011: 426) for primary school enrollment ratio.

heterogeneity (e.g., geographical characteristics). Figure 5.7 displays the partial correlation of historical conflict exposure and regional literacy in 1880 across Western Europe. There is a positive and significant relationship between the two variables. This evidence corroborates the within-Italy evidence, further suggesting that human capital accumulation was a channel through which the warfare-to-wealth effect was transmitted over time.

Local Political Institutions

Unlike human capital accumulation, there is less regional variation in political institutions that placed checks on royal power in nineteenth-

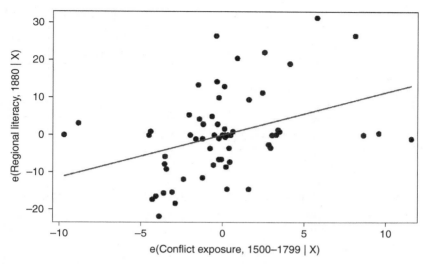

FIGURE 5.7 Historical Warfare (1500–1799) and Regional Literacy (1880) in Europe
Notes: Literacy rate is the percentage of the regional population that could read and write. Regional data are for Belgium, France, Germany (excluding East Germany), Italy, the Netherlands, Portugal, Spain, and the United Kingdom. Historical conflict exposure (1) sums the number of recorded major conflicts over 1500–1799 within each 150 km × 150 km grid cell and (2) averages this sum over all grid cells that overlap with each available region. Estimation method is OLS. Partial regression controls for country fixed effects.
Sources: Clodfelter (2002) for historical warfare and Tabellini (2010) for the literacy rate.

century Italy, making it somewhat difficult to analyze the channel that concerns the establishment of local privileges including self-governance and property rights protections from predatory outside rulers. However, we can still glean insights about the importance of political regime types during the pre-unitary period (1815–60). Piedmont established the only lasting pre-unitary parliamentary regime in 1848. Dincecco, Federico, and Vindigni (2011: 895–6) argue that King Victor Emmanuel II (reign, 1849–61) upheld the 1848 constitutional reform as part of his strategy for state expansion. Both business-minded urban elites (e.g., in Genoa) and the king benefitted from this political bargain. Urban elites gained formal political representation and a greater say over how public funds were to be spent (e.g., on transportation infrastructure), while the king secured new funds for the military (Dincecco, Federico, and Vindigni, 2011: 895–6). Consistent with this argument, Table 5.8 indicates that per

TABLE 5.8 *Political Regimes and Public Finances in Pre-Unitary Piedmont*

	Taxation	Military Spending	Nonmilitary Spending
Absolutist regime (1825–47)	4.27	1.93	2.79
Parliamentary regime (1848–58)	6.41	3.31	6.34
Percent increase after regime change	50%	72%	127%

Note: Taxation and spending figures are in gold grams per capita.
Source: Dincecco, Federico, and Vindigni (2011).

capita tax revenues in Piedmont increased by 50 percent in the parliamentary period (1848–58) relative to the absolutist period (1825–47). Similarly, per capita military expenditures increased by more than 70 percent, while per capita nonmilitary expenditures increased by more than 125 percent.

To further analyze the political institutions channel, we study the relationship between historical warfare and local self-governance in Italy between 1500 and 1800. This period displays greater variation in political institutions that checked royal power than does the pre-unitary period. To measure local self-governance, we compute the share of self-governing communes according to Bosker, Buringh, and van Zanden (2013) within each NUTS2 region for each century from 1500 to 1800, averaging this share over the whole period. Figure 5.8 plots the relationship between conflict exposure and the commune share at the regional level in early modern Italy. There is a clear difference between the north and the south. Recall from earlier that historical political fragmentation and instability was high in the north, making warfare more likely. In this context, rulers may have been more willing to strike political bargains with well-off urban elites (Putnam, 1993: 124; Tilly, 1994: 22–6), exchanging local freedoms, including self-governance and property rights protections, for new funds. In the south, however, bureaucratic centralization came early, reducing both political instability and the ruler's demand for new funds, while at the same time likely making repression a more attractive way to tax than bargaining. Accordingly, we observe both high conflict exposure and high self-governance in northern regions such as Emilia-Romagna, Liguria, Lombardy, and Piedmont but low conflict exposure and low self-governance in southern regions such as Apulia, Basilicata, Calabria, and others (see Figure 5.8).

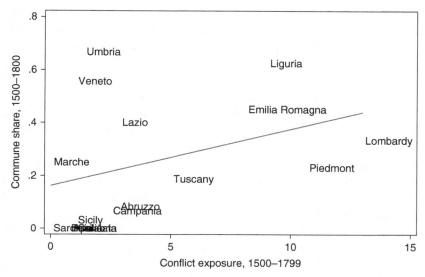

FIGURE 5.8 Historical Warfare and Urban Self-Governance in Italy, 1500–1800
Notes: Commune share (1) computes the share of urban centers that are self-governing communes within each NUTS2 region each century and (2) averages this share over 1500–1800. Historical conflict exposure (1) sums the number of recorded major conflicts over 1500–1799 within each 150 km × 150 km grid cell and (2) averages this sum over all grid cells that overlap with each NUTS2 region. "Veneto" refers to the regions of Veneto and Friuli Venezia Giulia.
Sources: Clodfelter (2002) for historical warfare and Bosker, Buringh, and van Zanden (2013) for self-governing communes.

Overall, the evidence for both parliamentary government in pre-unitary Piedmont and local self-governance in early modern Italy suggests that – in line with the historical discussion in Chapter 3 – political institutions that placed checks on royal power were another channel through which the city's historical role as a safe harbor could translate into local economic development.

Economic Agglomeration Effects

Finally, we analyze the channel that concerns economic agglomeration effects. Historical urbanization rates in the bureaucratically centralized south were surprisingly high (Malanima, 1998: 103–5). However, southern urban centers were agro-towns – large agricultural centers in which the majority of inhabitants were peasants (Malanima, 1998:

102–3). Hearder (1983: 126), for example, describes eighteenth-century Naples as follows: "She lived on the back of a desperately overworked, desperately poor, peasantry, who were given no civic rights."

Beyond historical urbanization rates, therefore, we must analyze the economic, political, and social character of urban centers in Italy, which was very different in the north versus the south (Putnam, 1993: 136; Malanima, 1998: 102–3). Malanima (1998: 102) explains as follows: "A city is, in fact, not only a relatively wide settlement, but also, and more importantly, a settlement whose inhabitants are mostly involved in activities different from those the peasants of the countryside are involved in. A city, to be a city indeed, cannot be a large village with a population of peasants. It must be a settlement inhabited by craftsmen, merchants, shop-keepers, political officials, sometimes the court, soldiers, and always the clergy." Only urban centers in northern Italy displayed such functional characteristics (Malanima, 1998: 102–3). Accordingly, we may expect (1) reductions in exchange costs for goods and labor, (2) an efficient division of labor, and (3) thick labor markets to have taken hold in the north but not necessarily in the south. This fundamental difference in the character of urban centers in northern versus southern Italy corresponds with historical differences in political fragmentation and warfare. As described earlier, political fragmentation and warfare was high in the north but low in the south. Overall, this evidence is broadly consistent with our argument that economic agglomeration effects were a third channel through which the warfare-to-wealth effect was transmitted over time.[16]

CHAPTER SUMMARY

This chapter performs a rigorous statistical analysis of the warfare-to-wealth effect, the results of which strongly support the argument that the city's historical role as a safe harbor translated into local economic development. Thus, to answer the question posed at the start of this chapter, the statistical evidence suggests that the safe harbor effect did in fact "turn into" the warfare-to-wealth effect in Europe. Human capital accumulation, local political institutions, and economic agglomeration effects all stand out as channels that helped mediate the relationship between the city's role as safe harbor and local development over the long run. Do our results imply that the logic of "warfare to wealth" is universal? To answer that question, we analyze the European development experience in comparative perspective in Chapter 6.

6

Warfare to Wealth in Comparative Perspective

The previous four chapters have analyzed urban Europe's historical path from warfare to wealth. Warfare was a central feature of Europe's historical landscape. To mitigate the high rural costs of warfare, rural inhabitants migrated to urban centers. Over time, the city's historical role as a safe harbor translated into local economic development. The historical evidence in Chapters 2 and 3, along with the statistical analyses in Chapters 4 and 5, show strong support for this argument.

Is the logic of "warfare to wealth" universal? Historical warfare was common across the globe, but many world regions remain poor today. To better understand the political economy context in which the warfare-to-wealth effect may take hold, this chapter performs a comparative analysis. We focus on two diverse parts of the world: China and sub-Saharan Africa. There are several reasons why China and sub-Saharan Africa make for meaningful foils for Europe. The first concerns economic diversity. An important literature seeks to explain the "Great Divergence" whereby Europe took off economically but China fell behind after 1800 (see Chapter 1). Yet China has experienced rapid economic development over the past 30 years (Zhu, 2012: 103). Sub-Saharan Africa, however, remains the "development challenge of our time" (Akyeampong et al., 2014: 1). In addition to widespread poverty, civil conflicts and wars are common there (Blattman and Miguel, 2010: 4). The second reason concerns geographical comparability. Europe, China, and sub-Saharan Africa make for relatively similar geographical units of analysis in terms of physical size.[1] The third reason concerns geographical diversity. Europe and China are located at different ends of Eurasia, north of the equator, while a good portion of sub-Saharan Africa is located in the Southern Hemisphere.

TABLE 6.1 *Historical Comparisons: Europe versus China and Sub-Saharan Africa*

	Warfare	Political Fragmentation	Land-Labor Ratio	Warfare to Wealth?
Europe	Common	High	Low	Most likely
China	Common	Low	Low	Less likely
Sub-Saharan Africa	Common	High	High	Less likely

Note: See text for historical evidence and sources.

We contrast China and sub-Saharan Africa with Europe on the basis of two important historical features: political fragmentation and the land-labor ratio. Table 6.1 summarizes the differences between Europe, China, and sub-Saharan Africa along these dimensions. What distinguishes Europe is not historical warfare itself, which was relatively common across all three world regions. Rather, the historical combination of high political fragmentation and a low land-labor ratio makes Europe unique. In China, the land-labor ratio was low, but political fragmentation was low too. In sub-Saharan Africa, the opposite was the case, because both political fragmentation and the land-labor ratio were high. In what follows, we show how historical differences in political fragmentation and the land-labor ratio can help explain why the warfare-to-wealth effect took hold in Europe but not in China or sub-Saharan Africa. We do not think of the results of this analysis as the last word on this topic, however. Rigorous study of the long-run economic consequences of warfare in world regions beyond Europe remains an important area for future research. We view the evidence in this chapter as a first step in such a research agenda.

WAR FREQUENCY

Warfare was a main feature of Europe's historical landscape (see Chapter 2). However, military conflict itself does not necessarily distinguish preindustrial Europe from other world regions. Hoffman (2015: 70), for example, estimates that China fought interstate wars in 56 percent of all years between 1500 and 1800, while England fought 53 percent of the time, France fought 52 percent of the time, and Spain fought 81 percent of the time. Similarly, warfare was common in precolonial sub-Saharan Africa (Thornton, 1999: 1–18; Reid, 2012: 1–17; Bates, 2014: 426–8; Besley and Reynal-Querol, 2014: 323–6).

TABLE 6.2 *Nomadic Invasion: Western Europe versus China*

	Western Europe	China
800s	Magyar	Uygur
900s	—	Khitan
1000s	—	—
1100s	—	Jurchen
1200s	—	Mongol
1300s	—	Tatar
1400s	—	Oirot
1500s	—	—
1600s	—	Manchu
1700s	—	—
Totals	1	7

Note: Nomad invader name listed.
Sources: Chaliand (2005), as reported by Ko, Koyama, and Sng (2014).

There were important historical differences in the contours of warfare across Europe, China, and sub-Saharan Africa, which we will analyze ahead. Still, military conflict itself – a basic ingredient for the warfare-to-wealth effect to take hold – was present across all three historical contexts. To help explain why historical warfare did not always translate into economic development, we first analyze differences in political fragmentation between Europe and China.

POLITICAL FRAGMENTATION: EUROPE VERSUS CHINA

According to Tilly (1992: 45), there were upward of 500 states in Europe circa 1500. Furthermore, average state size was small – roughly the size of modern-day El Salvador or Armenia (Tilly, 1992: 45). Early modern China, by contrast, was huge in size (Rosenthal and Wong, 2011: 12; Hoffman, 2015: 74–5). Unlike rulers in preindustrial Europe, moreover, rulers in China were able to establish lasting authority over large amounts of territory by the late thirteenth century (Rosenthal and Wong, 2011: 12–13, 17–24; Blockmans and t'Hart, 2013: 425).[2]

Given the high level of political fragmentation and the small average state size in preindustrial Europe, attack threats could emanate from multiple directions. China, by contrast, faced an overwhelmingly unidirectional threat from nomads from the Eurasian Steppe (Hoffman, 2015:

70–1). From 800 to 1700, there were seven invasions by steppe nomads in China, but only one in Western Europe (Table 6.2). Similarly, more than 95 percent of early modern China's wars were fought against nomads (Hoffman, 2015: 70–1). City walls provide further evidence of the unidirectional nature of historical attack threats in China. Ioannides and Zhang (2015) assemble data on city wall characteristics for more than 900 urban centers during the Qing dynasty (1644–1911). They find that city walls located along the steppe were significantly taller and thicker than non-steppe walls (see Ioannides and Zhang, 2015: 16–20), reflecting greater attack threats by nomad invaders.

Consequences for Urbanization

The preceding discussion suggests that even if historical warfare was common across both Europe and China, the contours of conflict were different because of the varying levels of political fragmentation and the diverse types of attack threats – namely, multidimensional versus unidimensional – to which they gave rise. Our formal model (as summarized in Chapter 3) helps us interpret the consequences of such differences for historical city population growth. Beyond the recurrent nomadic threat, early modern China can be thought of as a relatively peaceful empire that promoted domestic trade, delivered basic public services, and charged low taxes (Rosenthal and Wong, 2011: 209–15; Hoffman, 2015: 51; von Glahn, 2016: 345–7). In the spirit of the model's first prediction, rural–urban migration may take place in peacetime, because the urban productivity gain can make the city an attractive choice. This prediction is consistent with the historical evidence suggesting that urbanization rates in medieval China were relatively high (Xu, van Leeuwen, and van Zanden, 2015). Still, in the spirit of the model's second and third predictions, historical rural–urban migration ought to have been higher overall in Europe than in China since greater conflict risk – which we interpret here in terms of political fragmentation and multidimensional threats – made city relocation more likely (i.e., to mitigate the rural costs of warfare). The historical evidence supports this view. Winter (2013: 405) writes that the "divergent trends noted from at least the sixteenth century onwards suggest that the overall proportion of people involved in urban migration was lower in Ming-Qing China than in contemporaneous Europe." By the start of the 1800s, the urbanization rate in Western Europe was 13 percent, but only 5 percent in China (Winter, 2013: 405).[3]

In fact, historical rulers in China may have taken advantage of the relatively high level of bureaucratic centralization to limit urbanization. Dense urban populations – particularly when located near centers of government power – can mobilize more quickly against incumbent regimes than can dispersed rural populations (Wallace, 2014: 4–5; Glaeser and Millett Steinberg, 2016: 9–10). To reduce threats of revolt, autocratic regimes may have the incentive to restrict rural–urban migration (Wallace, 2014: 6–7). In modern-day China, for example, the government has implemented a variety of economic, fiscal, and social reforms to make rural life more attractive (Wallace, 2014: 6–7).

Consequences for Local Political Institutions

Over the long run, the relatively high and enduring level of bureaucratic centralization in early modern China may have reduced the potential for local political and legal innovations that could have promoted greater economic development. Blockmans and t'Hart (2013: 434) argue that the historical balance of power in China "gravitated towards the central ruler, which precluded the development of autonomous communities." In politically fragmented Europe, by contrast, the fiscal pressures of warfare oftentimes induced sovereign rulers to bargain with well-off urban entrepreneurs over new tax funds, the "price" of which was the granting of local political and legal freedoms including self-governance and property rights protections from outside predation (see Chapter 3). Stasavage (2016: 155, 159) argues that political fragmentation and warfare fostered the historical development of parliamentary government in Europe, but only because such rulers could not rely upon an alternative governance strategy based on bureaucratic centralization and coercive resource extraction as in China. Self-governance by business-oriented urban elites – along with property rights that were safe from outside predation – may have promoted a legal environment in Europe that was favorable to investment and trade (see Chapter 3). Furthermore, due to political fragmentation, urban elites in Europe could play rulers against each other and threaten to switch allegiances from one polity to another if their appeals for greater political and legal autonomy were overlooked (see Chapter 3). Our historical and quantitative analyses (in Chapters 3 and 5, respectively) suggest that local privileges were one channel through which the warfare-to-wealth effect took hold in Europe. Given the relatively high level of historical bureaucratic centralization in China, however, this channel was less likely to emerge there.

LAND-LABOR RATIO: EUROPE VERSUS SUB-SAHARAN AFRICA

Precolonial sub-Saharan Africa was politically fragmented and average state size was small. Thornton (1999: 3–4), for example, writes that "probably more than half of the people in Atlantic Africa lived in polities that measured around 50 kilometers across and had only a few thousand inhabitants, comparable in size to an American county or perhaps to a parish in older European political organizations." Ethnic diversity was high even within precolonial African empires (Herbst, 2000: 44). Thus, in terms of political fragmentation (high) and state size (small), precolonial sub-Saharan Africa did not appear to differ dramatically from preindustrial Europe.

Rather, an important historical difference between sub-Saharan Africa and Europe in 1500 was the land-labor ratio, which was approximately 14 people per square kilometer in Europe (and 13 people per square kilometer in China) but only 2 people per square kilometer in sub-Saharan Africa (Herbst, 2000: 16).[4] When the land-labor ratio was relatively low, territory was scarce, making it more likely that the city would function as a safe harbor in wartime, ceteris paribus. If the land-labor ratio was high enough, then rural inhabitants may have preferred to migrate to virgin rural land far from the conflict's epicenter rather than seek safety behind urban fortifications. Herbst (2000: 39) calls this phenomenon the "primacy of exit," writing, "The combinations of large amounts of open land and rain-fed agriculture meant that, in precolonial Africa, control of territory was often not contested because it was often easier to escape from rulers than to fight them." The general absence of a map-making tradition in precolonial Africa attests to the lack of importance of land ownership – and to the potential for rural–rural migration to escape political turmoil (Herbst, 2000: 39). While Europeans did not typically distinguish between land occupancy and land ownership (see Chapter 2), it was possible for land to be controlled by one state but owned by another in sub-Saharan Africa (Herbst, 2000: 40–1).

Consequences for Urbanization

The preceding discussion suggests that even if precolonial warfare was common in sub-Saharan Africa, differences in the land-labor ratio reduced the importance of the city's role as a safe harbor in wartime relative to Europe. To further elucidate this point, we now tweak our formal model (the technical details are in the Model Appendix). Say that – unlike an individual who lives in the countryside in preindustrial Europe –

a rural individual in precolonial sub-Saharan Africa has two realistic migration options in the face of nearby conflict: relocate to virgin rural land (a new alternative option in the African context) or to the city (the original option as described in Chapter 3). Given high-enough rural costs of nearby conflict, this individual will prefer to migrate rather than stay in the original countryside location. To decide between her migration choices, this individual must compare (1) the relocation cost of rural–rural migration plus the cost of farming virgin land against (2) the relocation cost of rural–urban migration plus the urban graveyard cost (plus any urban productivity gain). The historical cost of farming virgin land in sub-Saharan Africa was very low (Herbst, 2000: 39), making it more likely that condition (1) would be a less-costly migration solution than condition (2) in the face of nearby conflict. Put differently, in the precolonial sub-Saharan African context, this individual would likely prefer the "primacy of exit" in response to conflict threats: namely, to flee to virgin rural land rather than to the city.

The historical evidence supports this prediction of the model. Relative to Europe, urbanization in precolonial sub-Saharan Africa was very low. Describing urbanization trends in 1500, Weil (2014: 94–5) writes that "extraordinarily few cities appear" beyond a handful of urban centers in the west of the continent. In 1500, there were nearly 80 urban centers with at least 20,000 inhabitants in Europe but only 22 such centers in sub-Saharan Africa (Table 6.3). Similarly, while Europe had nearly 20 urban centers with at least 50,000 inhabitants in 1500, sub-Saharan Africa only had two. Without steady rural–urban migration in precolonial sub-Saharan Africa, the warfare-to-wealth effect was less likely to take hold.

Political borders in sub-Saharan Africa became well defined from the colonial period onward (Besley and Reynal-Querol, 2014: 326). In terms of the modeling tweak described earlier, strong political borders would likely increase the cost of rural–rural migration, making rural–urban

TABLE 6.3 *Number of Urban Centers in 1500: Europe versus Sub-Saharan Africa*

	Europe	Sub-Saharan Africa
20,000–50,000 inhabitants	78	22
50,000+ inhabitants	19	2

Source: Weil (2014)

migration (within a given sovereign territory) a more attractive choice. Furthermore, according to Reid (2012: 398–407), there was an African military revolution over the long nineteenth century (1770s–1920s) that was akin to that in early modern Europe (Parker, 1996). Interestingly, there is evidence for a safe harbor effect in this context. Describing eastern and central Africa, for example, Reid (2012: 118) writes, "Armed urbanization proceeded apace, and fortified villages and towns became commonplace across a region formerly characterized by dispersed patterns of settlement." However, both Bates (2014) and Reid (2014) argue that the imperial "peace" implemented by European powers in the late 1800s retarded the process by which warfare could have promoted indigenous African economic and political development.

Consequences for Enduring Warfare

Over time, the high historical land-labor ratio may have contributed to an "enduring-warfare effect" from past to present rather than to the warfare-to-wealth effect. Precolonial sub-Saharan Africa was land-rich and labor-scarce. Thus, unlike in Europe, where the main goal of warfare was to gain new territory (see Chapter 2), a main goal in sub-Saharan Africa was to capture slaves. Scholars highlight this feature of sub-Saharan Africa's historical landscape. Herbst (2000: 42–3), for example, writes, "Warfare tended to be concentrated on seizing booty since it was hard to hold onto territory. As most farmers had nothing to seize, the most valuable treasure was slaves (i.e., the farmers themselves). Due to the slave trade, capturing people who later could be sold to the Europeans or Omanis or other Africans was, in fact, one of the most profitable activities that could be undertaken at particular times in many parts of the continent." Similarly, Reid (2012: 5) states, "One of the key vectors in Africa's military past has been the drive to maximize and control productive and reproductive labor; coercion has often been required to control people in a relatively land-rich environment..." Finally, Thornton (1999: 16) argues that "ownership of slaves in Africa was virtually equivalent to owning land in Western Europe or China." The most common style of historical warfare in Africa – known as the "raiding war" (Reid, 2012: 4–5) – reflects Africa's high land-labor ratio.[5] Unlike traditional campaign-style warfare in Europe, characterized by large-scale operations and set-piece battles, the raiding style of warfare in Africa was characterized by repeated small attacks on the enemy's resources – human, animal, and physical (Reid, 2012: 4–5).

The raiding war may have been more likely to engender open-ended conflict, particularly in combination with important historical events such as the transatlantic slave trade.[6] Whatley and Gillezeau (2011) argue that the transatlantic slave trade made individuals more valuable to African states as potential slaves than as potential taxpayers. In turn, African states had greater incentives to carry out slave raids rather than bargain with local social groups over policy concessions in exchange for greater revenues as in Europe (Whatley and Gillezeau, 2011). Whatley and Gillezeau link the transatlantic slave trade to the establishment of large numbers of small and independent villages, which exacerbated ethnic divisions. Note that this logic is the opposite of the "war makes states" paradigm (Tilly, 1975, 1992) often thought to characterize the European historical experience. Indeed, ethnic fragmentation may fuel civil conflict (Montalvo and Reynal-Querol, 2005). Similarly, social groups that have a history of fighting may be less trustful of each other, promoting future conflict (Nunn and Wantchekon, 2011; Besley and Reynal-Querol, 2014). Furthermore, previous combat experience can endow social groups with "martial capital" that may be transmitted vertically to future generations, thereby making conflict more likely to endure (Jha and Wilkinson, 2012). All three factors – ethnic fragmentation, a history of fighting, and combat experience – may be more likely to promote sustained conflict if the state remains too weak to act as an impartial third-party mediator (Bates, 2010: 57–66). More than half of sub-Saharan African nations today, for example, are highly or extremely fragile (Table 6.4).

Overall, this logic suggests that the high historical land-labor ratio in sub-Saharan Africa – particularly in combination with major historical

TABLE 6.4 *State Fragility: Western Europe versus Sub-Saharan Africa*

	Western Europe	Sub-Saharan Africa
No fragility	100%	2%
Low–moderate fragility	0%	46%
High–extreme fragility	0%	52%

Note: Fragility is the percentage of nations in Western Europe or sub-Saharan Africa in 2008 that fall within each category of Marshall and Cole's (2009) state fragility index.
Sources: Marshall and Cole (2009), as reported by Besley and Persson (2011).

events, including the transatlantic slave trade – may promote enduring warfare rather than wealth creation. Scholars highlight the negative legacy of precolonial conflict in sub-Saharan Africa. Bates (2008: 85) writes that "past conquests by monarchs and warriors created territorial disputes that reverberate to this day ..." Similarly, Reid (2012: 10) states, "The past was very much present in the organization of violence, even during the revolutionary upheaval of the nineteenth century and the self-consciously modernist struggles of the mid-twentieth century." The statistical evidence in Besley and Reynal-Querol (2014) supports this view. They find a significant correlation between precolonial conflict and recent conflict in Africa whereby each additional year of conflict between 1400 and 1700 translates into an extra two months of modern-day civil conflict over the period from colonial independence to today. Furthermore, Besley and Reynal-Querol find that greater precolonial conflict predicts lower current per capita GDP and greater current ethnic identification (at the expense of national identity). This evidence is consistent with our argument that, given the specific historical political economy context of sub-Saharan Africa, an enduring-warfare effect from past to present may have been more likely to take hold there than the warfare-to-wealth effect.

WHY WARFARE-TO-WEALTH TOOK HOLD IN EUROPE

The comparative analysis in previous sections suggests why the warfare-to-wealth effect was more likely to take hold in Europe than in China or sub-Saharan Africa. Military conflict was present across all three world regions. However, only in preindustrial Europe was steady warfare combined with high political fragmentation and a low land-labor ratio. Relative to China, high political fragmentation in Europe induced greater conflict risk in the form of multidimensional attack threats, making rural–urban migration more likely. Furthermore, political fragmentation often induced European rulers to grant local political and legal freedoms in exchange for new tax funds, thereby promoting a business environment that was conducive to economic development. Credible threats by urban elites to switch allegiances from one city or polity to another further enhanced their bargaining power relative to rulers.[7]

Relative to sub-Saharan Africa, the low land-labor ratio in Europe made it more likely that the city would function as a safe harbor from conflict threats rather than encourage migration to faraway virgin lands.

The low land-labor ratio, moreover, was the basis by which warfare could "make" states in Europe, because, unlike in sub-Saharan Africa, European territory was valuable (Herbst, 2000: 13–15). According to the "war makes states" paradigm (Tilly, 1975, 1992), historical European states undertook institutional reforms to increase extractive capacity and finance military efforts (see Chapter 1). As the fiscal and military strength of states grew, they became better able to reduce civil conflict, using both repression and enticement. On the one hand, European states could enforce local peace agreements and demilitarize local warlords (Bates, 2010: 46–50). On the other hand, states could establish national-level parliaments that gave local elites a formal voice in government decision making (Bates, 2010: 52–4). Thus, over time, military competition between European states over scarce territory could promote domestic peace within each of them (see Chapter 1). To echo Morris (2014: 8), "war made governments, and governments made peace." Western European nations today are very stable (Table 6.4). Over the long run, the nation-state's growing ability to secure peace – along with fundamental nineteenth-century changes to the nature of warfare – reduced the city's traditional importance as a safe harbor in Europe (see Chapter 1).

CHAPTER SUMMARY

This chapter analyzes the universality of the warfare-to-wealth effect, the process by which the city's historical role as a safe harbor translated into local economic development in Europe. We suggest that the warfare-to-wealth effect was most likely to take hold in a historical political economy context in which political fragmentation was high and the land-labor ratio was low. To help make this case, we compare preindustrial Europe to early modern China and precolonial sub-Saharan Africa. In China, the land-labor ratio was low, but political fragmentation was low too. By contrast, high political fragmentation in Europe induced greater conflict risk in the form of multi-dimensional attack threats, making city relocation more likely. Furthermore, political fragmentation often induced European rulers to grant local political and legal privileges, promoting an urban legal environment favorable to economic activity, whereas the relatively high level of bureaucratic centralization in China may have reduced the potential for local institutional innovations that fostered investment and trade. In sub-Saharan Africa, the context was the opposite of that in China: political fragmentation and the land-labor ratio were each high. The city's historical role as a safe harbor was less important in this context than in Europe, because rural inhabitants in sub-Saharan Africa could instead escape to virgin rural land far from the epicenter of conflict. Furthermore, the high land-labor ratio may have induced persistent warfare rather than wealth creation, by promoting slave raids and exacerbating ethnic divisions – particularly in combination with important historical events such as the transatlantic slave trade. Thus, relative to China and sub-Saharan Africa, Europe seems unique. Only in Europe was steady warfare combined with high political fragmentation and a low land-labor ratio, producing a political economy context in which (1) rural–urban migration in response to conflict threats was large and sustained and (2) the warfare-to-wealth effect was most likely to take hold. As described at the start of this chapter, we view the results of our study as a first step in a research agenda that rigorously examines the long-run economic consequences of warfare in world regions beyond Europe. We look forward to further analysis of this topic.

Epilogue

Over the past millennium, real per capita GDP in Western Europe has grown roughly 30-fold.[1] Modern Europe's economic backbone is the urban belt – the corridor of urban regions that spans southern England, Belgium and the Netherlands, eastern France and western Germany, and northern Italy. However, things were not always this way. The urbanization rate in Europe after the fall of the Carolingian Empire more than 1,000 years ago was roughly 3 percent (van Bavel, Bosker, Buringh, and van Zanden, 2013: 394). We have argued that to truly explain how Europe became prosperous, we must understand how it became urban. As Glaeser and Joshi-Ghani (2015: xv) write, "Urbanization is undoubtedly a key driver of development – cities provide the national platform for shared prosperity."

Scholars describe the economic effects of contemporary civil warfare as "development in reverse" (Collier et al., 2003: 13–32). In historical Europe, however, we have argued that warfare "turned into" wealth – at least over the long run. The fall of Charlemagne's empire over the ninth century gave rise to a high level of political fragmentation in Europe, making instability and warfare more likely. Historical warfare inflicted numerous costs on rural populations. The city held two traditional defensive advantages over rural areas: fortification and scale. Thus, to mitigate the high rural costs of conflict, rural populations migrated to urban centers. Over time, the city's historical role as a safe harbor translated into local economic development through channels such as the establishment of local privileges including self-governance and private property rights protections from predatory outside rulers, technological innovation and human capital accumulation, and economic agglomeration effects. Overall, our study of the military origins of urban prosperity in Europe provides a new way to think about the process of long-run economic and political development.

To make our argument, we have taken advantage of a wide range of social science methods. First, we have constructed a novel quantitative database that spans a millennium, from the aftermath of the fall of Charlemagne's empire to today. This database provides a rich new perspective. Second, we have presented a large body of historical evidence in support of our argument. This evidence integrates, in innovative ways, previous scholarship from demography, economics, economic history, political science, and sociology. Third, we have developed a simple formal model that elucidates the decision-making process of would-be migrants in the historical countryside. This model produces predictions about optimal migration decisions that corroborate the historical evidence and help guide our statistical analyses. Fourth, we have performed rigorous statistical tests of both the safe harbor effect and the warfare-to-wealth effect. These analyses not only enable us to maximize the informative content of our database, but also to systematically account for potential confounding factors such as geographical endowments. The statistical results show robust support for the safe harbor effect and the warfare-to-wealth effect alike. Finally, we have analyzed urban Europe's historical path from warfare to wealth relative to China and sub-Saharan Africa – two world regions that differ in economic and political terms from Europe but that are similar in physical size. This comparative perspective expands our understanding of the different ways in which historical warfare can influence long-run economic development. What appears to have made Europe unique was the historical combination of high political fragmentation and a low land-labor ratio. We look forward to future research that further analyzes the long-run economic consequences of warfare in world regions beyond Europe.

IMPLICATIONS FOR DEVELOPMENT TODAY

We now conclude our analysis with two historical lessons for development today: the unintended consequences of political fragmentation and the importance of migration.

Unintended Consequences of Political Fragmentation

High historical political fragmentation in Europe drives the core dynamics of warfare, rural–urban migration, and economic and political development at play in this book. But where did high political fragmentation in

Europe come from? We have described the "accidental" way in which the Carolingian Empire was partitioned over the ninth century (see Chapters 1 and 2). This book's period of analysis starts in the aftermath of Charlemagne's fall. However, even Charlemagne's empire was short-lived (Ganshof, 1971: 17–27). Before that, Western Europe was politically fragmented from the time of the fall of the Roman Empire (Hoffman, 2015: 107). An exogenous shock – the Germanic invasions – may account for the Roman Empire's fall (Wickham, 1984: 18).

Overall, the high political fragmentation characteristic of Europe appears to have been a function of historical happenstance rather than any master plan. Given (1) the arduous historical process by which nation-states in Europe established uniform domestic legal and fiscal institutions (Epstein, 2000; Dincecco 2011, 2015) and (2) the economic benefits (e.g., greater domestic trade and labor specialization à la Adam Smith) of such nondiscriminatory national institutions, high political fragmentation in Europe can probably best be thought of as a vice that inadvertently became a virtue over the long run.[2] The nineteenth century saw the establishment of effective national governments in Europe (see Chapter 1). In turn, European nations were able to overcome the economic costs associated with high political fragmentation, while still reaping the unexpected benefits derived from it (i.e., better governance, technological innovation, human capital accumulation, greater productivity).

This lesson about unintended consequences affirms the scholarly consensus that historical events are important causes of modern development patterns (Nunn, 2009), but with a twist: the historical path to economic development does not always proceed in a straightforward manner. Depending on the interplay of different historical factors, warfare may lead to wealth in one context – as in Europe – but economic stagnation or civil conflict in another (see Table 6.1).

The Importance of Migration

The transformation from countryside to city brings great economic expectations. In this book, we show how warfare – via the safe harbor effect – was a main driver of this transformation in Europe, the world region in which the process of modern economic development first began.

Clearly, we do not advocate military conflict as a means to promote urbanization today.[3] In this regard, a key lesson of our book does not concern warfare, but rather the importance of migration, which can have significant economic effects. Clemens (2011: 85) finds that the potential gains from lifting modern-day policy barriers to labor mobility between nations are large – ranging from 50 to 150 percent of world GDP. Similarly, Lewis and Peri (2015: 681–2) document a positive relationship between present-day immigration and economic productivity on the one hand and higher earnings for native-born workers on the other. Our book shows how rural–urban migration – even if warfare-related – can have major consequences for economic development over the long stretch of history. In the modern era, effective policy rather than warfare is the best way to encourage migration. Yet the economic results should be the same today as they were historically: to foster prosperity through better governance, technological innovation and human capital accumulation, and greater productivity.

Data Appendix

APPENDIX TABLE A.1 *Military Conflicts in Europe, 1000–1799*

No.	Conflict Name	Year	Nearby Settlement	Country	Type	Duration
1	London	1010	London	England	Siege	Multiday
2	London	1013	London	England	Siege	Multiday
3	Struma	1014	Klyuch	Bulgaria	Battle	One day
4	Clontarf	1014	Dublin	Ireland	Battle	One day
5	London	1016	London	England	Battle	Multiday
6	Otford	1016	Otford	England	Battle	Multiday
7	Pontlevoy	1016	Pontlevoy	France	Battle	One day
8	Cannae	1018	Canne Della Battaglia	Italy	Battle	Multiday
9	Montboyau	1026	Saint-Cyr-sur-Loire	France	Siege	Multiday
10	Stiklestad	1030	Stiklestad	Norway	Battle	One day
11	Monte Maggio	1041	Canne della Battaglia	Italy	Battle	One day
12	Venosa	1041	Venosa	Italy	Battle	One day
13	Brionne	1047–50	Brionne	France	Siege	Multiyear
14	Val-es-Dunes	1047	Caen	France	Battle	Multiday
15	Domfront	1051–2	Domfront	France	Siege	Multiyear
16	Arques-la-Bataille	1052–3	Arques-la-Bataille	France	Siege	Multiyear
17	Saint-Aubin-sur-Scie	1053	Saint-Aubin-sur-Scie	France	Battle	One day
18	Civitate	1053	San Paolo di Civitate	Italy	Battle	One day
19	Mortemer	1054	Mortemer	France	Battle	Multiday
20	Cleobury	1056	Cleobury	England	Battle	One day
21	Lumphanan	1057	Lumphanan	England	Battle	One day
22	Varaville	1057	Varaville	France	Battle	Multiday

(continued)

114

23	Reggio	1060	Reggio di Calabria	Italy	Siege	Multiday
24	Messina	1061	Messina	Italy	Siege	Multiday
25	Mayenne	1063	Domfront	France	Siege	Multiday
26	Cerami	1063	Cerami	Italy	Battle	Multiday
27	Dinan	1064	Dinan	France	Siege	Multiday
28	Dol	1064	Dol-de-Bretagne	France	Siege	Multiday
29	Gate Fulford	1066	York	England	Battle	One day
30	Hastings	1066	Hastings	England	Battle	One day
31	Stamford Bridge	1066	Stamford Bridge	England	Battle	One day
32	Exeter	1068	Exeter	England	Siege	Multiday
33	Bari	1068–71	Bari	Italy	Siege	Multiyear
34	York	1069	York	England	Siege	Multiday
35	Ely	1071	Isle of Ely	England	Siege	Multiday
36	Cassel	1071	Cassel	France	Battle	One day
37	Hohenburg	1075	Bad Langensalza	Germany	Battle	One day
38	Skyhill	1079	Ramsey	England	Battle	Multiday
39	Flarchheim	1080	Flarchheim	Germany	Battle	One day
40	Hohen-Molsen	1080	Hohenmölsen	Germany	Battle	One day
41	Dyrrhachium	1081	Durres	Albania	Battle	One day
42	Dyrrhachium	1081–2	Durres	Albania	Siege	Multiyear
43	Larissa	1083	Larissa	Greece	Battle	Multiday
44	Larissa	1083	Larissa	Greece	Siege	Multiday
45	Toledo	1084–5	Toledo	Spain	Siege	Multiday
46	Zalaka	1086	Badajoz	Spain	Battle	One day
47	Mount Levunium	1091	Pazardzhik	Bulgaria	Battle	One day
48	Cuarte	1094	Valencia	Spain	Battle	Multiday

(continued)

No.	Conflict Name	Year	Nearby Settlement	Country	Type	Duration
49	Huseca	1094	Huesca	Spain	Siege	Multiday
50	Bamburgh	1095	Bamburgh	England	Siege	Multiday
51	Huesca	1096	Huesca	Spain	Siege	Multiday
52	Tinchebrai	1105–6	Tinchebrai	France	Siege	Multiyear
53	Candé	1106	Candé	France	Siege	Multiday
54	Tinchebrai	1106	Tinchebrai	France	Battle	Multiday
55	Sepulveda	1111	Sepulveda	Spain	Battle	One day
56	Alencon	1118	Alencon	France	Siege	Multiday
57	Zaragoza	1118	Zaragoza	Spain	Siege	Multiday
58	Bremule	1119	Gaillardbois-Cressenville	France	Battle	Multiday
59	Bourgtherould	1124	Bourgtheroulde-Infreville	France	Battle	Multiday
60	Brionne	1124	Brionne	France	Siege	Multiday
61	Standard	1138	Northallerton	England	Battle	One day
62	Wallingford	1139	Wallingford	England	Siege	Multiday
63	Ourique	1139	Ourique	Portugal	Battle	One day
64	Weinsberg	1140	Weinsberg	Germany	Battle	One day
65	Lincoln	1141	Lincoln	England	Battle	One day
66	Winchester	1141	Winchester	England	Other	One day
67	Weinsberg	1141	Weinsberg	Germany	Siege	Multiday
68	Oxford	1142	Oxford	England	Siege	Multiday
69	Wilton	1142	Wilton	England	Battle	Multiday
70	Burwell	1144	Burwell	England	Siege	Multiday
71	Faringdon	1145	Faringdon	England	Siege	Multiday
72	Lisbon	1147	Lisbon	Portugal	Siege	Multiday

(continued)

73	Montreuil-Bellay	1149–51	Montreuil-Bellay	France	Siege	Multiday
74	Wallingford	1152–3	Wallingford	England	Siege	Multiday
75	Muradel	1157	Ciudad Real	Spain	Battle	One day
76	Milan	1158–62	Milan	Italy	Siege	Multiyear
77	Fornham	1173	Bury St Edmunds	England	Battle	One day
78	Rebellion of Alnwick	1173–4	Alnwick	England	Other	Multiyear
79	Alessandria	1174–5	Alessandria	Italy	Siege	Multiyear
80	Legnano	1176	Legnano	Italy	Battle	One day
81	Strymon	1185	Komotini	Greece	Battle	One day
82	Thessalonika	1185	Thessalonika	Greece	Siege	Multiday
83	Gisors	1193	Gisors	France	Siege	Multiday
84	Freteval	1194	Freteval	France	Battle	One day
85	Alarcos	1195	Ciudad Real	Spain	Battle	One day
86	Gisors	1198	Gisors	France	Battle	One day
87	Chateau-Galliard	1203–4	Les Andelys	France	Siege	Multiyear
88	Toulouse	1211	Toulouse	France	Siege	Multiday
89	Las Navas de Tolosa	1212	Despeñaperros Natural Park	Spain	Battle	One day
90	Muret	1213	Muret	France	Battle	One day
91	Bouvines	1214	Bouvines	France	Battle	One day
92	Rochester	1215	Rochester	England	Siege	Multiday
93	Lincoln	1217	Lincoln	England	Battle	One day
94	Lincoln	1217	Lincoln	England	Siege	Multiday
95	Toulouse	1217–8	Toulouse	France	Siege	Multiyear
96	Bedford	1224	Bedford	England	Siege	Multiday
97	Thessalonika	1224	Thessalonika	Greece	Siege	Multiday

(continued)

No.	Conflict Name	Year	Nearby Settlement	Country	Type	Duration
98	Klokotnitsa	1230	Klokotnitsa	Bulgaria	Battle	Multiday
99	Cortenuova	1237	Cortenuova	Italy	Battle	One day
100	Brescia	1238	Brescia	Italy	Siege	Multiday
101	Liegnitz	1241	Legnickie Pole	Poland	Battle	One day
102	Saintes	1242	Saintes	France	Battle	One day
103	Montsegur	1243–4	Montségur	France	Siege	Multiyear
104	Parma	1247–8	Parma	Italy	Siege	Multiyear
105	Pelagonia	1259	Kastoria	Greece	Battle	Multiday
106	Largs	1263	Largs	Scotland	Battle	One day
107	Lewes	1264	Lewes	England	Battle	One day
108	Evesham	1265	Evesham	England	Battle	One day
109	Benevento	1266	Benevento	Italy	Battle	One day
110	Tagliacozzo	1268	Tagliacozzo	Italy	Battle	One day
111	Marchfeld	1278	Dürnkrut	Austria	Battle	One day
112	Sicilian Vespers	1282	Palermo	Italy	Other	Multiday
113	Dunbar	1296	Dunbar	Scotland	Battle	One day
114	Stirling	1297	Stirling	Scotland	Battle	One day
115	Falkirk	1298	Falkirk	Scotland	Battle	One day
116	Courtrai	1302	Courtrai	Belgium	Battle	One day
117	Mons-en-Pevele	1304	Mons-en-Pevele	France	Battle	One day
118	Methven	1306	Methven	Scotland	Battle	One day
119	Loudoun Hill	1307	Darvel	Scotland	Battle	One day
120	Bannockburn	1314	Bannockburn	Scotland	Battle	One day
121	Morgarten	1315	Lake Aegeri	Switzerland	Battle	One day

(*continued*)

122	Faughart	1318	Faughart	England	Battle	One day
123	Myton	1319	Myton-On-Swale	England	Battle	One day
124	Boroughbridge	1322	Boroughbridge	England	Battle	One day
125	Muehldorf	1322	Mühldorf am Inn	Germany	Battle	One day
126	Cassel	1328	Cassel	France	Battle	One day
127	Pelekanos	1329	Pelekanos	Greece	Battle	One day
128	Kustendil	1330	Kustendil	Bulgaria	Battle	One day
129	Dupplin Moor	1332	Scone	Scotland	Battle	One day
130	Halidon Hill	1333	Berwick-Upon-Tweed	England	Battle	One day
131	Rio Salado	1340	Tarifa	Spain	Battle	One day
132	Morlaix	1342	Morlaix	France	Battle	One day
133	Algeciras	1342–4	Algeciras	Spain	Siege	Multiyear
134	Neville's Cross	1346	Durham	England	Battle	One day
135	Caen	1346	Caen	France	Siege	Multiday
136	Calais	1346–7	Calais	France	Siege	Multiyear
137	Crecy	1346	Crecy-en-Ponthieu	France	Battle	One day
138	Saint-Pol de Leon	1346	Saint-Pol de Leon	France	Battle	One day
139	Roche-Derrien	1347	Roche-Derrien	France	Battle	One day
140	Roche-Derrien	1347	Roche-Derrien	France	Siege	Multiday
141	Eppila	1348	Épila	Spain	Battle	Multiday
142	Mauron	1352	Mauron	France	Battle	One day
143	Breteuil	1356	Breteuil	France	Siege	Multiday
144	Poitiers	1356	Maupertuis	France	Battle	One day
145	Rennes	1356–7	Rennes	France	Siege	Multiyear
146	Jacquerie	1358	Saint-Leu-d'Esserent	France	Other	Multiday
147	Cascina	1364	Cascina	Italy	Battle	One day

(continued)

No.	Conflict Name	Year	Nearby Settlement	Country	Type	Duration
148	Najera	1367	Najera	Spain	Battle	One day
149	Cascina	1369	Cascina	Italy	Battle	Multiday
150	Montiel	1369	Ciudad Real	Spain	Battle	One day
151	Thurie	1370	Albi	France	Siege	Multiday
152	Chernomen	1371	Ormenio	Greece	Battle	One day
153	La Rochelle	1372	La Rochelle	France	Siege	Multiday
154	Revolt in Bologna	1375	Bologna	Italy	Other	Multiday
155	Revolt in Orvieto	1375	Orvieto	Italy	Other	Multiday
156	Revolt in Perugia	1375	Perugia	Italy	Other	Multiday
157	Revolt in Viterbo	1375	Viterbo	Italy	Other	Multiday
158	Excomm of Florence	1376	Florence	Italy	Other	Multiday
159	Sack of Cesena	1377	Cesena	Italy	Other	Multiday
160	Uprising in Florence	1378	Florence	Italy	Other	Multiday
161	Peasant's Revolt	1381	Blackheath	England	Other	Multiday
162	Roosebeke	1382	Courtrai	Belgium	Battle	One day
163	Aljubarrota	1385	Aljubarrota	Portugal	Battle	One day
164	Sempach	1386	Sempach	Switzerland	Battle	One day
165	Radcot Bridge	1387	Radcot	England	Battle	One day
166	Castagnaro	1387	Castagnaro	Italy	Battle	One day
167	Otterburn	1388	Otterburn	England	Battle	One day
168	Kosovo	1389	Pristina	Kosovo	Battle	One day
169	Alessandria	1391	Alessandria	Italy	Battle	One day
170	Rovine	1395	Rovine	Romania	Battle	One day
171	Nicopolis	1396	Nikopol	Bulgaria	Battle	One day

(continued)

172	Nicopolis	1396	Nikopol	Bulgaria	Siege	Multiday
173	Homildon Hill	1402	Wooler	England	Battle	One day
174	Pilleth	1402	Knighton	Wales	Battle	One day
175	Shrewsbury	1403	Shrewsbury	England	Battle	One day
176	Bramham Moor	1408	Bramham	England	Battle	One day
177	Tannenberg	1410	Grunwald	Poland	Battle	One day
178	Agincourt	1415	Agincourt	France	Battle	One day
179	Harfleur	1415	Harfleur	France	Siege	Multiday
180	Kalamata	1415	Kalamata	Greece	Battle	Multiday
181	Valmont	1416	Valmont	France	Battle	One day
182	Caen	1417	Caen	France	Siege	Multiday
183	Falaise	1418–9	Falaise	France	Siege	Multiyear
184	Rouen	1418–9	Rouen	France	Siege	Multiyear
185	Vysehrad	1420	Prague	Czech Rep	Battle	One day
186	Saaz	1421	Zatec	Czech Rep	Battle	One day
187	Saaz	1421	Zatec	Czech Rep	Siege	Multiday
188	Bauge	1421	Bauge	France	Battle	One day
189	Meaux	1421–2	Meaux	France	Siege	Multiyear
190	Deutschbrod	1422	Havlíčkův Brod	Czech Rep	Siege	Multiday
191	Arbedo	1422	Arbedo-Castione	Switzerland	Battle	One day
192	Cravant	1423	Cravant	France	Battle	One day
193	Verneuil	1424	Verneuil	France	Battle	One day
194	Aussitz	1426	Ustí nad Labem	Czech Rep	Battle	Multiday
195	Orleans	1428–9	Orleans	France	Siege	Multiyear
196	Herrings	1429	Rouvray-Saint-Denis	France	Battle	One day
197	Patay	1429	Patay	France	Battle	One day

(continued)

APPENDIX TABLE A.1 (continued)

No.	Conflict Name	Year	Nearby Settlement	Country	Type	Duration
198	Beauvais	1430	Savignies	France	Battle	One day
199	Thessalonika	1430	Thessalonika	Greece	Siege	Multiday
200	Anghiari	1440	Anghiari	Italy	Battle	One day
201	Varna	1444	Varna	Bulgaria	Battle	Multiday
202	Varna	1444	Varna	Bulgaria	Siege	Multiday
203	St. Jakob	1444	Münchenstein	Switzerland	Battle	One day
204	Caravaggio	1448	Caravaggio	Italy	Battle	One day
205	Kosovo	1448	Pristina	Kosovo	Battle	Multiday
206	Rouen	1449	Rouen	France	Siege	Multiday
207	Cade's Rebellion	1450	Blackheath	England	Other	Multiday
208	Caen	1450	Caen	France	Siege	Multiday
209	Falaise	1450	Falaise	France	Siege	Multiday
210	Formigny	1450	Formigny	France	Battle	One day
211	Castillon	1453	Castillon-la-Bataille	France	Battle	One day
212	St. Albans	1455	St. Albans	England	Battle	One day
213	Blore Heath	1459	Market Drayton	England	Battle	One day
214	Northampton	1460	Northampton	England	Battle	One day
215	Wakefield	1460	Sandal Magna	England	Battle	One day
216	Mortimer's Cross	1461	Wigmore	England	Battle	One day
217	St. Alband	1461	St. Albans	England	Battle	One day
218	Towton	1461	Towton	England	Battle	One day
219	Hedgeley Moor	1464	Glanton	England	Battle	One day
220	Hexham	1464	Hexham	England	Battle	One day
221	Monthery	1465	Monthery	France	Battle	One day

(continued)

222	Liege	1468	Liege	Belgium	Siege	Multiday
223	Edgecote Moor	1469	Banbury	England	Battle	One day
224	Barnet	1471	High Barnet	England	Battle	One day
225	London	1471	London	England	Siege	Multiday
226	Twekesbury	1471	Tewkesbury	England	Battle	One day
227	Beauvais	1472	Beauvais	France	Siege	Multiday
228	Neuss	1474-5	Neuss	France	Siege	Multiyear
229	Toro	1476	Toro	Spain	Battle	Multiday
230	Grandson	1476	Grandson	Switzerland	Battle	One day
231	Morat	1476	Morat	Switzerland	Battle	One day
232	Nancy	1477	Nancy	France	Battle	One day
233	Battle of Campormoto	1482	Frosinone	Italy	Battle	One day
234	Sack of Adria	1482	Adria	Italy	Other	One day
235	Sack of Argenta	1482	Argenta	Italy	Other	One day
236	Sack of Comacchio	1482	Comacchio	Italy	Other	One day
237	Siege of Ferrara	1482-4	Ferrara	Italy	Other	Multiyear
238	Siege of Ficarolo	1482	Ficarolo	Italy	Siege	Multiday
239	Siege of Rovigo	1482	Rovigo	Italy	Siege	Multiday
240	Loja	1482	Loja	Spain	Battle	One day
241	Bosworth	1485	Market Bosworth	England	Battle	One day
242	Stoke	1487	East Stoke	England	Battle	One day
243	Granada	1491-2	Granada	Spain	Siege	Multiyear
244	Fornovo	1495	Fornovo di Taro	Italy	Battle	One day
245	Seminara	1495	Seminara	Italy	Battle	One day
246	Atella	1496	Orta di Atella	Italy	Battle	Multiday
247	Dornach	1499	Dornach	Switzerland	Battle	One day

(continued)

No.	Conflict Name	Year	Nearby Settlement	Country	Type	Duration
248	First Milan	1500	Milan	Italy	Siege	Multiday
249	Barletta	1502–3	Barletta	Italy	Siege	Multiyear
250	Cerignola	1503	Cerignola	Italy	Battle	One day
251	First Naples	1503	Naples	Italy	Siege	Multiday
252	Formia	1503	Formia	Italy	Battle	One day
253	Gaeta	1503	Gaeta	Italy	Siege	Multiday
254	Garigliano River	1503	Gaeta	Italy	Battle	One day
255	Agnadello	1509	Agnadello	Italy	Battle	One day
256	Padua	1509	Padua	Italy	Siege	Multiday
257	Vicenza	1510	Vicenza	Italy	Siege	Multiday
258	Battle of Brescia	1511	Brescia	Italy	Battle	One day
259	Bologna	1511	Bologna	Italy	Siege	Multiday
260	Sack of Brescia	1511	Brescia	Italy	Other	Multiday
261	Ravenna	1512	Ravenna	Italy	Siege	Multiday
262	Second Milan	1512	Milan	Italy	Siege	Multiday
263	Flodden Edge	1513	Branxton	England	Battle	One day
264	Battle of the Spurs	1513	Enguinegatte	France	Battle	One day
265	Therouanne	1513	Therouanne	France	Siege	Multiday
266	First Novara	1513	Novara	Italy	Siege	Multiday
267	Marignano (Melegnano)	1515	Melegnano	Italy	Battle	Multiday
268	Bath of Blood	1520	Stockholm	Sweden	Other	Multiday
269	Bogesand	1520	Ulricehamm	Sweden	Battle	One day
270	Siege of Stockholm	1520	Stockholm	Sweden	Siege	Multiday
271	Rhodes	1521	Rhodes Island	Greece	Siege	Multiday

(continued)

272	Third Milan	Milan	Italy	Siege	One day
273	Belgrade	Belgrade	Serbia	Siege	Multiday
274	Villalar	Villalar de Los Comuneros	Spain	Other	One day
275	Bicocca	Bicocca	Italy	Battle	One day
276	Landstuhl	Landstuhl	Germany	Siege	Multiday
277	Second Novara	Novara	Italy	Siege	Multiday
278	Palma	Palma de Mallorca	Spain	Siege	Multiday
279	Danish Surrender	Stockholm	Sweden	Siege	Multiday
280	Marseille	Marseille	France	Siege	Multiday
281	Sesia	Novara	Italy	Battle	One day
282	Frankenhausen	Bad Frankenhausen	Germany	Battle	One day
283	Weinsberg	Weinsberg	Germany	Battle	Multiday
284	Battle of Pavia	Pavia	Italy	Battle	Multiday
285	Siege of Pavia	Pavia	Italy	Siege	Multiday
286	Buda	Budapest	Hungary	Siege	Multiday
287	Mohacs	Mohács	Hungary	Battle	One day
288	Peterwardein	Peterwardein	Serbia	Siege	Multiday
289	Rome	Rome	Italy	Other	One day
290	Genoa	Genoa	Italy	Other	Multiday
291	Landriano	Landriano	Italy	Battle	One day
292	Second Naples	Naples	Italy	Siege	Multiday
293	Vienna	Vienna	Austria	Siege	Multiday
294	Buda	Budapest	Hungary	Siege	Multiyear
295	Florence	Florence	Italy	Siege	Multiday
296	Gavinana	San Marcello Pistoiese	Italy	Battle	One day
297	Guns	Kőszeg	Hungary	Siege	Multiday

(continued)

No.	Conflict Name	Year	Nearby Settlement	Country	Type	Duration
298	Coron	1532–3	Koroni	Greece	Siege	Multiyear
299	Essek	1537	Osijek	Croatia	Siege	Multiday
300	Valpo	1537	Valpovo	Croatia	Battle	One day
301	Corfu	1537	Corfu Island	Greece	Siege	Multiday
302	Taranto	1537	Taranto	Italy	Siege	Multiday
303	Castel Nuovo	1539	Naples	Italy	Siege	Multiday
304	Solway Moss	1542	Solway Moss (Gretna)	England	Battle	One day
305	Boulogne	1544	Boulogne-sur-Mer	France	Siege	Multiday
306	Ceresole	1544	Ceresole Alba	Italy	Battle	One day
307	Ancrum Moor	1544	Jedburgh	Scotland	Battle	One day
308	Kinlochlochy	1544	Laggan	Scotland	Battle	One day
309	Muhlberg	1547	Muhlberg	Germany	Battle	One day
310	Pinkie Cleugh	1547	Musselburgh	Scotland	Battle	One day
311	Metz	1552	Metz	France	Siege	Multiday
312	Bastia	1553	Bastia	France	Siege	Multiday
313	Sievershausen	1553	Lehrte	Germany	Battle	One day
314	Marciano	1553	Marciano della Chiana	Italy	Battle	One day
315	Siena	1553–4	Siena	Italy	Siege	Multiyear
316	St. Quentin	1557	St. Quentin	France	Siege	Multiday
317	Calais	1558	Calais	France	Siege	Multiday
318	Dunkirk	1558	Dunkirk	France	Other	One day
319	Gravelines	1558	Gravelines	France	Battle	One day
320	Dreux	1562	Dreux	France	Battle	One day
321	Le Havre	1562	Le Havre	France	Siege	Multiday

(continued)

322	Rouen	Rouen	1562	France	Other	One day
323	Vassy	Vassy	1562	France	Battle	One day
324	Orleans	Orleans	1563	France	Siege	Multiday
325	Malta	Valletta	1565	Malta	Siege	Multiday
326	Szigeth	Szigetvár	1566	Hungary	Siege	Multiday
327	Meaux	Meaux	1567	France	Other	One day
328	Paris	Paris	1567	France	Siege	Multiday
329	Jodoigne	Jodoigne	1568	Belgium	Battle	One day
330	Jemmingen	Jemmingen	1568	Germany	Battle	One day
331	Heiligerlee	Heiligerlee	1568	Netherlands	Battle	One day
332	Granada	Granada	1568	Spain	Other	One day
333	Jarnac	Jarnac	1569	France	Battle	One day
334	Moncontour	Moncontour	1569	France	Battle	One day
335	Poitiers	Poitiers	1569	France	Siege	Multiday
336	Roche L'Abeille	La Roche-L'Abeille	1569	France	Battle	One day
337	Ohanez	Ohanes	1569	Spain	Battle	Multiday
338	Galera	Galera	1570	Spain	Siege	Multiday
339	Seron	Serón	1570	Spain	Siege	Multiday
340	Mons	Mons	1572	Belgium	Siege	Multiday
341	Paris	Paris	1572	France	Other	Multiday
342	Brill	Brielle	1572	Netherlands	Siege	Multiday
343	Haarlem	Haarlem	1572–3	Netherlands	Siege	Multiyear
344	Alkmaar	Alkmaar	1573	Netherlands	Siege	Multiday
345	Leyden	Leiden	1574	Netherlands	Siege	Multiday
346	Mookerhyde	Mook en Middelaar	1574	Netherlands	Battle	One day
347	Antwerp	Antwerp	1576	Belgium	Other	One day

(continued)

127

No.	Conflict Name	Year	Nearby Settlement	Country	Type	Duration
348	Zierikzee	1576	Zierikzee	Netherlands	Siege	Multiday
349	Gemblours	1578	Bembloux	Netherlands	Battle	One day
350	Maastricht	1579	Maastricht	Netherlands	Siege	Multiday
351	Alcantara	1580	Alcantara	Portugal	Battle	One day
352	Antwerp	1584–5	Antwerp	Belgium	Siege	Multiyear
353	Zutphen	1585	Zutphen	Netherlands	Siege	Multiday
354	Coutras	1587	Coutras	France	Battle	One day
355	Sluys	1587	Sluis	Netherlands	Siege	Multiday
356	Paris	1588	Paris	France	Siege	Multiday
357	Arques	1589	Arques-la-Bataille	France	Battle	One day
358	Paris	1589	Paris	France	Siege	Multiday
359	Dreux	1590	Dreux	France	Siege	Multiday
360	Ivry	1590	Ivry-la-Bataille	France	Battle	One day
361	Paris	1590	Paris	France	Siege	Multiday
362	Caudebec	1592	Caudebec-en-Caux	France	Battle	Multiday
363	Paris	1594	Paris	France	Siege	Multiday
364	Biscuits	1594	Enniskillen	Ireland	Battle	One day
365	Fontaine-Francaise	1595	Fontaine-Francaise	France	Battle	One day
366	Guirgevo	1595	Guirgiu	Romania	Battle	One day
367	Kerestes	1596	Mezőkeresztes	Hungary	Battle	Multiday
368	Tournhour	1597	Turnhout	Belgium	Battle	One day
369	Yellow Ford	1598	Armagh	Ireland	Battle	One day
370	Nieuport	1600	Nieuwpoort	Belgium	Battle	One day
371	Ostend	1601–4	Ostend	Belgium	Siege	Multiyear

(*continued*)

372	Kinsale	1601	Kinsale	Ireland	Siege	Multiday
373	Sablat	1619	Budweis	Czech Rep	Battle	One day
374	White Hill	1620	Prague	Czech Rep	Battle	One day
375	Cecora	1620	Ţuţora	Romania	Battle	Multiday
376	Jassy	1620	Iaşi	Romania	Battle	One day
377	Fleurus	1622	Fleurus	Belgium	Battle	One day
378	Hochst	1622	Frankfurt am Main	Germany	Battle	One day
379	Wimpfen	1622	Bad Wimpfen	Germany	Battle	One day
380	Stadtlohn	1623	Stadtlohn	Germany	Battle	One day
381	Breda	1624	Breda	Netherlands	Siege	One day
382	Bridge of Dessau	1625	Dessau	Germany	Battle	One day
383	Lutter	1626	Lutter am Barenberge	Germany	Battle	Multiday
384	Stralsund	1626	Stralsund	Germany	Siege	Multiday
385	La Rochelle	1627–8	La Rochelle	France	Siege	Multiyear
386	Tezew	1627	Tczew	Poland	Battle	Multiday
387	Wolgast	1628	Wolgast	Germany	Battle	One day
388	Magdeburg	1630–1	Magdeburg	Germany	Siege	Multiyear
389	Breitenfeld	1631	Leipzig	Germany	Battle	One day
390	Frankfurt-on-the-Oder	1631	Frankfurt am der Oder	Germany	Siege	Multiday
391	Werben	1631	Werben (Elbe)	Germany	Battle	Multiday
392	Lutzen	1632	Lutzen	Germany	Battle	One day
393	Nuremburg	1632	Nuremburg	Germany	Battle	Multiday
394	River Lech	1632	Rain	Germany	Battle	Multiday
395	Nordlingen	1634	Nordlingen	Germany	Battle	One day
396	Wittstock	1636	Wittstock	Germany	Battle	One day
397	Tornavento	1636	Oleggio	Italy	Battle	One day

(continued)

129

APPENDIX TABLE A.1 *(continued)*

No.	Conflict Name	Year	Nearby Settlement	Country	Type	Duration
398	Croquant	1637	La Sauvetat	France	Other	One day
399	Leucate	1637	Leucate	France	Siege	Multiday
400	Breda	1637	Breda	Netherlands	Siege	Multiday
401	Breisach	1638	Breisach	Germany	Siege	Multiday
402	Fuenterrabia	1638	Hondarribia (Guipúzcoa)	Spain	Siege	Multiday
403	Rheinfelden	1638	Rheinfelden	Switzerland	Battle	Multiday
404	Nu-Pied	1639	Avranches	France	Other	One day
405	Bridge of Dee	1639	Aberdeen	Scotland	Battle	One day
406	Durham	1640	Durham	England	Siege	Multiday
407	Newburn	1640	Newburn	England	Battle	One day
408	Newcastle	1640	Newcastle Upon Tyne	England	Siege	Multiday
409	Casale	1640	Casale Monferrato	Italy	Battle	One day
410	Edgehill	1642	Edgehill	England	Battle	One day
411	Turnham Green	1642	London	England	Battle	One day
412	Second Breitenfeld	1642	Leipzig	Germany	Battle	One day
413	Lerida	1642	Lerida	Spain	Battle	One day
414	Bristol	1643	Bristol	England	Siege	Multiday
415	First Newbury	1643	Newbury	England	Battle	One day
416	Lansdown	1643	Bath	England	Battle	One day
417	Roundway Down	1643	Devizes	England	Battle	One day
418	Stratton	1643	Bude	England	Battle	One day
419	Rocroi	1643	Rocroi	France	Siege	One day
420	Bolton	1644	Bolton	England	Siege	Multiday
421	Cheriton	1644	Cheriton (Winchester)	England	Battle	One day

(continued)

422	Cropredy Bridge	Cropredy	1644	England	Battle	One day
423	Lostwithiel	Lostwithiel	1644	England	Battle	One day
424	Marston Moor	Long Marston	1644	England	Battle	One day
425	Second Newbury	Newbury	1644	England	Battle	One day
426	York	York	1644	England	Siege	Multiday
427	Freiburg	Freiburg im Breisgau	1644	Germany	Battle	Multiday
428	Tippermuir	Perth	1644	Scotland	Battle	One day
429	Montijo	Montijo	1644	Spain	Battle	One day
430	Jankau	Jankov	1644	Czech Rep	Battle	One day
431	Langport	Langport	1645	England	Battle	One day
432	Naseby	Naseby	1645	England	Battle	One day
433	Allerheim	Allerheim	1645	Germany	Battle	One day
434	Mergentheim	Bad Mergentheim	1645	Germany	Battle	One day
435	Alford	Alford	1645	Scotland	Battle	One day
436	Auldearn	Auldearn	1645	Scotland	Battle	One day
437	Inverlochy	Fort William	1645	Scotland	Battle	One day
438	Kilsyth	Kilsyth	1645	Scotland	Battle	One day
439	Philiphaugh	Selkirk	1645	Scotland	Battle	One day
440	Benburb	Benburb	1646	Ireland	Battle	One day
441	Dunganhill	Summerhill	1647	Ireland	Battle	One day
442	Masaniello	Naples	1647–8	Italy	Other	Multiday
443	Lerida	Lerida	1647	Spain	Battle	One day
444	Colchester	Colchester	1648	England	Siege	Multiday
445	Pembroke Castle	Pembroke	1648	England	Siege	Multiday
446	Preston	Preston	1648	England	Battle	Multiday
447	Lens	Lens	1648	France	Battle	One day

(continued)

131

No.	Conflict Name	Year	Nearby Settlement	Country	Type	Duration
448	Zusmarshausen	1648	Zusmarshausen	Germany	Battle	One day
449	Fronde de la Parlement	1649	Charenton-le-Pont	France	Other	One day
450	Fronde de la Parlement	1649	Paris	France	Siege	Multiday
451	Drogheda	1649	Drogheda	Ireland	Siege	Multiday
452	Rathmines	1649	Dublin	Ireland	Battle	One day
453	Wexford	1649	Wexford	Ireland	Siege	Multiday
454	Clonmen	1650	Clonmel	Ireland	Siege	Multiday
455	Carbiesdale	1650	Ardgay	Scotland	Battle	One day
456	Dunbar Ridges	1650	Dunbar	Scotland	Battle	Multiday
457	Worcester	1651	Worcester	England	Battle	One day
458	Dundee	1651	Dundee	Scotland	Siege	Multiday
459	Inverkeithing	1651	Inverkeithing	Scotland	Battle	One day
460	Perth	1651	Perth	Scotland	Siege	Multiday
461	Frond of the Princes	1652	Paris	France	Other	One day
462	Dunottar Castle	1652	Stonehaven	Scotland	Siege	Multiday
463	Arras	1654	Arras	France	Siege	Multiday
464	Siege of Warsaw	1655	Warsaw	Poland	Siege	Multiday
465	Valenciennes	1656	Valenciennes	France	Siege	Multiday
466	Battle of Warsaw	1656	Warsaw	Poland	Battle	Multiday
467	Sandomierz	1656	Sandomierz	Poland	Battle	One day
468	First Villmergen	1656	Villmergen	Switzerland	Battle	One day
469	Fredericksodde	1657	Fredericia	Denmark	Siege	One day
470	Copenhagen	1658	Copenhagen	Denmark	Siege	Multiday
471	The Dunes	1658	Dunkirk	France	Battle	One day

(continued)

132

472	Nyborg	1659	Nyborg	Denmark	Battle	Multiday
473	Ameixal	1663	Estremoz	Portugal	Battle	One day
474	Montes Claros	1663	Vila Viçosa	Portugal	Battle	One day
475	Neuhausel	1663	Neuhausel	Slovak Rep	Siege	Multiday
476	St. Gotthard	1664	Szentgotthárd	Hungary	Battle	One day
477	Villaviciosa	1665	Vila Viçosa	Portugal	Battle	One day
478	Lille	1667	Lille	France	Siege	Multiday
479	Maastricht	1673	Maastricht	Germany	Siege	Multiday
480	Seneffe	1674	Seneffe	Belgium	Battle	One day
481	Enzheim	1674	Entzheim	France	Battle	One day
482	Sinsheim	1674	Sinsheim	Germany	Battle	One day
483	Turkheim	1674	Turkheim	Germany	Battle	One day
484	Torrebens	1675	Rennes	France	Other	Multiday
485	Fehrbellin	1675	Fehrbellin	Germany	Battle	One day
486	Sasbach	1675	Sasbach (Ortenau)	Germany	Battle	One day
487	Philipsburg	1676	Philipsburg	Germany	Siege	Multiday
488	Messina	1676	Messina	Italy	Battle	One day
489	Lund	1676	Lund	Sweden	Battle	One day
490	Landskronz	1677	Landskrona	Sweden	Battle	One day
491	St. Denis	1678	Mons	Belgium	Battle	One day
492	Bothwell Bridge	1679	Hamilton	Scotland	Battle	One day
493	Drumclog	1679	Darvel	Scotland	Battle	One day
494	Khalenberg	1683	Vienna	Austria	Battle	One day
495	Vienna	1683	Vienna	Austria	Siege	Multiday
496	Parkany	1683	Stúrovo	Slovak Rep	Battle	One day
497	First Buda	1684	Budapest	Hungary	Siege	Multiday

(continued)

133

No.	Conflict Name	Year	Nearby Settlement	Country	Type	Duration
498	Luxembourg	1684	Luxembourg City	Luxembourg	Battle	Multiday
499	Norton St. Phillips	1685	Norton St. Phillip	England	Battle	One day
500	Sedgemoor	1685	Westonzoyland	England	Battle	One day
501	Second Buda	1686	Budapest	Hungary	Siege	Multiday
502	Athens	1687	Athens	Greece	Siege	Multiday
503	Harkany	1687	Harkany	Hungary	Battle	One day
504	First Belgrade	1688	Belgrade	Serbia	Siege	Multiday
505	Walcourt	1689	Walcourt	Belgium	Battle	One day
506	Enniskillen	1689	Enniskillen	Ireland	Siege	Multiday
507	Londonderry	1689	Londonderry	Ireland	Siege	Multiday
508	Newtown Butler	1689	Clones	Ireland	Battle	One day
509	Killiecrankie	1689	Killiecrankie	Scotland	Battle	One day
510	Fleurus	1690	Fleurus	Belgium	Battle	One day
511	River Boyne	1690	Drogheda	Ireland	Battle	One day
512	Storm of Limerick	1690	Limerick	Ireland	Siege	Multiday
513	Staffarda	1690	Revello	Italy	Battle	One day
514	Zernyest	1690	Zărneşti	Romania	Battle	One day
515	Cromdale	1690	Grantown-on-Spey	Scotland	Battle	One day
516	Second Belgrade	1690	Belgrade	Serbia	Siege	Multiday
517	Hal	1691	Halle	Belgium	Siege	Multiday
518	Leuze	1691	Leuze-en-Hainaut	Belgium	Battle	One day
519	Mons	1691	Mons	Belgium	Siege	Multiday
520	Aughrim	1691	Aughrim	Ireland	Battle	One day
521	Fall of Limerick	1691	Limerick	Ireland	Siege	Multiday

(continued)

522	Szalankemen	Stari Slankamen	Serbia	Battle	One day
523	Ripoli	Ripoli	Spain	Siege	Multiday
524	First Namur	Namur	Belgium	Siege	Multiday
525	Steenkerke	Veurne	Belgium	Battle	One day
526	Neerwinden	Neerwinden (Tienen)	Belgium	Battle	One day
527	Marsaglia	Marsaglia	italy	Battle	One day
528	Third Belgrade	Belgrade	Serbia	Siege	Multiday
529	Chios	Chios Island	Greece	Siege	Multiyear
530	Second Namur	Namur	Belgium	Siege	Multiday
531	Lippa	Lipova	Romania	Battle	One day
532	Zenta	Senta	Serbia	Battle	One day
533	Barcelona	Barcelona	Spain	Siege	Multiday
534	Chiari	Chiari	Italy	Battle	One day
535	Cremona	Cremona	Italy	Siege	Multiday
536	Liege	Liège	Belgium	Siege	Multiday
537	Cevennes	Le Pont-de-Montvert	France	Other	One day
538	First Landau	Landau in der Pfalz	Germany	Siege	Multiday
539	Friedlingen	Freiburg im Breisgau	Germany	Battle	One day
540	Kaiserswerth	Düsseldorf	Germany	Siege	Multiday
541	Luzzara	Luzzara	Italy	Battle	One day
542	Klissow	Kliszów	Poland	Battle	One day
543	Warsaw	Warsaw	Poland	Siege	Multiday
544	Bonn	Bonn	Germany	Siege	Multiday
545	Hochstadt	Hochstadt	Germany	Battle	One day
546	Second Landau	Landau in der Pfalz	Germany	Siege	Multiday
547	Speyerbach	Speyer	Germany	Battle	One day

(continued)

No.	Conflict Name	Year	Nearby Settlement	Country	Type	Duration
548	Bergen Op Zoom	1703	Bergen op Zoom	Netherlands	Battle	One day
549	Pultusk	1703	Pultusk	Poland	Battle	One day
550	Blenheim	1704	Blindheim	Germany	Battle	One day
551	Schellenberg Hill	1704	Donauwörth	Germany	Battle	One day
552	Third Landau	1704	Landau in der Pfalz	Germany	Siege	Multiday
553	First Rock of Gibraltar	1704	Rock of Gibraltar	Gibraltar	Battle	One day
554	Second Gibraltar	1704–5	Gibraltar City	Gibraltar	Siege	Multiday
555	Punitz	1704	Punitz	Poland	Battle	One day
556	Thorn	1704	Toruń	Poland	Siege	Multiday
557	Cassano	1705	Cassano d'Adda	Italy	Battle	One day
558	First Barcelona	1705–6	Barcelona	Spain	Siege	Multiyear
559	Menin	1706	Menen	Belgium	Siege	Multiday
560	Ramillies	1706	Ramillies	Belgium	Battle	One day
561	Battle of Turin	1706	Turin	Italy	Battle	One day
562	Calcinato	1706	Calcinato	Italy	Battle	One day
563	Siege of Turin	1706	Turin	Italy	Siege	Multiday
564	Fraustadt	1706	Wschowa	Poland	Battle	One day
565	Alicante	1706	Alicante	Spain	Siege	Multiday
566	Cartagena	1706	Cartagena	Spain	Siege	Multiday
567	Madrid	1706	Mardid	Spain	Siege	Multiday
568	Mallorca	1706	Palma de Mallorca (city)	Spain	Siege	Multiday
569	Toulon	1707	Toulon	France	Siege	Multiday
570	Almansa	1707	Almansa (Albacete)	Spain	Battle	One day
571	Denia	1707	Denia	Spain	Siege	Multiday

(continued)

572	Ghent	1708–9	Ghent	Belgium	Siege	Multiday
573	Oudenarde	1708	Oudenaarde	Belgium	Battle	One day
574	Wynendael	1708	Wijnendale	Belgium	Battle	One day
575	Lille	1708	Lille	France	Siege	Multiday
576	Kolesd	1708	Kölesd	Hungary	Battle	One day
577	Trencin	1708	Trenčianska Turná	Slovak Rep	Battle	One day
578	Esaulov	1708	Eslöv	Sweden	Siege	One day
579	Mons	1709	Mons	Belgium	Siege	Multiday
580	Tournai	1709	Tournai	Belgium	Siege	Multiday
581	Malplaquet	1709	Taisnières-sur-Hon	France	Battle	One day
582	Aire	1710	Aire-sur-la-Lys	France	Siege	Multiday
583	Bethune	1710	Béthune	France	Siege	Multiday
584	First Douai	1710	Douai	France	Siege	Multiday
585	Brihuega	1710	Brihuega	Spain	Battle	One day
586	Saragossa	1710	Zaragoza	Spain	Battle	One day
587	Villaviciosa	1710	Villaviciosa de Tajuña	Spain	Battle	One day
588	Helsingborg	1710	Helsingborg	Sweden	Battle	Multiday
589	First Bouchain	1711	Bouchain	France	Siege	Multiday
590	Pruth River	1711	Stănilești	Romania	Battle	Multiday
591	Denain	1712	Denain	France	Battle	One day
592	Le Quesnoy	1712	Le Quesnoy	France	Siege	Multiday
593	Second Bouchain	1712	Bouchain	France	Siege	Multiday
594	Second Douai	1712	Douai	France	Siege	Multiday
595	Gadebusch	1712	Gadebusch	Germany	Battle	One day
596	Second Villmergen	1712	Villmergen	Switzerland	Battle	One day
597	Helsingfors	1713	Helsinki	Finland	Siege	Multiday

(continued)

APPENDIX TABLE A.I (continued)

No.	Conflict Name	Year	Nearby Settlement	Country	Type	Duration
598	Fourth Landau	1713	Landau in der Pfalz	Germany	Siege	Multiday
599	Freiburg	1713	Freiburg im Breisgau	Germany	Siege	Multiday
600	Speyer	1713	Speyer	Germany	Siege	Multiday
601	Tonning	1713	Tonning	Germany	Siege	Multiday
602	Napue	1714	Isokyrö	Finland	Battle	One day
603	Second Barcelona	1714	Barcelona	Spain	Siege	Multiday
604	Preston	1715	Preston	England	Battle	Multiday
605	Rugen	1715	Bergen auf Rügen	Germany	Siege	Multiday
606	Sheriffmuir	1715	Sherrifmuir	Scotland	Battle	One day
607	Corfu	1716	Corfu Island	Greece	Siege	Multiday
608	Fredrikshald	1716	Halden City	Norway	Battle	Multiday
609	Temesvar	1716	Timișoara	Romania	Siege	Multiday
610	Peterwardein	1716	Peterwardein	Serbia	Battle	One day
611	Belgrade	1717	Belgrade	Serbia	Siege	Multiday
612	First Messina	1718	Messina	Italy	Siege	Multiday
613	Fredrikshald	1718	Halden City	Norway	Siege	Multiday
614	Francavilla	1719	Francavilla di Sicilia	Italy	Battle	One day
615	Second Messina	1719	Messina	Italy	Siege	Multiday
616	Glenshiel	1719	Glen Shiel	Scotland	Battle	One day
617	Pontevedra	1719	Pontevedra	Spain	Siege	Multiday
618	San Sebastian	1719	San Sebastian	Spain	Battle	One day
619	Vigo	1719	Vigo	Spain	Siege	Multiday
620	Ceuta	1720–7	Ceuta	Spain	Siege	Multiyear
621	Gibraltar	1727	Gibraltar City	Gibraltar	Siege	Multiday

(continued)

138

622	Philipsburg	1734	Philipsburg	Germany	Siege	Multiday
623	Bitonto	1734	Bitonto	Italy	Battle	One day
624	Gustalla	1734	Guastalla	Italy	Battle	One day
625	Parma	1734	Parma	Italy	Battle	One day
626	Danzig	1734	Gdańsk	Poland	Siege	Multiday
627	Jassy	1739	Iaşi	Romania	Siege	Multiday
628	Belgrade	1739	Belgrade	Serbia	Siege	Multiday
629	Groszka	1739	Belgrade	Serbia	Battle	One day
630	Willmanstrand	1741	Lappeenranta	Finland	Battle	One day
631	Mollwitz	1741	Mahujowice	Poland	Battle	One day
632	Chotusitz	1742	Chotusice	Czech Rep	Siege	Multiday
633	First Prague	1742–3	Prague	Czech Rep	Siege	Multiday
634	Helsinki	1742	Helsinki	Finland	Siege	Multiday
635	Dettingen	1743	Karlstein am Main	Germany	Battle	One day
636	Compo Santo	1743	Camposanto (Modena)	Italy	Battle	One day
637	Second Prague	1744	Prague	Czech Rep	Siege	Multiday
638	Cuneo	1744	Cuneo	Italy	Siege	Multiday
639	Madonna del Olmo	1744	Cuneo	Italy	Battle	One day
640	Velletri	1744	Velletri	Italy	Battle	One day
641	Fontenoy	1745	Tournai	Belgium	Battle	One day
642	Siege of Tournai	1745	Tournai	Belgium	Siege	Multiday
643	Sohr	1745	Hajnice	Czech Rep	Battle	One day
644	Carlisle	1745	Carlisle	England	Siege	Multiday
645	Derby	1745	Derby	England	Siege	Multiday
646	Manchester	1745	Manchester	England	Siege	Multiday
647	Amberg	1745	Amberg	Germany	Battle	One day

(continued)

No.	Conflict Name	Year	Nearby Settlement	Country	Type	Duration
648	Gorlitz	1745	Görlitz	Germany	Battle	One day
649	Gross-Hennersdorf	1745	Herrnhut	Germany	Battle	One day
650	Kesselsdorf	1745	Kesselsdorf	Germany	Battle	One day
651	Bassignano	1745	Bassignana	Italy	Battle	One day
652	Hohenfreidberg	1745	Strzegom	Poland	Battle	One day
653	Edinburgh	1745	Edinburgh	Scotland	Siege	Multiday
654	Prestonpans	1745	Prestonpans	Scotland	Battle	One day
655	Stirling	1745	Stirling	Scotland	Siege	Multiday
656	Roucoux	1746	Liège	Belgium	Battle	One day
657	Battle of Piacenza	1746	Piacenza	Italy	Battle	One day
658	First Siege of Genoa	1746	Genova	Italy	Siege	Multiday
659	Revolt of Genoa	1746	Genova	Italy	Other	Multiday
660	Rottofreddo	1746	Rottofreno	Italy	Battle	One day
661	Siege of Piacenza	1746	Piacenza	Italy	Siege	Multiday
662	Culloden Moor	1746	Inverness	Scotland	Battle	One day
663	Lauffeld	1747	Riemst	Belgium	Battle	One day
664	Colle dell'Assietta	1747	Testa dell'Assietta	Italy	Battle	One day
665	Second Siege of Genoa	1747	Genova	Italy	Siege	Multiday
666	Bergen Op Zoom	1747	Bergen op Zoom	Netherlands	Siege	Multiday
667	Maastricht	1748	Maastricht	Netherlands	Siege	Multiday
668	Lobositz	1756	Lovosice	Czech Rep	Battle	One day
669	First Dresden	1756	Dresden	Germany	Siege	Multiday
670	Pirna	1756	Pirna	Germany	Siege	Multiday
671	Battle of Prague	1757	Prague	Czech Rep	Battle	One day

(continued)

672	Kolin	1757	Kolin	Czech Rep	Battle	One day
673	Siege of Prague	1757	Prague	Czech Rep	Siege	Multiday
674	First Berlin	1757	Berline	Germany	Siege	Multiday
675	Hastenbeck	1757	Hamelin	Germany	Battle	One day
676	Moys	1757	Görlitz	Germany	Battle	One day
677	Rossbach	1757	Roßbach	Germany	Battle	One day
678	Zittau	1757	Zittau	Germany	Battle	One day
679	Battle of Breslau	1757	Wroclaw	Poland	Battle	One day
680	First Liegnitz	1757	Legnica	Poland	Siege	Multiday
681	First Schweidnitz	1757	Swidnica	Poland	Siege	Multiday
682	Leuthen	1757	Lutynia	Poland	Battle	One day
683	Oppelin	1757	Opole	Poland	Siege	Multiday
684	Siege of Breslau	1757	Wroclaw	Poland	Siege	Multiday
685	Altliebe	1758	Domašov nad Bystřicí	Czech Rep	Battle	One day
686	Olmutz	1758	Olomouc	Czech Rep	Siege	Multiday
687	Crefeld	1758	Krefeld	Germany	Battle	One day
688	Hochkirch	1758	Hochkirch	Germany	Battle	One day
689	Elbing	1758	Elbląg	Poland	Siege	Multiday
690	Kustrin	1758	Kostrzyn nad Odrą	Poland	Siege	Multiday
691	Second Schweidnitz	1758	Swidnica	Poland	Siege	Multiday
692	Thorn	1758	Toruń	Poland	Siege	Multiday
693	Zorndorf	1758	Sarbinowo	Poland	Battle	One day
694	Bergen	1759	Frankfurt am Main	Germany	Battle	One day
695	Maxen	1759	Maxen	Germany	Battle	Multiday
696	Minden	1759	Minden	Germany	Battle	One day
697	Second Dresden	1759	Dresden	Germany	Siege	Multiday

(continued)

No.	Conflict Name	Year	Nearby Settlement	Country	Type	Duration
698	Kunersdorf	1759	Kunowice	Poland	Battle	One day
699	Zullichau (Kay)	1759	Kije	Poland	Battle	One day
700	Emsdorf	1760	Kirchhain	Germany	Battle	One day
701	Kloster-Kamp	1760	Kamp-Lintfort	Germany	Battle	One day
702	Second Berlin	1760	Berlin	Germany	Siege	Multiday
703	Third Dresden	1760	Dresden	Germany	Siege	Multiday
704	Torgau	1760	Torgau	Germany	Battle	One day
705	Warburg	1760	Warburg	Germany	Battle	One day
706	Wessel	1760	Wesel	Germany	Siege	Multiday
707	Kolberg	1760	Kołobrzeg	Poland	Siege	Multiday
708	Landshut	1760	Kamienna Góra	Poland	Siege	Multiday
709	Second Liegnitz	1760	Legnica	Poland	Battle	One day
710	Vellinghausen	1761	Welver	Germany	Battle	One day
711	Reichenbach	1762	Liberec	Czech Rep	Battle	One day
712	Cassel	1762	Kassel	Germany	Siege	Multiday
713	Lutterberg	1762	Staufenberg	Germany	Battle	One day
714	Wilhelmsthal	1762	Calden	Germany	Battle	One day
715	Burkersdorf	1762	Burkatów	Poland	Battle	One day
716	Freiburg	1762	Swiebodzice	Poland	Battle	One day
717	Third Schweidnitz	1762	Swidnica	Poland	Siege	Multiday
718	Borgo	1768	Borgo	France	Battle	Multiday
719	Cracow	1768	Kraków	Poland	Siege	Multiday
720	Ponte Nuovo	1769	Castello-di-Rostino	France	Battle	Multiday
721	Bucharest	1769	Bucharest	Romania	Siege	Multiday

(continued)

722	Jassy	1769	Iași	Siege	Romania	Multiday
723	Landskron	1771	Lanškroun	Battle	Czech Rep	One day
724	Kozludji	1774	Kozloduy (Shumen)	Battle	Bulgaria	One day
725	Silistra	1774	Silistra	Siege	Bulgaria	Multiday
726	Varna	1774	Varna	Siege	Bulgaria	Multiday
727	Nachod	1778	Náchod	Siege	Czech Rep	Multiday
728	Westminster	1780	London	Other	England	One day
729	Câmpeni	1784	Câmpeni	Other	Romania	One day
730	Jassy	1788	Iași	Siege	Romania	Multiday
731	Karansebes	1788	Caransebeş	Battle	Romania	One day
732	Turnhout	1789	Turnhout	Battle	Belgium	One day
733	Bastille	1789	Paris	Other	France	One day
734	Foscani	1789	Focşani	Battle	Romania	One day
735	Martinesti	1789	Râmnicu Sărat	Battle	Romania	One day
736	Mehadia	1789	Mehadia	Siege	Romania	Multiday
737	Belgrade	1789	Belgrade	Siege	Serbia	Multiday
738	Champs de Mars	1791	Paris	Other	France	One day
739	Brussels	1792	Brussels	Siege	Belgium	Multiday
740	Jemappes	1792	Jemappes	Battle	Belgium	One day
741	Tuileries Palace	1792	Paris	Other	France	One day
742	Valmy	1792	Valmy	Battle	France	One day
743	Menin	1793	Menen	Battle	Belgium	One day
744	Neerwinden	1793	Neerwinden	Battle	Belgium	One day
745	Chantonnay	1793	Chantonnay	Battle	France	One day
746	Chatillon-sur-Sevre	1793	Mauléon	Battle	France	One day
747	Cholet	1793	Cholet	Battle	France	One day

(continued)

No.	Conflict Name	Year	Nearby Settlement	Country	Type	Duration
748	Entrammes	1793	Entrammes	France	Battle	One day
749	First Angers	1793	Angers	France	Siege	Multiday
750	Fontenay-le-Comte	1793	Fontenay-le-Comte	France	Battle	One day
751	Froeschwiller	1793	Froeschwiller	France	Battle	One day
752	Geisberg	1793	Wissembourg	France	Battle	One day
753	Granville	1793	Granville	France	Siege	Multiday
754	Hondschoote	1793	Hondschoote	France	Battle	Multiday
755	Le Mans	1793	Le Mans	France	Battle	One day
756	Maubeuge	1793	Maubeuge	France	Siege	Multiday
757	Nantes	1793	Nantes	France	Siege	Multiday
758	Saumur	1793	Saumur	France	Siege	Multiday
759	Savenay	1793	Savenay	France	Battle	One day
760	Second Angers	1793	Angers	France	Siege	Multiday
761	Valenciennes (Famacs)	1793	Valenciennes	France	Battle	Multiday
762	Wattignies	1793	Wattignies-la-Victoire	France	Battle	Multiday
763	Kaiserslautern	1793	Kaiserslautern	Germany	Battle	Multiday
764	Charleroi	1794	Charleroi	Belgium	Siege	Multiday
765	Erquelinnes	1794	Erquelinnes	Belgium	Battle	One day
766	Fleurus	1794	Fleurus	Belgium	Battle	One day
767	Tournai	1794	Tournai	Belgium	Battle	One day
768	Lambusart	1794	Lambersart	France	Battle	One day
769	Le Cateau (Troisvilles)	1794	Beaumont-en-Cambrésis	France	Battle	One day
770	Saorgio	1794	Saorge	France	Battle	One day
771	Tourcoing	1794	Tourcoing	France	Battle	One day

(continued)

772	Cracow	Kraków	1794	Poland	Siege	Multiday
773	Kobilka	Kobilka	1794	Poland	Battle	One day
774	Krupshchitse	Krupczyce	1794	Poland	Battle	One day
775	Maciejowice	Jaciejowice	1794	Poland	Battle	One day
776	Raclawice	Racławice (Miechów)	1794	Poland	Battle	One day
777	Szczezekrina	Szczekociny	1794	Poland	Battle	One day
778	Warsaw	Warsaw	1794	Poland	Siege	Multiday
779	Campmany	Capmany	1794	Spain	Battle	Multiday
780	Paris	Paris	1795	France	Other	One day
781	Quiberon	Quiberon	1795	France	Battle	One day
782	Mainz	Mainz	1795	Germany	Battle	One day
783	Mannheim	Mannheim	1795	Germany	Siege	Multiday
784	Loano	Loano	1795	Italy	Battle	Multiday
785	Amberg	Amberg	1796	Germany	Battle	One day
786	Biberach	Biberach	1796	Germany	Battle	One day
787	Malsch	Malsch	1796	Germany	Battle	One day
788	Neresheim	Neresheim	1796	Germany	Battle	One day
789	Uckerath	Bonn	1796	Germany	Battle	One day
790	Wetzlar	Wetzlar	1796	Germany	Battle	One day
791	Wurzberg	Würzburg	1796	Germany	Battle	One day
792	Arcola	Arcole	1796	Italy	Battle	Multiday
793	Bassano	Bassano del Grappa	1796	Italy	Battle	Multiday
794	Borghetto	Valeggio sul Mincio	1796	Italy	Battle	One day
795	Bridge of Lodi	Lodi	1796	Italy	Battle	One day
796	Caldiero	Caldiero	1796	Italy	Battle	One day
797	Calliano	Calliano	1796	Italy	Battle	Multiday

(continued)

145

APPENDIX TABLE A.1 *(continued)*

No.	Conflict Name	Year	Nearby Settlement	Country	Type	Duration
798	Castiglione	1796	Castiglione delle Stiviere	Italy	Battle	One day
799	Cembra	1796	Cembra	Italy	Battle	Multiday
800	Dego	1796	Dego	Italy	Battle	Multiday
801	Lonato	1796	Lonato del Garda	Italy	Battle	Multiday
802	Mantua	1796	Mantova	Italy	Siege	Multiday
803	Milan	1796	Milan	Italy	Siege	Multiday
804	Montenotte	1796	Cairo Montenotte	Italy	Battle	One day
805	Roveredo	1796	Roveredo	Switzerland	Battle	Multiday
806	Diersheim	1797	Rheinau	Germany	Battle	Multiday
807	Lahn (Neuwied)	1797	Neuwied	Germany	Battle	One day
808	La Favorita	1797	Mantua	Italy	Battle	One day
809	Malborghetto (Tarvis)	1797	Tarvisio	Italy	Battle	One day
810	Rivoli	1797	Rivoli Veronese	Italy	Battle	Multiday
811	Arklow	1798	Arklow	Ireland	Battle	One day
812	Ballymore	1798	Ballymore Eustace	Ireland	Battle	One day
813	Ballynamuck	1798	Ballinamuck	Ireland	Battle	One day
814	Castlebar	1798	Castlebar	Ireland	Siege	Multiday
815	Enniscorthy	1798	Enniscorthy	Ireland	Other	One day
816	Granard	1798	Granard	Ireland	Other	One day
817	Killala	1798	Killala	Ireland	Siege	Multiday
818	Longford	1798	Longford	Ireland	Other	One day
819	New Ross	1798	New Ross	Ireland	Other	One day
820	Scullabogue	1798	New Ross	Ireland	Other	One day
821	Vinegar Hill	1798	Enniscorthy	Ireland	Other	One day

(continued)

146

822	Civita Castellana	1798	Civita Castellana	Italy	Battle	One day
823	Rome	1798	Rome	Italy	Siege	Multiday
824	Malta	1798	Valletta	Malta	Battle	One day
825	Valletta	1798–1800	Valletta	Malta	Siege	Multiyear
826	Feldkirch	1799	Feldkirch	Austria	Siege	Multiday
827	Nauders	1799	Nauders	Austria	Battle	One day
828	Ostrach	1799	Ostrach	Germany	Battle	One day
829	Stockach	1799	Stockach	Germany	Battle	One day
830	Capri	1799	Capri (city)	Italy	Siege	Multiday
831	Capua	1799	Capua	Italy	Siege	Multiday
832	Cassano	1799	Cassano d'Adda	Italy	Battle	One day
833	First Milan	1799	Milan	Italy	Siege	Multiday
834	Genola	1799	Genola	Italy	Battle	One day
835	Magnano	1799	Castell d'Azzano	Italy	Battle	One day
836	Mantua	1799	Mantova	Italy	Siege	Multiday
837	Naples	1799	Naples	Italy	Siege	Multiday
838	Novi	1799	Novi Ligure	Italy	Battle	One day
839	Peschiera	1799	Peschiera del Garda	Italy	Siege	Multiday
840	Tauffers	1799	Taufers im Münstertal	Italy	Battle	One day
841	Trebbia	1799	Piacenza	Italy	Battle	Multiday
842	Turin	1799	Turin	Italy	Siege	Multiday
843	First Bergen	1799	Bergen	Netherlands	Battle	One day
844	Groet Keeten (Texel)	1799	Callantsoog	Netherlands	Battle	Multiday
845	Kastrikum	1799	Castricum	Netherlands	Battle	One day
846	Second Bergen (Alkmaar)	1799	Alkmaar	Netherlands	Battle	One day

(continued)

APPENDIX TABLE A.1 *(continued)*

No.	Conflict Name	Year	Nearby Settlement	Country	Type	Duration
847	Zyper-Sluis	1799	Camperduin	Netherlands	Battle	One day
848	Chur	1799	Chur	Switzerland	Battle	Multiday
849	Dottingen (Amsteg)	1799	Döttingen	Switzerland	Battle	One day
850	First Zurich	1799	Zurich	Switzerland	Battle	One day
851	Klontal	1799	Klöntalersee	Switzerland	Battle	Multiday
852	Maienfeld	1799	Maienfeld	Switzerland	Battle	Multiday
853	Muettental	1799	Muotathal (Muttenthal)	Switzerland	Battle	Multiday
854	Second Zurich	1799	Zurich	Switzerland	Battle	One day
855	St. Gotthard Pass	1799	Airolo	Switzerland	Battle	One day
856	Third Zurich	1799	Zurich	Switzerland	Battle	One day

Note: See Chapter 2 for construction methods for historical conflict database.
Sources: Bradbury (2004) and Clodfelter (2002).

	Dependent Variable: Conflict Exposure
Riverport	−0.185
	(0.113)
	[0.100]
Seaport (non-Atlantic)	−0.269
	(0.201)
	[0.180]
Atlantic port	−0.150
	(0.192)
	[0.433]
Roman road hub	0.100
	(0.127)
	[0.431]
Terrain ruggedness	−0.001
	(0.001)
	[0.395]
Elevation	−0.001
	(0.000)
	[0.013]
Cultivation likelihood	0.064
	(0.341)
	[0.851]
Barley suitability	2.602
	(0.714)
	[0.000]
Potato suitability	0.120
	(0.039)
	[0.002]
Urban network (first lag)	0.063
	(0.046)
	[0.169]
Self-governing commune (first lag)	0.118
	(0.143)
	[0.408]
Archbishop seat (first lag)	−0.258
	(0.170)
	[0.130]
Sovereign capital (first lag)	1.165
	(0.251)
	[0.000]
University seat (first lag)	0.161
	(0.185)
	[0.384]
Observations	4,672

Notes: Estimation method is logit. Regression includes century fixed effects. Robust standard errors clustered at grid cell level in parentheses, followed by corresponding p-values in brackets. See Chapter 4 for variable descriptions and sources.

APPENDIX TABLE B.2 *Descriptive Statistics for Chapter 4 Analysis*

	Obs	Mean	Std dev	Min	Max
City population (1,000s)	3,293	17.342	32.456	1	948
Log city population	3,293	2.372	0.919	0	6.854
Number of conflicts (by grid cell)	3,293	1.206	2.743	0	20
Conflict exposure	3,293	0.363	0.481	0	1
Conflict exposure (ordered)	3,293	0.580	0.823	0	2
Battle exposure	3,293	0.262	0.440	0	1
Siege exposure	3,293	0.210	0.407	0	1
Riverport	3,293	0.615	0.487	0	1
Seaport	3,293	0.208	0.406	0	1
Seaport (Atlantic)	3,293	0.093	0.291	0	1
Seaport (non-Atlantic)	3,293	0.114	0.318	0	1
Roman road hub	3,293	0.288	0.453	0	1
Terrain ruggedness	3,293	69.037	75.665	0.466	559.45
Elevation (meters)	3,293	169.650	210.752	-4	1,333
Barley suitability	3,134	0.057	0.094	0	0.461
Potato suitability	3,293	6.465	2.983	0	9.842
Hanseatic city	3,293	0.064	0.245	0	1
Urban network	3,293	2.819	3.694	0	27
Historical capital	3,293	0.211	0.408	0	1
Archbishop	3,293	0.115	0.320	0	1

Note: See Chapter 4 for variable descriptions and sources.

APPENDIX TABLE C.1 *Historical Conflict Exposure Ranked by (NUTS2) Region, 1500–1799*

No.	ID	Region	Country	Conflict Exposure
1	BE10	Région de Bruxelles-Capitale	Belgium	34.000
2	BE31	Prov. Brabant Wallon	Belgium	34.000
3	BE23	Prov. Oost-Vlaanderen	Belgium	31.500
4	NL34	Zeeland	Netherlands	31.500
5	BE25	Prov. West-Vlaanderen	Belgium	29.000
6	BE32	Prov. Hainaut	Belgium	22.667
7	BE21	Prov. Antwerpen	Belgium	21.000
8	BE22	Prov. Limburg	Belgium	21.000
9	BE24	Prov. Vlaams-Brabant	Belgium	21.000
10	NL31	Utrecht	Netherlands	21.000
11	NL33	Zuid-Holland	Netherlands	21.000
12	NL41	Noord-Brabant	Netherlands	21.000
13	FR30	Nord – Pas-de-Calais	France	16.333
14	BE33	Prov. Liége	Belgium	14.667
15	DE11	Stuttgart	Germany	13.000
16	DE12	Karlsruhe	Germany	13.000
17	ITC4	Lombardia	Italy	13.000
18	ITC2	Valle d'Aosta	Italy	12.500
19	NL22	Gelderland	Netherlands	12.500
20	BE35	Prov. Namur	Belgium	12.250
21	DEB3	Rheinhessen-Pfalz	Germany	12.000
22	NL32	Noord-Holland	Netherlands	12.000
23	DE14	Tübingen	Germany	11.250
24	ITC1	Piemonte	Italy	10.667
25	FR23	Haute-Normandie	France	10.000
26	DEB1	Koblenz	Germany	9.250
27	DE13	Freiburg	Germany	9.000
28	ITC3	Liguria	Italy	9.000
29	ITH2	Provincia Autonoma di Trento	Italy	9.000
30	FR22	Picardie	France	8.750
31	FR42	Alsace	France	8.667
32	DE71	Darmstadt	Germany	8.400
33	ITH5	Emilia-Romagna	Italy	8.167
34	DE26	Unterfranken	Germany	8.000
35	DEA1	Düsseldorf	Germany	8.000
36	DEA2	Köln	Germany	8.000
37	NL42	Limburg (NL)	Netherlands	8.000
38	UKM2	Eastern Scotland	United Kingdom	8.000
39	CZ05	Severovychod	Czech Republic	7.600
40	FR10	Île de France	France	7.333
41	DED2	Dresden	Germany	7.000
42	DED5	Leipzig	Germany	7.000

(continued)

APPENDIX TABLE C.I *(continued)*

No.	ID	Region	Country	Conflict Exposure
43	PL51	Dolnoslaskie	Poland	7.000
44	PL43	Lubuskie	Poland	6.800
45	UKM5	North Eastern Scotland	United Kingdom	6.750
46	DEA5	Arnsberg	Germany	6.500
47	UKD1	Cumbria	United Kingdom	6.500
48	UKJ1	Berkshire, Buckinghamshire, Oxfordshire	United Kingdom	6.500
49	UKJ3	Hampshire, Isle of Wight	United Kingdom	6.500
50	CZ02	Stredni Cechy	Czech Republic	6.250
51	CZ07	Stredni Morava	Czech Republic	6.250
52	AT34	Vorarlberg	Austria	6.000
53	CZ04	Severozapad	Czech Republic	6.000
54	DE72	Gießen	Germany	6.000
55	DE73	Kassel	Germany	6.000
56	UKM3	South Western Scotland	United Kingdom	6.000
57	DEA3	Münster	Germany	5.750
58	DED4	Chemnitz	Germany	5.667
59	DE30	Berlin	Germany	5.500
60	DEB2	Trier	Germany	5.500
61	PL52	Opolskie	Poland	5.500
62	UKH3	Essex	United Kingdom	5.500
63	UKJ4	Kent	United Kingdom	5.500
64	ITH3	Veneto	Italy	5.250
65	BE34	Prov. Luxembourg	Belgium	5.000
66	DE25	Mittelfranken	Germany	5.000
67	ITF2	Molise	Italy	5.000
68	ITI1	Toscana	Italy	5.000
69	UKG3	West Midlands	United Kingdom	5.000
70	FR24	Centre	France	4.833
71	DEG0	Thüringen	Germany	4.750
72	DE40	Brandenburg	Germany	4.714
73	CZ01	Praha	Czech Republic	4.500
74	NL21	Overijssel	Netherlands	4.500
75	UKC2	Northumberland, Tyne, Wear	United Kingdom	4.500
76	UKF2	Leicestershire, Rutland, Northamptonshire	United Kingdom	4.500
77	UKH2	Bedfordshire, Hertfordshire	United Kingdom	4.500
78	UKI2	Outer London	United Kingdom	4.500
79	UKJ2	East Surrey, West Sussex	United Kingdom	4.500
80	HU33	Dél-Alföld	Hungary	4.400
81	DE22	Niederbayern	Germany	4.333
82	DEA4	Detmold	Germany	4.333

(continued)

APPENDIX TABLE C.1 *(continued)*

No.	ID	Region	Country	Conflict Exposure
83	UKK1	Gloucestershire, Wiltshire, Bristol/Bath	United Kingdom	4.333
84	DE27	Schwaben	Germany	4.250
85	DE24	Oberfranken	Germany	4.200
86	PL41	Wielkopolskie	Poland	4.125
87	CZ03	Jihozápad	Czech Republic	4.000
88	DE94	Weser-Ems	Germany	4.000
89	NL23	Flevoland	Netherlands	4.000
90	ES63	Ciudad Autónoma de Ceuta	Spain	4.000
91	UKC1	Tees Valley, Durham	United Kingdom	4.000
92	UKD3	Greater Manchester	United Kingdom	4.000
93	UKG1	Herefordshire, Worcestershire, Warwickshire	United Kingdom	4.000
94	CZ06	Jihovýchod	Czech Republic	3.667
95	PL11	Łódzkie	Poland	3.667
96	DE23	Oberpfalz	Germany	3.500
97	HU10	Közép-Magyarország	Hungary	3.500
98	UKE3	South Yorkshire	United Kingdom	3.500
99	UKE4	West Yorkshire	United Kingdom	3.500
100	UKF1	Derbyshire, Nottinghamshire	United Kingdom	3.500
101	UKK2	Dorset, Somerset	United Kingdom	3.500
102	FR51	Pays de la Loire	France	3.400
103	UKN0	Northern Ireland	United Kingdom	3.400
104	UKH1	East Anglia	United Kingdom	3.333
105	DE92	Hannover	Germany	3.250
106	DEE0	Sachsen-Anhalt	Germany	3.250
107	PL33	Swietokrzyskie	Poland	3.250
108	FR53	Poitou-Charentes	France	3.200
109	IE02	Southern, Eastern	Ireland	3.125
110	AT13	Wien	Austria	3.000
111	Dec-00	Saarland	Germany	3.000
112	HU21	Közép-Dunántúl	Hungary	3.000
113	IE01	Border, Midland, Western	Ireland	3.000
114	NL12	Friesland	Netherlands	3.000
115	PL22	Slaskie	Poland	3.000
116	SK02	Západné Slovensko	Slovak Republic	3.000
117	UKI1	Inner London	United Kingdom	3.000
118	ITI4	Lazio	Italy	2.833
119	FR41	Lorraine	France	2.800
120	ITF1	Abruzzo	Italy	2.800
121	UKG2	Shropshire, Staffordshire	United Kingdom	2.800
122	DE91	Braunschweig	Germany	2.750

(continued)

APPENDIX TABLE C.1 *(continued)*

No.	ID	Region	Country	Conflict Exposure
123	SK01	Bratislavský kraj	Slovak Republic	2.750
124	UKL2	East Wales	United Kingdom	2.750
125	AT12	Niederösterreich	Austria	2.667
126	AT33	Tirol	Austria	2.667
127	HU23	Dél-Dunántúl	Hungary	2.667
128	ITH1	Provincia Autonoma di Bolzano	Italy	2.667
129	RO42	Vest	Romania	2.667
130	SK03	Stredné Slovensko	Slovak Republic	2.600
131	CZ08	Moravskoslezsko	Czech Republic	2.500
132	DE80	Mecklenburg-Vorpommern	Germany	2.500
133	ITF3	Campania	Italy	2.500
134	ES62	Región de Murcia	Spain	2.500
135	UKK4	Devon	United Kingdom	2.500
136	PL12	Mazowieckie	Poland	2.429
137	PL21	Malopolskie	Poland	2.400
138	AT31	Oberösterreich	Austria	2.333
139	PL42	Zachodniopomorskie	Poland	2.333
140	UKE2	North Yorkshire	United Kingdom	2.333
141	DE21	Oberbayern	Germany	2.250
142	PL32	Podkarpackie	Poland	2.167
143	AT11	Burgenland	Austria	2.000
144	FR21	Champagne-Ardenne	France	2.000
145	FR25	Basse-Normandie	France	2.000
146	PL61	Kujawsko-Pomorskie	Poland	2.000
147	UKD4	Lancashire	United Kingdom	2.000
148	UKD6	Cheshire	United Kingdom	2.000
149	UKD7	Merseyside	United Kingdom	2.000
150	HU32	Észak-Alföld	Hungary	1.800
151	UKM6	Highlands, Islands	United Kingdom	1.769
152	DK02	Sjælland	Denmark	1.750
153	FR82	Provence-Alpes-Côte d'Azur	France	1.667
154	HU31	Észak-Magyarország	Hungary	1.667
155	HR04	Kontinentalna Hrvatska	Croatia	1.500
156	FR43	Franche-Comté	France	1.500
157	FR52	Bretagne	France	1.500
158	FR63	Limousin	France	1.500
159	HU22	Nyugat-Dunántúl	Hungary	1.500
160	PL62	Warminsko-Mazurskie	Poland	1.500
161	UKE1	East Yorkshire, Northern Lincolnshire	United Kingdom	1.500
162	UKF3	Lincolnshire	United Kingdom	1.500
163	ITI2	Umbria	Italy	1.333

(continued)

APPENDIX TABLE C.1 *(continued)*

No.	ID	Region	Country	Conflict Exposure
164	RO21	Nord-Est	Romania	1.333
165	FR71	Rhône-Alpes	France	1.300
166	ES51	Cataluña	Spain	1.286
167	FR61	Aquitaine	France	1.167
168	ES52	Comunidad Valenciana	Spain	1.167
169	RO31	Sud–Muntenia	Romania	1.143
170	ES61	Andalucía	Spain	1.100
171	AT22	Steiermark	Austria	1.000
172	AT32	Salzburg	Austria	1.000
173	BG32	Severen tsentralen	Bulgaria	1.000
174	BG33	Severoiztochen	Bulgaria	1.000
175	FR26	Bourgogne	France	1.000
176	FR81	Languedoc-Roussillon	France	1.000
177	DE50	Bremen	Germany	1.000
178	ITF6	Calabria	Italy	1.000
179	ITG1	Sicilia	Italy	1.000
180	ITH4	Friuli-Venezia Giulia	Italy	1.000
181	NL11	Groningen	Netherlands	1.000
182	NL13	Drenthe	Netherlands	1.000
183	PT15	Algarve	Portugal	1.000
184	RO22	Sud-Est	Romania	1.000
185	RO32	Bucuresti–Ilfov	Romania	1.000
186	SK04	Východné Slovensko	Slovak Republic	1.000
187	ES21	País Vasco	Spain	1.000
188	ES22	Comunidad Foral de Navarra	Spain	1.000
189	FR62	Midi-Pyrénées	France	0.857
190	PL63	Pomorskie	Poland	0.833
191	PT18	Alentejo	Portugal	0.833
192	RO41	Sud-Vest Oltenia	Romania	0.833
193	SE23	Västsverige	Sweden	0.833
194	ES42	Castilla-la Mancha	Spain	0.818
195	ITF4	Puglia	Italy	0.800
196	FR83	Corse	France	0.750
197	ITF5	Basilicata	Italy	0.750
198	ES23	La Rioja	Spain	0.750
199	UKK3	Cornwall, Isles of Scilly	United Kingdom	0.750
200	UKL1	West Wales, The Valleys	United Kingdom	0.750
201	ES24	Aragón	Spain	0.714
202	AT21	Kärnten	Austria	0.667
203	DK01	Hovedstaden	Denmark	0.667
204	DK03	Syddanmark	Denmark	0.667
205	DK04	Midtjylland	Denmark	0.667

(continued)

APPENDIX TABLE C.1 *(continued)*

No.	ID	Region	Country	Conflict Exposure
206	FI1B	Helsinki-Uusimaa	Finland	0.667
207	DE93	Lüneburg	Germany	0.667
208	PT11	Norte	Portugal	0.667
209	ES43	Extremadura	Spain	0.667
210	DK05	Nordjylland	Denmark	0.600
211	DEF0	Schleswig-Holstein	Germany	0.600
212	SE11	Stockholm	Sweden	0.600
213	SE21	Småland med öarna	Sweden	0.545
214	ES41	Castilla y León	Spain	0.538
215	BG34	Yugoiztochen	Bulgaria	0.500
216	FR72	Auvergne	France	0.500
217	EL25	Peloponnisos	Greece	0.500
218	PL31	Lubelskie	Poland	0.500
219	PL34	Podlaskie	Poland	0.500
220	PT16	Centro	Portugal	0.500
221	PT17	Área Metropolitana de Lisboa	Portugal	0.500
222	RO12	Centru	Romania	0.500
223	SI01	Vzhodna Slovenija	Slovenia	0.500
224	ES13	Cantabria	Spain	0.500
225	ES30	Comunidad de Madrid	Spain	0.500
226	ES53	Illes Balears	Spain	0.500
227	SE22	Sydsverige	Sweden	0.500
228	SE12	Östra Mellansverige	Sweden	0.444
229	FI1 C	Etelä-Suomi	Finland	0.375
230	BG31	Severozapaden	Bulgaria	0.333
231	EL30	Attiki	Greece	0.333
232	RO11	Nord-Vest	Romania	0.333
233	ES11	Galicia	Spain	0.333
234	ES12	Principado de Asturias	Spain	0.333
235	SE31	Norra Mellansverige	Sweden	0.333
236	FI19	Länsi-Suomi	Finland	0.250
237	SI02	Zahodna Slovenija	Slovenia	0.250
238	BG42	Yuzhen tsentralen	Bulgaria	0.200
239	BG41	Yugozapaden	Bulgaria	0.167
240	EL24	Sterea Ellada	Greece	0.167
241	SE33	Övre Norrland	Sweden	0.059
242	FI1D	Pohjois-ja Itä-Suomi	Finland	0.040
243	HR03	Jadranska Hrvatska	Croatia	0.000
244	FI20	Åland	Finland	0.000
245	DE60	Hamburg	Germany	0.000
246	EL11	Anatoliki Makedonia, Thraki	Greece	0.000
247	EL12	Kentriki Makedonia	Greece	0.000

(continued)

APPENDIX TABLE C.1 *(continued)*

No.	ID	Region	Country	Conflict Exposure
248	EL13	Dytiki Makedonia	Greece	0.000
249	EL14	Thessalia	Greece	0.000
250	EL21	Ipeiros	Greece	0.000
251	EL22	Ionia Nisia	Greece	0.000
252	EL23	Dytiki Ellada	Greece	0.000
253	EL41	Voreio Aigaio	Greece	0.000
254	EL42	Notio Aigaio	Greece	0.000
255	EL43	Kriti	Greece	0.000
256	ITG2	Sardegna	Italy	0.000
257	ITI3	Marche	Italy	0.000
258	SE32	Mellersta Norrland	Sweden	0.000

Notes: Historical conflict exposure (1) sums the number of recorded major conflicts over 1500–1799 within each 150 km × 150 km grid cell and (2) averages this sum over all grid cells that overlap with each NUTS2 region. See Chapter 5 for further details.
Sources: Clodfelter (2002) for military conflicts and Eurostat (http://ec.europa.eu/eurostat) for NUTS2 regions.

APPENDIX TABLE C.2 *Descriptive Statistics for Chapter 5 Analysis*

	Obs	Mean	Std dev	Min	Max
Panel A: Eurostat (2015)					
Per capita GDP, 2001–5 (PPS)	258	20,445	7,931	4,520	70,080
Log per capita GDP, 2001–5 (PPS)	258	9.842	0.436	8.416	11.157
Log population density, 2005	176	5.074	1.234	1.194	9.133
High-tech employment, 2005	176	4.063	1.875	0.890	10.490
Log per capita R&D spending, 2005 (PPS)	176	5.205	1.335	1.569	7.495
Historical conflict exposure, 1500–1799	258	4.291	5.816	0	34
Historical conflict exposure, 1300–1699	258	2.968	3.807	0	21
Historical conflict exposure, 1000–1799	258	5.866	6.755	0	35
Log population density, 1500	258	0.004	0.017	0	0.186
Log population density, 1300	258	0.003	0.015	0	0.193
Log population density, 1000	258	0.001	0.005	0	0.073
Area (1,000 sq km)	258	16.195	21.732	0.019	226.739
Primary river	258	0.364	0.482	0	1
Landlocked	258	0.535	0.500	0	1
Roman road hub	258	0.411	0.493	0	1
Terrain ruggedness	258	1.128	1.302	0.012	7.466
Elevation (meters)	258	312.620	307.874	-2.637	2,091.345
General cultivation likelihood	258	0.620	0.244	0.003	0.993
Barley suitability	246	0.064	0.092	0	0.461
Potato suitability	246	0.113	0.165	0	0.795
Wheat suitability	246	0.106	0.137	0	0.934

(continued)

	N	Mean	SD	Min	Max
Distance to Mainz (1,000 km)	258	0.806	0.483	0.035	2.121
Distance to Wittenberg (1,000 km)	258	0.873	0.499	0.057	2.296
Distance to nearest university, 1500 (1,000 km)	258	1.989	0.690	0.444	3.547
Panel B: Nordhaus et al. (2011)					
Per capita GCP, 2005 (2005 USD)	998	24.430	9.985	3.434	69.583
Log per capita GCP, 2005 (2005 USD)	998	3.092	0.495	1.234	4.243
Historical conflict exposure, 1500–1799	998	0.567	1.631	0	19
Log population density, 1500	998	0.001	0.003	0	0.041
Area (1,000 sq km)	998	4.324	3.085	0.006	9.862
Primary river	998	0.197	0.398	0	1
Landlocked	998	0.524	0.499	0	1
Roman road hub	998	0.222	0.416	0	1
Terrain ruggedness	998	1.321	1.489	0.010	7.590
Elevation (meters)	998	348.090	391.072	−1.269	2,755.611
General cultivation likelihood	998	0.525	0.327	0.001	0.998

Note: See Chapter 5 for variable descriptions and sources.

Model Appendix

Say that individual j lives in the countryside, where she produces output $y_j > 0$.

There are two states of the world: the threat likelihood of nearby conflict may be low or it may be high. For simplicity, we normalize the low threat likelihood of nearby conflict to 0 (i.e., peacetime) and the high threat likelihood of nearby conflict to 1 (i.e., conflict).

Given this environment, individual j must make two sequential decisions.

First, individual j must decide whether to migrate from the countryside to the city. Let $f > 0$ be the relocation cost of rural–urban migration. Warfare inflicted many costs on rural populations (see Chapter 3), including property destruction by soldiers along the war march, the traditional duty of billeting soldiers, the loss of agricultural manpower, and money raising by the military. Accordingly, if nearby conflict occurs, then the output of any individual j that did not migrate to the city in response falls by w_j, where $0 < w_j \leq y_j$. If nearby conflict does not occur, however, then there is no such cost to stay in the countryside.

Second, if individual j does in fact decide to migrate to the city, then she must next decide whether to remain there temporarily or permanently. If individual j decides to return to the countryside, then she must pay an additional relocation cost $r > 0$, where $r = f$. However, if individual j decides to remain permanently in the city, then she must pay an urban graveyard cost $x > 0$. This cost reflects the historical fact that urban life expectancy was on average lower than rural life expectancy due to epidemics (see Chapter 3). Finally, the city's historical role as a safe harbor could translate into economic and political benefits for urban migrants through a variety of channels: the establishment of local privileges, including self-governance and property rights protections from predatory outside rulers, technological change and human capital accumulation, and economic agglomeration effects (see Chapter 3). Accordingly, the output of any individual j that permanently migrates to the city increases by productivity factor $t_j \geq 1$.

The model's timing is as follows:

1. Individual j, who lives in the countryside, produces output y_j.
2. This individual observes whether nearby conflict will or will not occur.
3. This individual decides whether to migrate to the city at relocation cost f. The output of any individual j that does not migrate to the city in response to nearby conflict falls by w_j. However, there is no such cost to stay in the countryside if nearby conflict does not occur.
4. Any individual j that does in fact migrate to the city must decide whether to remain there temporarily or permanently. Individual j can return to the countryside at relocation cost r or remain permanently in the city at urban graveyard cost x. Any individual j that permanently migrates to the city increases output by productivity factor t_j.

Figure A.1 illustrates the model and payoffs for individual j.

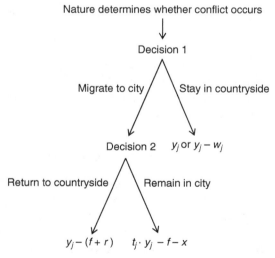

FIGURE A.1 Model and Payoffs for Individual j

OPTIMAL DECISIONS

We evaluate individual j's optimal migration decisions for two states of the world. First, we analyze such decisions under peacetime. Second, we analyze them under nearby conflict.

State of the World 1: Peacetime

We proceed by backwards induction, starting with individual j's decision whether to remain in the city temporarily or permanently (i.e., Decision 2 in Figure A.1). Individual j prefers to remain there permanently so long as the following condition is satisfied.

$$
\begin{aligned}
t_j \cdot y_j - f - x &> y_j - (f + r) \\
\Rightarrow (t_j \cdot y_j - y_j) + r &> x
\end{aligned}
\tag{A.1}
$$

Condition (A.1) indicates that individual j prefers to remain in the city permanently so long as the urban productivity gain $t_j \cdot y_j - y_j$ is large enough and/or the relocation cost to return to the countryside r is high enough and/or the urban graveyard cost x is small enough. If condition (A.1) holds, then individual j will decide to migrate to the city at the first stage if

$$
\begin{aligned}
t_j \cdot y_j - f - x &> y_j \\
\Rightarrow (t_j \cdot y_j - y_j) - f &> x
\end{aligned}
\tag{A.2}
$$

According to condition (A.2), individual j will permanently relocate to the city so long as the urban productivity gain (i.e., net of the rural–urban relocation cost f) outweighs the urban graveyard cost. Thus, permanent urban migration may be an attractive choice even in peacetime. The greater the net urban productivity gain for individual j, then the more likely permanent peacetime urban migration will be (i.e., holding constant the urban graveyard cost).

State of the World 2: Nearby Conflict

The analysis in the previous section indicates that, under the state of the world in which there is peacetime, individual j may still prefer to permanently migrate to the city if the net urban productivity gain is large enough (alternatively, if the urban graveyard cost is low enough). We now evaluate how individual j's optimal migration decisions change under the state of the world in which there is nearby conflict.

Given condition (A.1) from earlier, individual *j* prefers to permanently remain in the city if the urban productivity gain is large enough and/or the relocation cost to return to the countryside is high enough and/or the urban graveyard cost is small enough. If condition (A.1) holds, then individual *j* will decide to migrate to the city in the first place so long as

$$t_j \cdot y_j - f - x > y_j - w_j$$
$$\Rightarrow (t_j \cdot y_j - y_j) - f + w_j > x \tag{A.3}$$

This condition indicates that the likelihood that individual *j* will permanently relocate to the city is increasing in the urban productivity gain (i.e., net of the rural–urban relocation cost) and the conflict-induced rural production loss but decreasing in the urban graveyard cost. If condition (A.1) does not hold, then individual *j* will still decide to temporarily migrate to the city to escape the costs of conflict in the countryside so long as the conflict-induced production loss w_j exceeds the migration-related relocation costs $f + r$.

Is individual *j* more likely to permanently relocate to the city under nearby conflict than under peacetime? To answer, we compare conditions (A.2) and (A.3), which we reproduce here.

$$(t_j \cdot y_j - y_j) - f > x \tag{A.2}$$

$$(t_j \cdot y_j - y_j) - f + w_j > x \tag{A.3}$$

Given $w_j > 0$, this comparison indicates that the condition under which individual *j* permanently migrates to the city is more likely to hold under nearby conflict. Thus, nearby conflict does in fact alter individual *j*'s optimal migration calculus. Furthermore, as the conflict-induced rural production loss for individual *j* increases, permanent urban migration becomes more likely (i.e., holding constant the urban graveyard cost).

We provide a summary of the model's main predictions in Chapter 3.

EXTENSIONS

Target Effect

Up to this point, we have assumed that conflict costs only affect the countryside. This assumption is historically accurate, since warfare inflicted greater costs on rural versus urban populations in Europe (see Chapter 3). We now extend our analysis to evaluate a target effect

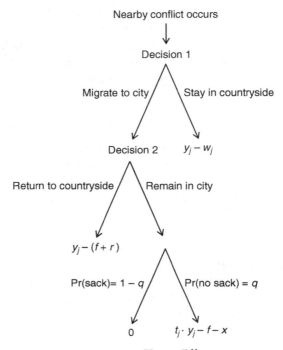

Nearby conflict occurs

Decision 1

Migrate to city / \ Stay in countryside

Decision 2 $y_j - w_j$

Return to countryside / \ Remain in city

$y_j - (f + r)$

Pr(sack)= $1 - q$ / \ Pr(no sack) = q

0    $t_j \cdot y_j - f - x$

FIGURE A.2 Target Effect

whereby nearby conflict could negatively affect urban centers as well as the countryside (see Chapter 3). We show that the model's predictions should remain valid in the presence of such an effect.

To evaluate the target effect, we add a third stage to our model, which Figure A.2 illustrates. Let q be the probability that the city avoids a sack in wartime, where $0 < q \le 1$. Thus, $1 - q$ is the probability of a successful sack. We assume that any individual j who lives in the city loses all output in such an event.[1]

At the final stage, individual j prefers to permanently remain in the city in the presence of a target effect rather than return to the countryside so long as

$$q(t_j \cdot y_j - f - x) > y_j - (f + r) \tag{A.4}$$

This condition indicates that individual j's incentive to permanently remain in the city is increasing in the probability that the city avoids a wartime sack. If condition (A.4) holds, then individual *j* prefers to migrate to the city in the first place to escape the rural costs of conflict if

$$q(t_j \cdot y_j - f - x) > y_j - w_j \qquad (A.5)$$

Similar to the previous logic, individual *j*'s initial incentive to migrate to the city – and remain there permanently – is increasing in the likelihood that the city avoids a wartime sack.

Successful urban sacks were rare in European history (see Chapter 3), implying that the probability q was very high (i.e., $q \approx 1$). Thus, the model's predictions from the previous section should remain valid in the presence of a target effect.

Rural–Rural Migration

In precolonial sub-Saharan Africa, the land-labor ratio was very high (see Chapter 6). In this context, individual *j* may have had two realistic migration options in the face of nearby conflict: relocate to virgin rural land (the new alternative option) or to the city (the original option). Figure A.3 illustrates the revised model, where $f_R > 0$ is the relocation cost of rural–rural migration and $f_U > 0$ is the relocation cost of rural–urban migration. Similarly, $x_R > 0$ is the cost of farming virgin land, while $x_U > 0$ is the urban graveyard cost.

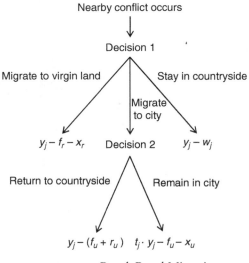

FIGURE A.3 Rural–Rural Migration

Given high-enough rural costs of conflict w_j, individual j will prefer to either migrate to virgin rural land or to the city rather than stay in her original countryside location. Individual j prefers rural–rural migration to (permanent) urban migration if

$$y_j - f_r - x_r > t_j \cdot y_j - f_u - x_u$$
$$\Rightarrow (f_u + x_u) > (f_r + x_r) + (t_j \cdot y_j - y_j) \qquad \text{(A.6)}$$

For ease of exposition, we set urban productivity factor $t_j = 1$. Thus, condition (A.6) reduces to

$$(f_u + x_u) > (f_r + x_r)$$

Historically, the cost of farming virgin land in sub-Saharan Africa was very low (see Chapter 6), making it more likely that condition (A.6) would be satisfied (i.e., holding constant all other costs). Thus, in this context, individual j would likely prefer the "primacy of exit" in the face of nearby conflict: namely, to flee to virgin rural land rather than to the city.[2,3]

Notes

I INTRODUCTION

1. By Europe, we mean the whole continent, including major islands but excluding Russia and Turkey.
2. We analyze north-south differences in Italy in detail in Chapter 5.
3. If we travel even further back in time, we see that the Carolingian Empire itself was short-lived (Ganshof, 1971: 17–27). Prior to Charlemagne, Western Europe was politically fragmented from the time of the fall of the Roman Empire (Hoffman, 2015: 107; Stasavage, 2016: 156–8).
4. Dekle and Eaton (1998), Glaeser and Maré (2001), Rosenthal and Strange (2004), Combes et al. (2010), and Greenstone, Hornbeck, and Moretti (2010) show evidence that the relationship between urbanization and greater productivity is in fact casual.
5. Jones (2003: 124–5) also highlights the economic importance of the sustained balance of power among sovereign states in medieval Europe. Numerous scholars have analyzed why the European states system did not succumb to hegemony by a single powerful polity, including Spruyt (1994a), Fearon (1997), Hui (2004), Schweller (2004), Levy and Thompson (2005), Wohlforth et al. (2007), and Møller (2014).
6. Cox (2016b) links political fragmentation to the development of local parliamentary governance and its spillover effects on free trade, due to credible exit options by merchants. Similarly, Gelderblom (2013: 1–18) argues that political fragmentation induced urban governments to make political innovations in order to attract trade. Stasavage (2016) contends that, given political fragmentation, historical rulers had the incentive to strike political bargains with constituents through representative government because coercion was not viable.
7. Rosenthal (1992: 100–21), Epstein (2000: 12–37), Dincecco (2011: 10–23), Grafe (2012: 213–40), and Dincecco and Katz (2016) highlight the economic costs of historical institutional fragmentation in Europe.

8. Recent works in this tradition include Polèse (2009: 67–75), Nunn and Qian (2011), Haber (2012), Motamed, Florax, and Masters (2014), Abramson and Boix (2015), Andersen, Jensen, and Skovsgaard (2015), and Boix (2015: 209–15).

9. Similarly, scholars including North and Weingast (1989), Pincus and Robinson (2011), Acemoglu and Robinson (2012: 102–4), and Cox (2016a: 100–16) analyze the relationship between the Glorious Revolution–era institutional reforms and the Industrial Revolution in England.

10. Abramson and Boix (2015) argue that parliamentary institutions were consequences rather than causes of historical economic development in Europe. Stasavage (2016: 153–54) offers the following counterargument to this claim. In 1000, per capita GDP in England was much lower than in China, somewhat lower than in the Abbasid Empire, and somewhat higher than in the Byzantine Empire. Still, only preindustrial England developed representative government. This evidence suggests that economic development alone cannot explain historical political development in Europe. Boucoyannis (2015) describes the origins of parliament in medieval England, which she links to war-related tax needs.

11. This literature includes Tilly (1975, 1992: 67–95), Mann (1986), Brewer (1989: 88–134), Downing (1992), Burke (1997: 11–29), Ertman (1997: 74–87), Besley and Persson (2009), and Gennaioli and Voth (2015).

12. Scholars argue that Tilly's logic does not always prevail in non-European contexts – see Centeno (2002) for Latin America and Herbst (2000) and Osafo-Kwaako and Robinson (2013) for sub-Saharan Africa. By contrast, Thies (2005, 2007) finds qualified support for Tilly's argument for both Latin America and sub-Saharan Africa.

13. In this regard, our book complements Strayer (1970), Blockmans (1975), Levi (1988: 95–121), Spruyt (1994b: 77–108), Blaydes and Chaney (2013), and Blaydes and Paik (2016), all of whom highlight the medieval roots of modern state development.

14. This argument is similar in spirit to Elias (2000: 185–362), Gat (2006: 401–42), Bates (2010: 34–56), Besley and Persson (2011: 1, 10), O'Brien (2011), Pinker (2011: 59–80), Fearon and Laitin (2014), and Turchin (2016).

15. In this respect, our book may help shed new light on the historical roots of the "democratic peace," the empirical regularity that modern democratic regimes tend to interact in peaceful ways with each other (Levy, 1988; Maoz and Abdolali, 1989; Dafoe, Oneal, and Russett, 2013).

16. Both Rosenthal and Wong (2011: 215–21) and Hoffman (2015: 19–66) argue that endemic warfare in Europe drove historical advances in military technology there, enabling European nations to colonize other world regions in the first place. Acemoglu, Johnson, and Robinson (2002) focus on the negative institutional effects of European colonization for civilizations in the Americas, which they link to a reversal in the global income distribution between 1500 and today, while Acemoglu, Johnson, and Robinson (2005) highlight the consequences of Atlantic trade for domestic political institutions in Europe itself (we discuss this work in detail in a previous section of this chapter).

17. To explain the Great Divergence, both Rosenthal and Wong (2011: 208–27) and Voightländer and Voth (2013a, 2013b) do in fact highlight political fragmentation and warfare. We contrast our analysis with these important works in a previous section of this chapter.

2 THE IMPORTANCE OF WARFARE

1. Similarly, Hoffman (2015: 22) estimates that European powers were at war in more than 70 percent of all years between 1550 and 1600, 60 percent of all years over the 1600s, and nearly 40 percent of all years during the 1700s.
2. Tilly (1992: 74–5) provides a similar account of the importance of warfare to government budgets in early modern Europe. For a description of military costs, see Nef (1968: 203–5).
3. Similarly, Schultz and Weingast (1998) argue that the ability of parliamentary regimes in European history to finance budget deficits through public debt (due to their superior creditworthiness) provided an important military advantage.
4. We base this account on Stasavage (2011: 95–100).
5. Scholars including Spruyt (1994a), Fearon (1997), Hui (2004), Schweller (2004), Levy and Thompson (2005), Wohlforth et al. (2007), and Møller (2014) have analyzed why the competing states system in medieval Europe never gave way to domination by a single hegemonic polity.
6. Hoffman's calculations exclude civil wars. However, including civil wars does not change the results, except for in the case of Britain. Namely, the likelihood that the British monarch would lose his throne after defeat in war rose from 0 percent to 29 percent once civil wars are included (Hoffman, 2015: 27).
7. Iyigun (2008) analyzes the relationship between Ottoman conquests and intra-European conflicts between Catholics and Protestants in early modern Europe.
8. By contrast, Hale (1985: 22) downplays the importance of the profits (e.g., rents) that landowners could earn.
9. We describe our computational method in detail in Chapter 4.
10. Technically, the battle in 1018 was the Second Battle of Cannae. The first was fought more than 1,000 years before (in 216 BCE), when Hannibal, the famed Carthaginian general, defeated the Romans (Bradbury, 2004: 148).
11. Another reason to prefer Bradbury and Clodfelter is that both works have been published, while Brecke remains a working paper.
12. Furthermore, in contrast to Brecke (1999), few scholars have made use of Jaques's dictionary. One notable exception is Gennaioli and Voth (2015).

3 EUROPE'S URBAN RISE

1. Beyond Rome, Constantinople was the only other large non-Muslim city in 1000 (van Bavel, Bosker, Buringh, and van Zanden, 2013: 392).
2. Van Bavel, Bosker, Buringh, and van Zanden define Western Europe as Germany, Switzerland, Italy, and all zones to their west.

3. Winter (2013: 407–11) provides a pyramid of historical urban migration patterns. The main source of a city's migrants was typically the surrounding countryside. However, migrants could also travel long distances (Moch, 2003: 31). Another migration pattern was between cities (Winter, 2013: 408). However, this type of migration was too small to explain the total increase in urban populations in preindustrial Europe (Winter, 2013: 408).

4. By comparison, this rate was approximately 3 percent in 1000 (van Bavel, Bosker, Buringh, and van Zanden, 2013: 394).

5. For example, according to Tracy, (2000a: 1), there is a single word ("cheng") in classical Chinese for "city" and "wall."

6. The fortification length required to encircle a round city equals $2\sqrt{\pi AN}$, where N denotes the urban population and A denotes the fixed space that each inhabitant takes up (Glaeser and Shapiro, 2002: 209).

7. Hale (1985: 188) describes Landucci's account.

8. Benedict (1991: 75) estimates that rural inhabitants made up nearly 70 percent of the total Huguenot population in France at the start of the 1600s. According to his calculations, which make use of parish vital records data, the population distribution of Huguenots in northern France in 1610 was roughly 71,000 urban, 18,000 small town, and 86,000 rural. For southern France, this distribution was roughly 121,000 urban, 82,000 small town, and 573,000 rural. Overall, the rural share of the total Huguenot population at this time was $\dfrac{86,000 + 573,000}{951,000} = 0.693$.

9. Settia (1987: 435) relates Salimbene da Parma's account.

10. Furthermore, according to Friedrichs (1995: 300), "No city was every completely destroyed by warfare." This observation is consistent with Livi-Bacci's (2000: 36) claim that although some early modern towns saw relative decay, examples of outright disappearance were scarce.

11. Even on the odd chance that warfare permanently destroyed a city's economy, another city could take advantage of out-migration from this location. For example, the sack of Antwerp in 1576 prompted a flood of high-skilled migration to Amsterdam (Moch, 2003: 29, 53–4).

12. It was not always the case that conflict zones saw population losses in wartime (Hohenberg and Lees, 1995: 81). For example, Gutmann (1980: 200) finds that wartime population levels were flat, but never declining, in the early modern Low Countries.

13. Similarly, Friedrichs (1995: 300) writes, "Even Magdeburg was repopulated by a straggling remnant of its former inhabitants and eventually became a substantial city again."

14. Other epidemics included cholera, influenza, smallpox, and typhus (Friedrichs, 1995: 130; Voightländer and Voth, 2013b: 779).

15. Voightländer and Voth (2013b) model the relationships between the Black Death, urbanization, and warfare in early modern Europe. They argue that – consistent with the historical evidence – such relationships were positive (we describe this argument in Chapter 1).

16. Blockmans and t'Hart (2013: 430–3) describe the most common political, legal, and fiscal privileges of medieval towns. Friedrichs (1995: 266–71)

describes the manner in which urban public administrations were organized.

17. Stasavage (2014) argues that urban autonomy in preindustrial Europe reduced economic growth over the long run, because commercial elites were able to block technological innovations through the implementation of entry limits into their professions. We discuss Stasavage's results in the next section.

18. Similarly, Mokyr (2007: 24) portrays the ability of dissident scholars to migrate across sovereign borders in early modern Europe, enabling their ideas to not only survive, but to flourish.

19. Rural invention did in fact take place, including the medieval invention of the heavy plow (White, 1962: 41–57; Mokyr, 1995: 19–20). Towns became more important innovation hubs from the 1300s onward (Mokyr, 1995: 19).

20. It is well established that technological change and human capital accumulation play important roles in economic growth. See Romer (1990), Lucas (2009), and Gennaioli, La Porta, Lopez-de-Silanes, and Shleifer (2013). Beyond human capital accumulation, scholars highlight the relationships between historical urbanization and social capital formation. Examples include Guiso, Sapienza, and Zingales (2008) and Greif and Tabellini (2015).

21. Ciccone (2002) shows evidence for significant agglomeration effects in modern-day Europe.

22. There were four major urban economic sectors: food processing, cloth and leather good manufacturing, building construction, and tool and household item manufacturing (Friedrichs, 1995: 94–5).

23. In the Model Appendix we extend our model to evaluate a target effect whereby nearby conflict could negatively affect urban centers as well as the countryside. We show that the model's predictions still remain valid in the presence of such an effect.

24. In the model, the conflict-induced rural production loss and urban productivity factor differ by individuals. Thus, it is not likely that all individuals in the countryside will *permanently* migrate to the city in response to high threats of nearby conflict. Put differently, at least some individuals will likely stay in the countryside and produce food. Even if the vast majority of individuals do in fact permanently migrate to the city, however, we can rely on the fact that historical food production was endogenous in the medium run, if not the short run (as described in a previous section).

25. If the domestic security situation improved, then artisanal goods production in the countryside would likely become relatively more attractive, because the conflict-induced rural production loss would fall. An example is the growth of the putting-out industry in England following the end of the Civil War in the mid-1600s (as described in the previous section).

4 EVALUATING THE SAFE HARBOR EFFECT

1. Bairoch, Batou, and Chèvre include populations for historical communes, faubourgs, hamlets, quarters, and suburbs that directly adjoined city centers (Dittmar, 2011: 1143). Following Bosker, Buringh, and van Zanden (2013:

data appendix, 1), we updated the population data for five major historical urban centers: Bruges, Cordoba, London, Palermo, and Paris.

2. The Bairoch, Batou, and Chèvre data do not include 1100. Thus, we interpolate (but never extrapolate) observations for 1100.

3. We only include grid cells that at least partially fall within the borders of modern-day nations for which there is at least one sample city. Among such grid cells, 196 include at least one sample city. Those that fall within the grid cells represent 94 percent of total sample conflicts between 1000 and 1799 (of which there are 856). We exclude grid cells for the other 6 percent of total conflicts that do not satisfy this criterion. Such conflicts were oftentimes very distant from any sample city.

4. The first observation of $P_{i,g,t}$ is 1100, because the first observation of $Conflict_{i,g,t-1}$ measures local conflict exposure over 1000–99.

5. They are: Albania, Austria, Belgium, Bulgaria, the Czech Republic, Denmark, France, Finland, Germany, Greece, Hungary, Ireland, Italy, Luxemburg, Malta, the Netherlands, Norway, Poland, Portugal, Romania, the Slovak Republic, Spain, Sweden, Switzerland, the United Kingdom, and the former Yugoslavia.

6. "Initial city populations" refers to the first available observation for each sample city.

7. We compute average city population growth as $\frac{\overline{P}_t - \overline{P}_{t-1}}{\overline{P}_{t-1}}$.

8. Voightländer and Voth (2013a: 178) analyze a sample of approximately 20 nations between 1300 and 1700. They find that the urbanization rate for a nation that saw an average of one war per year over 1300–1700 increased nearly eight percentage points faster than the urbanization rate for a nation that saw zero warfare over this period. A direct comparison of the magnitudes of our respective estimates is difficult, however, because Voightländer and Voth test national-level urbanization rates, whereas we focus on historical city population sizes.

9. We take the barley suitability variable ("high suitability") from Andersen, Jensen, and Skovsgaard (2015). They provide barley suitability at Eurostat's main unit of economic territory (NUTS2) as available, which we match to each sample city.

10. In historical China, Jia (2015) finds that the introduction of the drought-resistant sweet potato reduced peasant revolts.

11. We take the potato suitability variable from Nunn and Qian (2011). We follow their data construction procedure, matching potato suitability according to a global GIS raster file to the 150 km × 150 km grid cell in which each sample city falls.

12. This control is a "bad control" (Angrist and Pischke, 2009: 64–8) in the sense that urban networks may themselves have been conflict outcomes.

13. They are Bulgaria, the Czech Republic, Hungary, Poland, Romania, and the Slovak Republic. The other four Eastern European nations according to the UN (Belarus, Moldova, Russia, and Ukraine) are not part of our city sample.

14. Different samples yield similar results. For example, for 1200–1700 the point estimate is 0.095 (p-value = 0.022) for the fixed effects specification and 0.041

for the most stringent specification (p-value = 0.219). Similarly, for 1500–1700 the respective point estimates are 0.142 (p-value = 0.008) and 0.060 (p-value = 0.243).

15. We divide large countries – France, Germany, Italy, and Spain – into histori-cally relevant macroregions. For example, we divide Italy into the south and non-south. The notes to Figure 4.2 provide further details.

16. Other grid sizes yield similar results, although they are somewhat sensitive to the exclusion of specific regions. For example, for the 50 km × 50 km grid size, the point estimate for $Conflict_{i,g,t-1}$ is 0.064 (p-value = 0.082) for the most stringent specification (i.e., column 3 of Table 4.1) that excludes the northern French region of Nord-Pas-de-Calais (NUTS1 unit FR3). Otherwise, this point estimate is 0.048 (p-value = 0.190). Similarly, for the 100 km × 100 km grid size and the 200 km × 200 km grid size, the respective point estimates are 0.045 (p-value = 0.096) and 0.045 (p-value = 0.098) for the specification that excludes the southwest German region of Rhineland-Palatinate (NUTS1 unit DEB). Otherwise, these point estimates are 0.037 (p-value = 0.177) and 0.041 (p-value = 0.141).

17. This column and the following column of Table 4.4 use the benchmark grid cell size (i.e., 150 km × 150 km).

18. Bosker, Buringh, and van Zanden (2013: data appendix, 14–15) define plunder as the "near complete demolition, looting, carnage, or burning down of a city or the killing or deportation of the major part of its inhabitants."

19. Due to the panel's relatively small time component T (given 100-year intervals, $T = 7$), this approach is subject to Nickell (1981) bias. To address Nickell bias, we can use GMM estimation (Arellano and Bond, 1991), but GMM itself calls for strong assumptions (Angrist and Pischke, 2009: 245).

20. Still, according to Hale (1985: 191–6), the destructive effects of sieges were worse for the surrounding countryside than for the besieged city. He writes, "Outside the walls the effect on the peasant and village economy was literally devastating if the operation were a prolonged one; many lasted several months, some for years . . . Inside the walls there was, by contrast, a necessary collabora-tion between the populace and their garrison" (Hale, 1985: 191).

21. Famously, Venice was unwalled, relying instead on its unique topographical location across more than a hundred islands in the Venetian lagoon (Friedrichs, 1995: 22, 30).

22. However, once built, city walls typically endured through 1800 (Friedrichs, 1995: 25). Mintzker (2012: 85–101) describes the surge of defortification in Germany between 1789 and 1815.

23. For perspective, 6 ducats was enough to support a rural family in mid-sixteenth-century Italy (Pepper and Adams, 1986: 30).

24. Tracy's (2000b: 79) definition of a "walled city" includes (single or double) stone walls, gun platforms placed outside of walls, or bastioned traces.

25. Such mappings are approximations. Tracy (2000b: 85) shows data for 11 historical provinces. We exclude two historical provinces (East Prussia and Silesia) that do not fall within the borders of modern-day Germany. Of the

nine historical provinces that we include, we map Anhalt to the modern-day state of Saxony-Anhalt, Brandenburg to Brandenburg, Hesse to Hesse, Meckenburg and Pomerania to Mecklenburg-Vorpommern, Rhineland to Rhineland-Palatinate, Saxony (sometimes called "Old Saxony") to Lower Saxony, Schleswig-Holstein to Schleswig-Holstein, and Thuringia to Thuringia.

26. This map is to be found in the book's end pocket.

5 EVALUATING THE WARFARE-TO-WEALTH EFFECT

1. For example, the 2005 Urban Audit by Eurostat provides GDP data for far fewer cities than the 676 that we analyze in Chapter 4. Furthermore, such data do not always measure GDP for cities themselves, but rather for larger regional agglomerations.

2. The main results to be described ahead are similar in magnitude and significance for per capita GDP averages over different years (i.e., 2000–10, 2005, or 2008–10).

3. Per capita GDP data in PPS at the NUTS2 regional level are not available for Switzerland, which is not part of the European Union.

4. We harmonize observations across these three variables.

5. The main results are robust to alternative sample periods, which we will describe ahead.

6. We restrict our sample to regions for which per capita GDP data are also available (see Figure 5.2).

7. Appendix Table C.1 ranks regions by historical conflict exposure.

8. The demographic data are from Bairoch, Batou, and Chèvre (1988). We truncate all city populations <10, 000 at 0. We sum all city populations by region and then divide by regional area. We assign zeros to regions with no sample city populations. Finally, to include all observations, we add 1 before taking logs.

9. We include binary variables equal to 1 for regions that have a primary river, are landlocked, or were Roman road hubs. These data are from the European Environment Agency (2009), Natural Earth (2015), and Touring Club Italiano (2009), respectively. The terrain ruggedness and elevation data are from Nunn and Puga (2012). They are available for roughly 1 km × 1 km grid cells. The general cultivation likelihood data are from Ramakutty et al. (2002). They calculate the probability that a grid cell is cultivable based on climate and soil conditions and are available for roughly 55 km × 40 km grid cells. For the terrain ruggedness, elevation, and general cultivation likelihood variables, we average data values across all grid cells that overlap with each NUTS2 region.

10. Average per capita GDP over 2001–5 was 30,180 PPS in Lombardy and 14,540 PPS in Calabria (Eurostat, 2015), for a total difference of 15,640 PPS.

11. We take the agricultural suitability variables (coded at the NUTS2 regional level) from Anderson, Jensen, and Skovsgaard (2015). Here the sample size

falls by nearly 30 due to lost observations after we merge the Anderson, Jensen, and Skovsgaard data with our main database.

12. We measure all control variables in $X_{r,c}$ in the same manner as for NUTS2 regions, except now the relevant unit is a 1 degree longitude × 1 degree latitude grid cell.

13. Vecchi's regions are very similar to NUTS2 regions.

14. Veneto became part of Italy in 1866 and Rome in 1870 (Dincecco, Federico, and Vindigni, 2011: 897).

15. Tabellini's regions tend to be a good deal larger than the NUTS2 regions used for the within-Italy analysis. Tabellini defines the literacy rate as the share of the regional population that could read and write. The sample nations for which he has regional data are Belgium, France, Germany (excluding East Germany), Italy, the Netherlands, Portugal, Spain, and the United Kingdom.

16. More generally, the example of northern and southern Italy shows how raw urbanization rates and economic development need not always be correlated (Jedwab and Vollrath, 2015); the particular character of urbanization matters for development outcomes.

6 WARFARE TO WEALTH IN COMPARATIVE PERSPECTIVE

1. Pomeranz (2000: 7), Rosenthal and Wong (2011: 4–5), and von Glahn (2016: 359) all criticize historical comparisons based on modern-day political units such as Britain versus China, because Britain is far smaller in physical size.

2. We should not mistake the ability of rulers in early modern China to establish effective authority for a complete and utter "monopoly of violence" by them. Tong (1991: 43–75) shows that rebellions and banditry (among other types of collective violence) were common under both the Ming dynasty (1368–1644) and the late Qing dynasty (1796–1911).

3. Similarly, according to Xu, van Leeuwen, and van Zanden (2015: 15), the average urbanization rate for the 18 core provinces in China was 7 percent in 1776. The Xu, van Leeuwen, and van Zanden data for China include all urban centers with more than 2,000 inhabitants, whereas city population data for Europe (e.g., van Bavel, Bosker, Buringh, and van Zanden, 2013) often restrict the sample to urban centers with more than 10,000 inhabitants, making clean Europe-China comparisons somewhat difficult.

4. Weil (2014: 124–8) provides country-level estimates of historical population density in sub-Saharan Africa, the results of which strongly support Herbst's (2000) estimates.

5. This style of warfare also reflects geographical challenges related to Africa's rugged and vast terrain (Reid, 2012: 4).

6. Reid (2012: 5), for example, writes, "In many respects, the highly mobile, skirmishing style of combat has endured into the modern era."

7. Like preindustrial Europe, pre-Tokugawa (i.e., pre-1600) Japan combined warfare with high political fragmentation and a low land-labor ratio. The sixteenth century is called the Warring States ("Sengoku") period of

Japanese history, characterized by civil war between local power-holders (Rozman, 1973: 45). Population density in Japan circa 1500 was approximately 45 people per square kilometer (Herbst, 2000: 16). The historical evidence corroborates the city's role as a safe harbor in this context. Rozman (1973: 46) writes, "By the end of the sixteenth century Japan had entered perhaps the most remarkable period of urban development of any premodern country." Furthermore, urban self-governance was common in pre-Tokugawa Japan. In the words of Rozman (1973: 39), "Especially during the fifteenth and sixteenth centuries Japanese guilds achieved a measure of self-governance unknown in Chinese history. Forms of urban government approximated the 'free' cities of feudal Europe ..."

EPILOGUE

1. We derive this estimate from Maddison (2013), a well-known source for long-run GDP data. For Europe in 1000, Maddison only provides real per capita GDP data for England (757 international dollars), which we compare to his average figure for 12 Western European nations in 2010 (21,793 international dollars). For 1500, Maddison provides real per capita GDP data for 5 Western European regions (Belgium, Germany, center-north Italy, Holland, and England). Between 1500 and 2010, average real per capita GDP in Western Europe has grown 16-fold according to Maddison's data.

2. To be clear, political debates over regional and national sovereignty – think Brexit – still dog Europe even today. O'Rourke (2016) provides an analysis of the Brexit vote. Other contemporary examples include the independence movement in Catalonia (*New York Times*, 2016) and the Eurozone crisis and the lack of fiscal union (Eichengreen, 2014).

3. Europe's refugee crisis – the result of warfare in nations such as Syria – shows how military conflict still influences present-day migration patterns, however (Park, 2015).

MODEL APPENDIX

1. Alternatively, $1 - q$ may represent the likelihood of a conflict-related urban fire or epidemic outbreak (i.e., above and beyond the urban graveyard cost x).

2. If we allow $t_j > 1$, then condition (A.6) will still obtain, so long as the urban productivity gain is not too large. Historically, the urbanization rate in sub-Saharan Africa was very low (see Chapter 6), implying that rural–rural migration was the most attractive option in the face of nearby conflict.

3. Given a low-enough cost of farming virgin land, we can derive a similar "primacy of exit" prediction if we compare individual j's choice of rural–rural migration to temporary (i.e., versus permanent) urban migration.

Works Cited

Abramson, S. and C. Boix (2015). "The Roots of the Industrial Revolution: Political Institutions or (Socially-Embedded) Know-How?" Working paper, Princeton University.

Acemoglu, D. (2009). *Introduction to Modern Economic Growth*. Princeton, NJ: Princeton University Press.

Acemoglu, D., D. Cantoni, S. Johnson, and J. Robinson (2011). "The Consequences of Radical Reform: The French Revolution." *American Economic Review*, 101: 3286–307.

Acemoglu, D. and S. Johnson (2005). "Unbundling Institutions." *Journal of Political Economy*, 114: 949–95.

Acemoglu, D., S. Johnson, and J. Robinson (2002). "Reversal of Fortune: Geography and Institutions in the Making of the Modern World Income Distribution." *Quarterly Journal of Economics*, 117: 1231–94.

(2005). "The Rise of Europe: Atlantic Trade, Institutional Change, and Economic Growth." *American Economic Review*, 94: 546–79.

Acemoglu, D. and J. Robinson (2012). *Why Nations Fail*. London: Profile.

Airlie, S. (1998). "Private Bodies and the Body Politic in the Divorce Case of Lothar II." *Past and Present*, 161: 3–38.

Akyeampong, E., R. Bates, N. Nunn, and J. Robinson (2014). "Introduction: Africa – The Historical Roots of Its Underdevelopment." In E. Akyeampong, R. Bates, N. Nunn, and J. Robinson, eds., *Africa's Development in Historical Perspective*, pp. 1–32. Cambridge: Cambridge University Press.

Allen, R. (2009). *The British Industrial Revolution in Global Perspective*. Cambridge: Cambridge University Press.

Andersen, T., P. Jensen, and C. Skovsgaard (2015). "The Heavy Plough and the Agricultural Revolution in Medieval Europe." *Journal of Development Economics*, 118: 133–49.

Angrist, J. and J. S. Pischke (2009). *Mostly Harmless Econometrics*. Princeton, NJ: Princeton University Press.

Arellano, M. and S. Bond (1991). "Some Tests of Specification for Panel Data: Monte Carlo Evidence and an Application to Employment Equations." *Review of Economic Studies*, 58: 277–97.

Bairoch, P. (1988). *Cities and Economic Development*. Chicago: University of Chicago Press.

Bairoch, P., J. Batou, and P. Chèvre (1988). *La Population Des Villes Européenes*. Geneva: Librarie Droz.

Bates, R. (2008). *When Things Fell Apart*. Cambridge: Cambridge University Press.

(2010). *Prosperity and Violence* (Second Edition). New York: Norton.

(2014). "The Imperial Peace." In E. Akyeampong, R. Bates, N. Nunn, and J. Robinson, eds., *Africa's Development in Historical Perspective*, pp. 424–46. Cambridge: Cambridge University Press.

Becker, S. and L. Woessmann (2009). "Was Weber Wrong? A Human Capital Theory of Protestant Economic History." *Quarterly Journal of Economics*, 124: 531–96.

Benedict, P. (1991). "The Huguenot Population of France, 1600–1685: The Demographic Fate and Customs of a Religious Minority." *Transactions of the American Philosophical Society*, 81: 1–164.

Besley, T. and T. Persson (2009). "The Origins of State Capacity: Property Rights, Taxation, and Politics." *American Economic Review*, 99: 1218–44.

(2011). *The Pillars of Prosperity*. Princeton, NJ: Princeton University Press.

Besley, T. and M. Reynal-Querol (2014). "The Legacy of Historical Conflict: Evidence from Africa." *American Political Science Review*, 108: 319–36.

Blattman, C. and E. Miguel (2010). "Civil War." *Journal of Economic Literature*, 48: 3–57.

Blaydes, L. and E. Chaney (2013). "The Feudal Revolution and Europe's Rise: Political Divergence of the Christian West and the Muslim World before 1500 CE." *American Political Science Review*, 107: 16–34.

Blaydes, L. and C. Paik (2016). "The Impact of Holy Land Crusades on State Formation: War Mobilization, Trade Integration, and Political Development in Medieval Europe." *International Organization*, 70: 551–86.

Bleakley, H. and J. Lin (2015). "History and the Sizes of Cities." *American Economic Review: Papers and Proceedings*, 105: 558–63.

Blockmans, W. (1994). "Voracious States and Obstructing Cities: An Aspect of State Formation in Pre-Industrial Europe." In C. Tilly and W. Blockmans, eds., *Cities and the Rise of States in Europe, AD 1000 to 1800*, pp. 218–50. Boulder, CO: Westview Press.

Blockmans, W. and M. t'Hart (2013). "Power." In P. Clark, ed., *Oxford Handbook of Cities in World History*, pp. 421–37. Oxford: Oxford University Press.

Blondé, B. and I. van Damme (2013). "Early Modern Europe: 1500–1800." In P. Clark, ed., *Oxford Handbook of Cities in World History*, pp. 240–57. Oxford: Oxford University Press.

Blumenthal, U. R. (1988). *The Investiture Controversy*. Philadelphia: University of Pennsylvania Press.

Boix, C. (2015). *Political Order and Inequality*. Cambridge: Cambridge University Press.

Boone, M. (2013). "Medieval Europe." In P. Clark, ed., *Oxford Handbook of Cities in World History*, pp. 221–39. Oxford: Oxford University Press.

Bosker, M., E. Buringh, and J. L. van Zanden (2013). "From Baghdad to London: Unraveling Urban Development in Europe and the Arab World, 800–1800." *Review of Economics and Statistics*, 95: 1418–37.

Boucoyannis, D. (2015). "No Taxation of Elites, No Representation: State Capacity and the Origins of Representation." *Politics & Society*, 43: 303–32.

Bradbury, J. (2004). *The Routledge Companion to Medieval Warfare*. London: Routledge.

Brecke, P. (1999). "Violent Conflicts 1400 A.D. to the Present in Different Regions of the World." Paper presented at 1999 Meeting of Peace Science Society. www.cgeh.nl/data#conflict

Brenner, R. (1976). "Agrarian Class Structure and Economic Development in Pre-Industrial Europe." *Past and Present*, 70: 30–75.

Brewer, J. (1989). *The Sinews of Power*. New York: Knopf.

Burke, V. (1997). *The Clash of Civilizations*. Cambridge: Polity.

Caferro, W. (2008). "Warfare and Economy in Renaissance Italy, 1350–1450." *Journal of Interdisciplinary History*, 39: 167–209.

Cantoni, D. and N. Yuchtman (2014). "Medieval Universities, Legal Institutions, and the Commercial Revolution." *Quarterly Journal of Economics*, 129: 823–87.

Centeno, M. (2002). *Blood and Debt*. College Station, PA: Penn State University Press.

Chaliand, G. (2005). *Nomadic Empires*. New Brunswick, NJ: Transaction.

Chittolini, G. (1994). "Cities, 'City-States,' and Regional States in North-Central Italy." In C. Tilly and W. Blockmans, eds., *Cities and the Rise of States in Europe, AD 1000 to 1800*, pp. 28–43. Boulder, CO: Westview Press.

Ciccone, A. (2002). "Agglomeration Effects in Europe." *European Economic Review*, 46: 213–27.

Cipolla, C. (1965). *Guns, Sails, and Empires*. New York: Barnes and Noble.

Clemens, M. (2011). "Economics and Emigration: Trillion-Dollar Bills on the Sidewalk?" *Journal of Economic Perspectives*, 25: 83–106.

Clodfelter, M. (2002). *Warfare and Armed Conflicts* (Second Edition). Jefferson, NC: McFarland.

Collier, P., V. Elliot, H. Hegre, A. Hoeffler, M. Reynal-Querol, and N. Sambanis (2013). *Breaking the Conflict Trap: Civil War and Development Policy*. Washington, DC: World Bank and Oxford University Press.

Combes, P. P., G. Duranton, L. Gobillon, and S. Roux (2010). "Estimating Agglomeration Economies with History, Geology, and Worker Effects." In E. Glaeser, ed., *Agglomeration Economics*, pp. 15–66. Chicago: University of Chicago Press.

Cox, G. (2011). "War, Moral Hazard, and Ministerial Responsibility: England after the Glorious Revolution." *Journal of Economic History*, 71: 133–61.

(2016a). *Marketing Sovereign Promises*. Cambridge: Cambridge University Press.

(2016b). "Political Institutions, Economic Liberty, and the Great Divergence." Working paper, Stanford University.

Dafoe, A., J. Oneal, and B. Russett (2013). "The Democratic Peace: Weighing the Evidence and Cautious Inference." *International Studies Quarterly*, 57: 201–14.

D'Amico, S. (1994). *Le contrade e la città*. Milan: FrancoAngeli.

(2012). *Spanish Milan*. New York: Palgrave Macmillan.

Dekle, R. and J. Eaton (1998). "Agglomeration and Land Rents: Evidence from the Prefectures." *Journal of Urban Economics*, 46: 200–14.

De Long, B. and A. Shleifer (1993). "Princes and Merchants: European City Growth before the Industrial Revolution." *Journal of Law and Economics*, 36: 671–702.

Del Panta, L., M. Livi-Bacci, G. Pinto, and E. Sonnino. (1996). *La populazione italiana del medioevo a oggi*. Bari, IT: Editori Laterza.

De Moor, T. (2008). "The Silent Revolution: A New Perspective on the Emergence of Commons, Guilds, and Other Forms of Corporate Collective Action in Western Europe." *International Review of Social History*, 53: 179–212.

de Vries, J. (1984). *European Urbanization: 1500–1800*. Cambridge, MA: Harvard University Press.

Dincecco, M. (2010). "Fragmented Authority from Ancien Régime to Modernity: A Quantitative Analysis." *Journal of Institutional Economics*, 6: 305–28.

(2011). *Political Transformations and Public Finances*. Cambridge: Cambridge University Press.

(2015). "The Rise of Effective States in Europe." *Journal of Economic History*, 75: 901–18.

Dincecco, M., G. Federico, and A. Vindigni (2011). "Warfare, Taxation, and Political Change: Evidence from the Italian Risorgimento." *Journal of Economic History*, 71: 887–914.

Dincecco, M. and G. Katz (2016). "State Capacity and Long-Run Economic Performance." *Economic Journal*, 126: 189–218.

Dincecco, M. and M. Prado (2012). "Warfare, Fiscal Capacity, and Performance." *Journal of Economic Growth*, 17: 171–203.

Dittmar, J. (2011). "Information Technology and Economic Change: The Impact of the Printing Press." *Quarterly Journal of Economics*, 126: 1133–72.

Dollinger, P. (1964). *The German Hansa*. Palo Alto, CA: Stanford University Press.

Downing, B. (1992). *The Military Revolution and Political Change*. Princeton, NJ: Princeton University Press.

Eichengreen, B. (2014). "Is There a Fiscal Union in Europe's Future?" *Finanz und Wirtschaft*, February 18.

Elias, N. (2000). *The Civilizing Process* (Revised Edition). Oxford: Blackwell.

Encyclopædia Britannica. www.britannica.com

Epstein, S. (2000). *Freedom and Growth*. London: Routledge.

Ertman, T. (1997). *Birth of the Leviathan*. Cambridge: Cambridge University Press.

European Environment Agency (2009). "WISE Large Rivers and Large Lakes." www.eea.europa.eu/data-and-maps

Eurostat (2015). http://ec.europa.eu/eurostat

Fearon, J. (1997). "The Offense-Defense Balance and War since 1648." Working paper, Stanford University.

Fearon, J. and D. Laitin (2014). "Does Contemporary Armed Conflict Have Deep Historical Roots?" Working paper, Stanford University.

Fortis, M. (2015). "Lombardy: A Manufacturing Leader." *ItalyEurope24* by *Il Sole 24 Ore*, October 27.

Friedrichs, C. (1995). *The Early Modern City, 1450–1750.* London: Longman.

Fujita, M. and J. F. Thisse (2002). *Economics of Agglomeration.* Cambridge: Cambridge University Press.

Ganshof, F. (1971). "On the Genesis and Significance of the Treaty of Verdun (843)." In F. Ganshof, ed., *The Carolingians and the Frankish Monarchy*, pp. 289–302. Ithaca, NY: Cornell University Press.

Gat, A. (2006). *War in Human Civilization.* Oxford: Oxford University Press.

Gelderblom, O. (2013). *Cities of Commerce.* Princeton, NJ: Princeton University Press.

Gennaioli, N., R. La Porta, F. Lopez-de-Silanes, and A. Shleifer (2013). "Human Capital and Regional Development." *Quarterly Journal of Economics*, 128: 105–64.

Gennaioli, N. and H. J. Voth (2015). "State Capacity and Military Conflict." *Review of Economic Studies*, 82: 1409–48.

Glaeser, E. (2011). *Triumph of the City.* New York: Penguin.

Glaeser, E. and A. Joshi-Ghani (2015). "Rethinking Cities." In E. Glaeser and A. Joshi-Ghani, eds., *The Urban Imperative*, pp. xv–xlvii. Oxford: Oxford University Press.

Glaeser, E. and D. Maré (2001). "Cities and Skills." *Journal of Labor Economics*, 19: 316–42.

Glaeser, E. and B. Millett Steinberg (2016). "Transforming Cities: Does Urbanization Promote Democratic Change?" NBER Working Paper 22860.

Glaeser, E. and J. Shapiro (2002). "Cities and Warfare: The Impact of Terrorism on Urban Form." *Journal of Urban Economics*, 51: 205–24.

Grafe, R. (2012). *Distant Tyranny.* Princeton, NJ: Princeton University Press.

Greenstone, M., R. Hornbeck, and E. Moretti (2010). "Identifying Agglomeration Spillovers: Evidence from Winners and Losers of Large Plant Openings." *Journal of Political Economy*, 118: 536–98.

Greif, A. and G. Tabellini (2015). "The Clan and the Corporation: Sustaining Cooperation in China and Europe." Working paper, Bocconi University.

Guiso, L., P. Sapienza, and L. Zingales (2008). "Long-Term Persistence." NBER Working Paper 14278.

Gutmann, M. (1980). *War and Rural Life in the Early Modern Low Countries.* Princeton, NJ: Princeton University Press.

Haber, S. (2012). "Where Does Democracy Thrive: Climate, Technology, and the Evolution of Economic and Political Institutions." Working paper, Stanford University.

Hale, J. (1985). *War and Society in Renaissance Europe, 1450–1620.* Baltimore, MD: Johns Hopkins University Press.

Hearder, H. (1983). *Italy in the Age of the Risorgimento, 1790–1870.* London: Longman.

——— (2001). *Italy: A Short History* (Second Edition). Cambridge: Cambridge University Press.

Herbst, J. (2000). *States and Power in Africa*. Princeton, NJ: Princeton University Press.

Hicks, J. (1969). *A Theory of Economic History*. Oxford: Oxford University Press.

Hobbes, T. (1950). *Leviathan*. New York: E.P. Dutton.

Hoffman, P. (1996). *Growth in a Traditional Society*. Princeton, NJ: Princeton University Press.

(2015). *Why Did Europe Conquer the World?* Princeton, NJ: Princeton University Press.

Hohenberg, P. and L. Lees (1995). *The Making of Urban Europe, 1000–1994*. Cambridge, MA: Harvard University Press.

Hornung, E. (2014). "Immigration and the Diffusion of Technology: The Huguenot Diaspora in Prussia." *American Economic Review*, 104: 84–122.

Hui, V. (2004). "Toward a Dynamic Theory of International Politics: Insights from Comparing the Ancient Chinese and Early Modern European Systems." *International Organization*, 58: 175–205.

Ioannides, Y. and J. Zhang (2015). "Walled Cities in Late Imperial China." Working paper, Tufts University.

Iyigun, M. (2008). "Luther and Suleyman." *Quarterly Journal of Economics*, 123: 146–94.

Iyigun, M., N. Nunn, and N. Qian (2010). "Resources and Conflict in the Run-Up to Modern Europe." Working paper, University of Colorado.

Jaques, T. (2007). *Dictionary of Battles and Sieges*. Westport, CT: Greenwood Press.

Jedwab, R. and D. Vollrath (2015). "Urbanization without Growth in Historical Perspective." *Explorations in Economic History*, 58: 1–21.

Jha, S. and S. Wilkinson (2012). "Does Combat Experience Foster Organizational Skill? Evidence from Ethnic Cleansing during the Partition of South Asia." *American Political Science Review*, 106: 883–907.

Jia, R. (2015). "Weather Shocks, Sweet Potatoes, and Peasant Revolts in Historical China." *Economic Journal*, 124: 92–118.

Jones, E. (2003). *The European Miracle* (Third Edition). Cambridge: Cambridge University Press.

Ko, C. Y., M. Koyama, and T. H. Sng (Forthcoming). "Unified China and Divided Europe." *International Economic Review*.

Landes, D. (1998). *The Wealth and Poverty of Nations*. New York: Norton.

Levi, M. (1988). *Of Rule and Revenue*. Berkeley: University of California Press.

Levy, J. (1988). "The Origin and Prevention of Major Wars." *Journal of Interdisciplinary History*, 18: 653–73.

Levy, J. and W. Thompson (2005). "Hegemonic Threats and Great-Power Balancing in Europe, 1495–1999." *Security Studies*, 14: 1–33.

Lewis, E. and G. Peri (2015). "Immigration and the Economy of Cities and Regions." In G. Duranton, J. Henderson, and W. Strange, eds., *Handbook of Regional and Urban Economics*, pp. 625–85. Amsterdam, NL: Elsevier.

Livi-Bacci, M. (2000). *The Population of Europe*. Oxford: Blackwell.

Lucas, R. (2009). "Ideas and Growth." *Economica*, 76: 1–19.

Luzzati, M., E. Baldi, and I. Puccinelli. (2009). "Le variazioni nel popolamento di una città toscana fra le metà del '400 e I primi decenni del '500." *Geografie del Popolamento*: 9–12.

Machiavelli, N. (2010). *The Prince* (Second Edition). Chicago: University of Chicago Press.

Maddison Project (2013). www.ggdc.net/maddison/maddison-project/home .htm.

Malanima, P. (1998). "Italian Cities, 1300–1800: A Quantitative Approach." *Rivista di Storia Economica*, 14: 91–126.

Mann, M. (1986). "The Autonomous Power of the State: Its Origins, Mechanisms, and Results." In J. Hall, ed., *States in History*, pp. 109–36. Oxford: Oxford University Press.

Maoz, Z. and N. Abdolali (1989). "Regime Types and International Conflict, 1816–1976." *Journal of Conflict Resolution*, 33: 3–35.

Marshall, M. and B. Cole (2009). *Global Report: Conflict, Governance, and State Fragility*. Vienna, VA: Center for Systemic Peace.

Mintzker, Y. (2012). *The Defortification of the German City, 1689–1866*. Cambridge: Cambridge University Press.

Moch, L. (2003). *Moving Europeans*. Bloomington: Indiana University Press.

Mokyr, J. (1995). "Urbanization, Technological Progress, and Economic History." In H. Giersch, ed., *Urban Agglomeration and Economic Growth*, pp. 3–38. Berlin: Springer.

(2002). *The Gifts of Athena*. Princeton, NJ: Princeton University Press.

(2007). "The Market for Ideas and the Origins of Economic Growth in Eighteenth-Century Europe." *Tijdschrift voor Sociale en Economische Geschiedenis*, 4: 3–38.

Møller, J. (2014). "Why Europe Avoided Hegemony: A Historical Perspective on the Balance of Power." *International Studies Quarterly*, 58: 660–70.

(Forthcoming). "The Birth of Representative Institutions: The Case of the Crown of Aragon." *Social Science History*, 41: 175–200.

Montalvo, J. and M. Reynal-Querol (2005). "Ethnic Polarization, Potential Conflict, and Civil Wars." *American Economic Review*, 95: 796–816.

Morris, I. (2014). *War! What Is It Good For?* New York: Farrar, Straus, and Giroux.

Motamed, M., R. Florax, and W. Masters (2014). "Agriculture, Transportation, and the Timing of Urbanization: Global Analysis at the Grid Cell Level." *Journal of Economic Growth*, 19: 339–68.

Mumford, L. (1961). *The City in History*. New York: Harcourt Brace.

Natural Earth (2015). www.naturalearthdata.com

Nef, J. (1968). *War and Human Progress*. New York: Norton.

New York Times (2016). "Catalans Protest Spain's Legal Challenges to Secession." November 16.

Nickell, S. (1981). "Biases in Dynamic Models with Fixed Effects." *Econometrica*, 49: 1417–26.

Nordhaus, W., Q. Azam, D. Corderi, K. Hood, N. Victor, M. Mohammed, A. Miltner, and J. Weiss (2011). "Geographically-Based Economic Data Project." http://gecon.yale.edu

North, D. and B. Weingast (1989). "Constitutions and Commitment: The Evolution of Institutions Governing Public Choice in Seventeenth-Century England." *Journal of Economic History*, 49: 803–32.

Nunn, N. (2009). "The Important of History for Economic Development." *Annual Review of Economics*, 1: 65–92.

Nunn, N. and D. Puga (2012). "Ruggedness: The Blessing of Bad Geography in Africa." *Review of Economics and Statistics*, 94: 20–36.

Nunn, N. and N. Qian (2011). "The Potato's Contribution to Population and Urbanization: Evidence from a Historical Experiment." *Quarterly Journal of Economics*, 126: 593–650.

Nunn, N. and L. Wantchekon (2011). "The Slave Trade and the Origins of Mistrust in Africa." *American Economic Review*, 101: 3221–52.

O'Brien, P. (2011). "The Nature and Historical Evolution of an Exceptional Fiscal State and Its Possible Significance for the Precocious Commercialization and Industrialization of the British Economy from Cromwell to Nelson." *Economic History Review*, 64: 408–46.

Ogilvie, S. (2011). *Institutions and European Trade*. Cambridge: Cambridge University Press.

Onorato, M., K. Scheve, and D. Stasavage (2014). "Technology and the Era of the Mass Army." *Journal of Economic History*, 74: 449–81.

O'Rourke, K. (2016). "Brexit: This Backlash Has Been a Long Time Coming." *Vox*, August 7.

Osafo-Kwaako, P. and J. Robinson (2013). "Political Centralization in Pre-Colonial Africa." *Journal of Comparative Economics*, 41: 6–21.

Park, J. (2015). "Europe's Migrant Crisis." Council on Foreign Relations, September 23.

Parker, G. (1996). *The Military Revolution*. Cambridge: Cambridge University Press.

Pepper, S. and N. Adams. (1986). *Firearms and Fortifications*. Chicago: University of Chicago Press.

Peters, M. (2015). "War Finance and the Re-imposition of Serfdom after the Black Death." Working paper, Yale University.

Pincus, S. and J. Robinson (2011). "What Really Happened During the Glorious Revolution?" in S. Galiani and I. Sened, eds., *Institutions, Property Rights, and Economic Growth*, pp. 192–222. Cambridge: Cambridge University Press.

Pinker, S. (2011). *The Better Angels of Our Nature*. New York: Penguin.

Pinto, G. (1988). "La Guerra e le modificazioni dell'habitat nelle campagne dell'Italia centrale (Toscana e Umbria, Sec. XIV e XV)." In A. Bazzana, ed., *Guerre, fortification, et habitat dans le monde méditerranéen*, pp. 247–55. Madrid, SP: Casa de Velázquez.

Pirenne, H. (1969). *Medieval Cities*. Princeton, NJ: Princeton University Press.

Polèse, M. (2009). *The Wealth and Poverty of Regions*. Chicago: University of Chicago Press.

Pomeranz, K. (2000). *The Great Divergence*. Princeton, NJ: Princeton University Press.

Postan, M. (1972). *The Medieval Economy and Society*. London: Weidenfeld and Nicolson.

Putnam, R. (1993). *Making Democracy Work*. Princeton, NJ: Princeton University Press.

Ramankutty, N., J. Foley, J. Norman, and K. McSweeney (2002). "The Global Distribution of Cultivable Lands: Current Patterns and Sensitivity to Possible Climate Change." *Global Ecology and Biogeography*, 11: 377–92.

Reid, R. (2012). *Warfare in African History*. Cambridge: Cambridge University Press.

(2014). "The Fragile Revolution: Rethinking War and Development in Africa's Violent Nineteenth Century." In E. Akyeampong, R. Bates, N. Nunn, and J. Robinson, eds., *Africa's Development in Historical Perspective*, pp. 393–423. Cambridge: Cambridge University Press.

Reyerson, K. (1999). "Commerce and Communications." In D. Abulafia, ed., *New Cambridge Medieval History*, pp. 50–70. Cambridge: Cambridge University Press.

(2000). "Medieval Walled Space: Urban Development versus Defense." In J. Tracy, ed., *City Walls*, pp. 88–116. Cambridge: Cambridge University Press.

Rokkan, S. (1975). "Dimensions of State Formation and Nation-Building: A Possible Paradigm for Research on Variations within Europe." In C. Tilly, ed., *The Formation of National States in Western Europe*, pp. 562–600. Princeton, NJ: Princeton University Press.

Romer, P. (1990). "Endogenous Technological Change." *Journal of Political Economy*, 98: S71–S102.

Rosenthal, J. L. (1992). *The Fruits of Revolution*. Cambridge: Cambridge University Press.

Rosenthal, J. L. and R. B. Wong (2011). *Before and Beyond Divergence*. Cambridge, MA: Harvard University Press.

Rosenthal, S. and W. Strange (2004). "Evidence on the Nature and Sources of Agglomeration Economies." In J. Henderson and J.F. Thisse, eds., *Handbook of Regional and Urban Economics*, pp. 2120–71. Amsterdam, NL: Elsevier.

Rozman, G. (1973). *Urban Networks in Ch'ing China and Tokugawa Japan*. Princeton, NJ: Princeton University Press.

Schultz, K. and B. Weingast (1998). "Limited Governments, Powerful States." In R. Siverson, ed., *Strategic Politicians, Institutions, and Foreign Policy*, pp. 15–49. Ann Arbor: University of Michigan Press.

Schweller, R. (2004). "Unanswered Threats: A Neoclassical Realist Theory of Underbalancing." *International Security*, 29: 159–201.

Scoville, W. (1951). "Minority Migrations and the Diffusion of Technology." *Journal of Economic History*, 11: 347–60.

Settia, A. (1987). "Crisi della sicurezza e fortificazioni di rifugio nelle campagne dell'Italia settentrionale." *Studi Storici*, 28: 435–45.

Shirley, J. (1968). *A Parisian Journal, 1405–49*. Oxford: Clarendon.

Smith, A. (2008). *The Wealth of Nations*. Oxford: Oxford University Press.

Spruyt, H. (1994a). "Institutional Selection in International Relations: State Anarchy as Order." *International Organization*, 48: 527–57.

(1994b). *The Sovereign State and Its Competitors*. Princeton, NJ: Princeton University Press.

Stasavage, D. (2011). *States of Credit*. Princeton, NJ: Princeton University Press.

(2014). "Was Weber Right? City Autonomy, Political Oligarchy, and the Rise of Europe." *American Political Science Review*, 108: 337–54.

(2016). "Representation and Consent: Why They Arose in Europe and Not Elsewhere." *Annual Review of Political Science*, 19: 145–62.

Stoob, H. (1988). "Die Stadtbefestigung – vergleichende Überlegungen zur bürgerlichen Siedlungs – und Baugeschichte, besonders der frühen Neuzeit." In K. Krüger, *Europäische Städte im Zeitalter des Barock*, pp. 25–56, Cologne: Böhlau.

Strayer, J. (1970). *On the Medieval Origins of the Modern State*. Princeton, NJ: Princeton University Press.

Tabellini, G. (2010). "Culture and Institutions: Economic Development in the Regions of Europe." *Journal of the European Economic Association*, 8: 677–716.

Thies, C. (2005). "War, Rivalry, and State-Building in Latin America." *American Journal of Political Science*, 49: 451–65.

(2007). "The Political Economy of State-Building in Sub-Saharan Africa." *Journal of Politics*, 69: 716–31.

Thornton, J. (1999). *Warfare in Atlantic Africa, 1500–1800*. London: Routledge.

Tilly, C. (1975). "Reflections on the History of European State-Making." In C. Tilly, ed., *The Formation of States in Western Europe*, pp. 3–83. Princeton, NJ: Princeton University Press.

(1992). *Coercion, Capital, and European States, 990–1992*. Cambridge, MA: Blackwell.

(1994). "Entanglements of European Cities and States." In C. Tilly and W. Blockmans, eds., *Cities and the Rise of States in Europe, AD 1000 to 1800*, pp. 1–27. Boulder, CO: Westview Press.

Tong, J. (1991). *Disorder under Heaven*. Palo Alto, CA: Stanford University Press.

Touring Club Italiano (1989). *Atlante Enciclopedico Touring, Volume 4: Storia Antica e Medievale*. Milan: Touring Club Italiano.

Tracy, J. (2000a). "Introduction." In J. Tracy, ed., *City Walls*, pp. 1–18. Cambridge: Cambridge University Press.

(2000b). "To Wall or Not to Wall: Evidence from Medieval Germany." In J. Tracy, ed., *City Walls*, pp. 71–7. Cambridge: Cambridge University Press.

Treasure, G. (2013). *The Huguenots*. New Haven, CT: Yale University Press.

Turchin, P. (2016). *Ultrasociety*. Chaplin, CT: Beresta.

United Nations (2015). "World Urbanization Prospects: The 2014 Revision." Department of Economic and Social Affairs, Population Division.

van Bavel, B., M. Bosker, E. Buringh, and J. L. van Zanden (2013). "Economy." In P. Clark, ed., *Oxford Handbook of Cities in World History*, pp. 385–402. Oxford: Oxford University Press.

van Zanden, J. L. (2009). *The Long Road to the Industrial Revolution*. Leiden: Brill.

van Zanden, J. L., M. Bosker, and E. Buringh (2012). "The Rise and Decline of European Parliaments, 1188–1789." *Economic History Review*, 65: 835–61.

Vecchi, G. (2011). *In ricchezza e in povertà*. Bologna: Mulino.

Verhulst, A. (1999). *The Rise of Cities in Northwest Europe*. Cambridge: Cambridge University Press.

Voightländer, N. and Voth, H. J. (2013a). "Gifts of Mars: Warfare and Europe's Early Rise to Riches." *Journal of Economic Perspectives*, 27: 165–86.

——— (2013b). "The Three Horsemen of Riches: Plague, War, and Urbanization in Early Modern Europe." *Review of Economic Studies*, 80: 774–811.

von Glahn, R. (2016). *The Economic History of China*. Cambridge: Cambridge University Press.

Wallace, J. (2014). *Cities and Stability*. Oxford: Oxford University Press.

Weber, M. (1958). *The City*. New York: Free Press.

——— (1992). *The Protestant Ethic and the Spirit of Capitalism*. London: Routledge.

Weil, D. (2014). "The Impact of Malaria on African Development over the Long Durée." In E. Akyeampong, R. Bates, N. Nunn, and J. Robinson, eds., *Africa's Development in Historical Perspective*, pp. 89–130. Cambridge: Cambridge University Press.

Whatley, W. and R. Gillezeau (2011). "The Impact of the Transatlantic Slave Trade on Ethnic Stratification in Africa." *American Economic Review: Papers and Proceedings*, 101: 571–76.

White, L. (1962). *Medieval Technology and Social Change*. Oxford: Oxford University Press.

Wickham, C. (1984). "The Other Transition: From the Ancient World to Feudalism." *Past and Present*, 103: 3–36.

Winter, A. (2013). "Population and Migration." In P. Clark, ed., *Oxford Handbook of Cities in World History*, pp. 403–20. Oxford: Oxford University Press.

Wohlforth, W., R. Little, S. Kaufman, D. Kang, C. Jones, V. Hui, A. Eckstein, D. Deudney, and W. Brenner (2007). "Testing Balance-of-Power Theory in World History." *European Journal of International Relations*, 13: 155–85.

Wolfe, M. (2000). "Walled Towns during the French Wars of Religion." In J. Tracy, ed., *City Walls*, pp. 317–48. Cambridge: Cambridge University Press.

——— (2009). *Walled Towns and the Shaping of France*. New York: Palgrave Macmillan.

Woods, R. (2003). "Urban-Rural Mortality Differentials: An Unresolved Debate." *Population and Development Review*, 29: 29–46.

World Bank Open Data (2016). http://data.worldbank.org

Xu, Y., B. van Leeuwen, and J. L. van Zanden (2015). "Urbanization in China circa 1100–1900." CGEH Working Paper 63.

Zhang, D., H. Lee, C. Wang, B. Li, Q. Pei, J. Zhang, and Y. Anc (2011). "The Causality Analysis of Climate Change and Large-Scale Human Crisis." *Proceedings of the National Academy of Sciences*, 108: 17296–301.

Zhu, X. (2012). "Understanding China's Growth: Past, Present, and Future." *Journal of Economic Perspectives*, 26: 103–24.

Index

(*continued from page ii*)